BREAKING BARRIERS

How P-TECH Schools Create a Pathway From High School to College to Career

Stanley S. Litow • Tina Kelley

Foreword by Randi Weingarten
Afterword by Rashid Ferrod Davis

TEACHERS COLLEGE PRESS

TEACHERS COLLEGE | COLUMBIA UNIVERSITY

NEW YORK AND LONDON

Published by Teachers College Press,® 1234 Amsterdam Avenue, New York, NY 10027

Copyright © 2021 by Stanley S. Litow and Tina Kelley

Front cover photo by Feature Photo Service.

Some of the material in Chapter 8 about the New Brunswick school previously appeared in *New Jersey Monthly*.

Library of Congress Cataloging-in-Publication Data

Names: Litow, Stanley S., author. | Kelley, Tina, author.
Title: Breaking barriers : how P-TECH schools create a pathway from high
    school to college to career / Stanley S. Litow, Tina Kelley.
Description: New York, NY : Teachers College Press, 2021. | Includes
    bibliographical references and index.
Identifiers: LCCN 2021007251 (print) | LCCN 2021007252 (ebook) |
    ISBN 9780807765586 (paperback) | ISBN 9780807765593 (hardcover) |
    ISBN 9780807779699 (ebook)
Subjects: LCSH: College-school cooperation. | School-to-work transition. |
    P-TECH (School) | Educational equalization.
Classification: LCC LB2331.53 .L58 2021 (print) | LCC LB2331.53 (ebook) |
    DDC 373.2/8—dc23
LC record available at https://lccn.loc.gov/2021007251
LC ebook record available at https://lccn.loc.gov/2021007252

ISBN 978-0-8077-6558-6 (paper)
ISBN 978-0-8077-6559-3 (hardcover)
ISBN 978-0-8077-7969-9 (ebook)

Printed on acid-free paper
Manufactured in the United States of America

To my grandchildren and all those in their generation,
regardless of income or race, who deserve a bright future
—Stanley Litow

To all the students who were told to aim lower,
and to all the students who told us their stories
—Tina Kelley

Contents

Foreword

The COVID-19 pandemic has exposed the far-reaching impacts of education inequities that exist in America and that carry into the labor market where lower-income Black and Hispanic Americans and those without a college degree have been among the hardest hit by job losses. At the same time, science and industry have accomplished the enormous feat of developing a vaccine in record time. But students from low-income families are less likely to take a science-oriented core curriculum and less likely to meet college-readiness benchmarks, let alone complete college. This book looks at the success of the P-TECH model to deliver a high-quality education in which all students can earn both a high school diploma and a free community college degree, plus a place at the head of the line for a career with a bright future.

In my experience, children need a healthy environment in order to thrive; they need to feel safe, welcomed, challenged, inspired, and supported. Successful educational models, such as P-TECH or community schools, have figured out how to bring these elements together. By moving beyond the normal confines of the school and partnering with local stakeholders, these schools provide real solutions to the unique problems of the students and families they serve, taking another major step forward in reclaiming the promise of public education.

P-TECH schools are open enrollment and offer a fully integrated grade 9–14 program. By integrating high school and college coursework, students can begin college courses as soon as they are ready. Students also participate in a range of workplace opportunities that include mentoring, site visits, and paid internships—all designed to support students' academic and professional growth. Students can choose from a range of STEM fields, including information technology, advanced manufacturing, health care, and finance—all higher-wage fields that too long have been set aside only for those of privilege.

When I visited the first P-TECH school shortly after it opened, I was struck by the teachers' deep engagement and passion for learning.

They fervently believed that every student, regardless of income or race, could succeed. With its high expectations and effective student supports, P-TECH benefits students of all races, economic levels, and prior academic accomplishments. When a college education, necessary now more than ever, too often is a pipe dream, P-TECH delivers it, totally free, for all students.

The teachers I know join this profession because they want to change the world one student at a time. Teachers want to challenge students with problems they can analyze and solve, so they too can bring about change. Teachers want to have their voices heard and their expertise in how to run and inspire a classroom be the basis for improving school systems.

Any successful model listens to teachers, values their expertise, and trusts their creativity, idealism, and heart. P-TECH schools aspire to give teachers the freedom to hone their pedagogical techniques and to develop high-quality, problem-based learning. With the help of tutoring, mentoring, paid internships, and close collaboration with a community college and business partner, the schools help ensure students are college ready, often much earlier than their peers at traditional high schools. P-TECH students are more likely to thrive in college and complete a valuable, debt-free degree.

Too many children from disadvantaged backgrounds have been left behind. Too often they hear, "Kids like you don't go to college," or "Kids like you could never achieve career success." This must change—both in attitude and action, and P-TECH is a change agent. We've seen how some students who are academically behind enter a P-TECH high school and, thanks to high expectations and support, are able to graduate from college ahead of schedule.

But P-TECH offers a lesson that goes far beyond the walls of an individual school. It shows that public education works, and innovative, improved, and adaptable approaches to schooling that are 100% public are not only needed but also achievable and affordable. Unlike other school reforms, where outsiders with little experience in public education felt they had all the answers and diminished the knowledge of educators by offering simplistic fixes, P-TECH reminds us that the key stakeholders responsible for student success, teachers especially, must have a seat at the table and be included and heard. Teachers must be deeply involved in both the creation and replication of any major school design or improvement—as must parents, civil rights and community organizations, employers, and higher education institutions.

Public schools can and must be direct pathways to prosperity and pluralism. Teachers aspire to a world where schools are excellent for all, equitable for all, and empowering for all. That's the promise of this model, as well. And the model is spreading—from New York, Connecticut, Colorado, Texas, and Maryland to Australia, France, and Taiwan. P-TECH students defy all the stereotypes of who can succeed. We know what works; innovative models such as P-TECH offer a ladder of opportunity, a path out of poverty, and a long leap toward a more equitable future. We have the tools to build schools in which all children thrive. It's long past time we recognized that doing so is among our society's most important tasks.

—Randi Weingarten, president,
American Federation of Teachers (January 25, 2021)

Acknowledgments

The authors wish to express their gratitude to the people who supported the idea of P-TECH—on the blackboard, in the boardroom, and beyond. Special thanks are due to Sam Palmisano and the Business Council of New York State for their help in bringing this book to fruition, and to Ginni Rometty and Arvind Krishna for their vision in spreading the hope of brighter futures to more than 150,000 young people.

Stan Litow would like to thank the education leaders who stepped up and got behind P-TECH: Joel Klein, Arne Duncan, John King, Randi Weingarten, Ernie Logan, Don Haddad, and so many more; former mayors Mike Bloomberg and Rahm Emanuel; former president Barack Obama; governors who promoted the model; the amazing principals he worked most closely with, including Rashid Davis, Kevin Rothman, Karen Amaker, and Armando Rodriguez; and the new, inspiring school leaders who are perfecting P-TECH.

Tina Kelley would like to thank encouraging friends; first readers; teachers Sue Leloia, Margaret Price, Beatrice Loevy, Gary Quam, and William Gabrielson; Pete and Katie Newman; and, particularly, Drew Newman, for his noble yet humorous company during a tedious recuperation.

CHAPTER 1

What Is P-TECH?

In a negation of the American Dream, a child's zip code is currently a far better predictor of success in school and life than hard work, intelligence, or resilience. In this book, we tell the story of a school model that focuses on equity and works to prove that *all* young people—regardless of race, language proficiency, special education status, previous achievement, or poverty—can achieve academic excellence and career readiness, given the right supports. When school is a place of high aspirations, rigorous and relevant coursework, tutoring, mentoring, and a direct, supported path to college and a career, students of every ability can successfully complete high school and free community college, and follow career paths into the middle class and beyond.

Pathways in Technology Early College High School (P-TECH) is a collaboration among a public high school, a community college, and a business partner. It gives a smooth and supported 6-year route from 9th grade to a career with potential for significant growth, to regular- and low-performing students, not just those scoring high on entry tests or doing well in 8th grade. The innovative model, now in its 10th year, serves more than 150,000 students in nearly 250 schools in 12 states and 28 countries. It tackles thorny issues such as the achievement gap, dismal college completion rates, college debt, income inequality, and the need for skilled, diverse science, technology, engineering, and math (STEM) employees.

In his 2013 State of the Union address, then President Obama said of the model, "We need to give every American student opportunities like this."[1]

As a nation we have worked, at least on paper, to make our schools more integrated, yet our classrooms remain more segregated than ever, despite recent public school population shifts leaving White students in the minority.[2] We know that students learn best from teachers who look like them, but our school staffs remain woefully White. We have made great progress in increasing our high school graduation rates, just in time for a diploma to lose its value. But early results show that the new 6-year schools are beginning to address these challenges.

As the need for equity in education becomes more and more glaringly obvious, P-TECH works toward a fairer school in several crucial ways: Unlike many school innovations, it puts up no barriers to entry, so students do not need to pass tests that may be biased or may favor students whose families can afford tutors. Because students gain entry to model schools via lottery, not via test scores, grades, or teacher recommendations, the demographics of these schools have accurately reflected those of their communities. Teachers and principals of color have been either drawn to or actively recruited to the model.

P-TECH presents uniformly high expectations to every student, which saves them from the low standards educators in some traditional schools too often present to poor and/or minority students. The model gives access to a free, high-quality college degree in STEM to students who might not otherwise have it, creating a pool of qualified employees for businesses seeking to hire prepared and diverse workers. This way, the model addresses the nation's need for a skilled workforce that is both well-educated and well-integrated. In tech giants such as Microsoft and Google, only 2.7% and 3.6% of executives are Black, respectively.[3]

Currently, many jobs that do not truly need the skills that come with a 4-year degree still require one. Known as "degree inflation," this practice puts job seekers of color, who are less likely to have a bachelor's degree, at an increased disadvantage. By preparing students for "new collar" STEM jobs requiring just a 2-year degree, the model provides diverse graduates with an entrée into the workforce. None of the three dozen Brooklyn P-TECH graduates hired by founding partner IBM are White. An influx of talented new workers of color can build the pipeline for more diverse employees and leaders in the years ahead.

The model works to address the shortage of diverse and qualified workers by planning backwards, from the skills and degrees companies require of new employees, to the 2-year degrees available at community colleges, and back to the high school, where students are prepared to begin such college classes.

Although more low-income students and students of color are graduating high school,[4] their entry into meaningful careers is not keeping pace. A high school diploma is no longer a sufficient ticket into the workforce, and people with only a high school diploma are relegated to low-wage jobs with zero growth potential. People with a bachelor's degree or higher have an unemployment rate of only 4.8%, whereas 9% of those with only a high school diploma and 8.1% of those with some college credits are unemployed.[5] Increasingly, new workers need a college degree to earn competitive wages, but not everyone can afford one or the onerous debt that can come with it, especially in the aftermath of a pandemic.

Even if we made college free for everyone, which would clearly address affordability, many students—especially students from under-performing schools, students of color, and students in poverty—know that cost is not the only issue. Lack of preparation keeps far too many students from completing a college degree. Only two-thirds of 4-year public college students finish a 4-year degree in 6 years; that translates into 41% for Black students and 50% for Hispanic students,[6] while on-time community college completion rates for low-income students of color are in the single digits. And while 4-year college completion rates stagnate, 2-year public colleges are suffering from enrollment declines and big bills for remedial classes. The 6-year model can help address these problems.

Its success is seen not in the way its students meet individual standards or pass specific tests. The model's outcomes are far more comprehensive and, therefore, more powerful. They are measured, instead, in universally meaningful accomplishments: A high school diploma. A college degree. A job with a future.

When we began writing the story of P-TECH, we were attempting to explain how a new innovative model could address the biggest prob-lems in American education—inequity based on race and socioeconom-ic status, and low college completion rates, especially for at-risk young people, leading to growing income inequality. But as we were writing this story, the pandemic hit. As a result, all students have been set back, but low-income students and those of color have been most seriously affected. They often lacked access to devices and connectivity; they were less likely to have a supervised, quiet place to study; and when schools opened for hybrid learning, they were less likely to attend.

The coronavirus pandemic served to magnify inequities in the system—Black Americans were 2.6 times more likely to get sick and 2.1 times more likely to die when compared to Whites.[7] Poor people suffered job losses as the pandemic hit, with almost 40% of people with a household income under $40,000 losing their jobs in March or early April 2020.[8] Meanwhile, students of color are slipping further and further behind. While the pandemic caused serious col-lege enrollment decline overall, low-income freshman enrollment dropped 37% in the fall of 2020.[9] That trend is in the exact wrong direction.

The P-TECH story has become all the more relevant during the pandemic and will continue to be long after. The grade 9 to 14 model, which was generally better prepared for remote learning, will need to be expanded even more widely to address the growing gaps in educational quality and economic opportunity facing our nation.

We will tell P-TECH's story by describing the attributes that have led to very encouraging results and a rapidly expanding network. We will do so with the help of the model's teachers, administrators, founders, and especially its students, sharing insights and research that can be useful in classrooms around the country and the world. The model can work with little to no added government spending, no changes in collective bargaining agreements, and no changes in state or local regulations, while eliminating the need for costly remedial classes. Students do not need such classes because the high school curriculum is designed expressly to prepare them for the specific college courses needed for their degrees, and those degrees prepare them for the exact jobs the business partners need to fill. While P-TECH requires private sector engagement, it does not depend on philanthropy. The philosophy behind the model can empower teachers, students, school leaders, and larger communities—more college graduates earn higher incomes and pay more in taxes back to the schools and beyond. As seen in the story of how it grew and its preliminary successes, the model holds promise for creating more equitable and more effective schools, and it offers lessons for creating additional, successful reforms.

P-TECH'S ROOTS

The first school using the P-TECH model opened in 2011 in the Crown Heights section of Brooklyn. In the story of how it began, the seeds for its spread were already apparent.

It all started at the U.S. Open during a rain delay in the finals match between Rafael Nadal and Novak Djokovic on a Monday night in mid-September 2010. As they did every year, longtime friends Joel Klein, the chancellor of the New York City public schools, and Sam Palmisano, chief executive officer (CEO) of IBM, attended the tennis championships in Flushing. They knew each other from their long conversations when Klein headed up the Justice Department's antitrust division, leading the case against IBM's competitor, Microsoft.

Palmisano asked if IBM was doing enough to help the million-student district. Klein told him of the students' needs for links to jobs as the city recovered from the 2008 recession, the worst since the Great Depression, and he spoke of then mayor Michael Bloomberg's interest in providing more career opportunities for students in engineering and technology. Palmisano talked about IBM's workforce development work in Brazil and elsewhere, and Klein enthusiastically discussed the need for connecting schools and career opportunities. Palmisano said he would have the head of IBM's corporate foundation and former deputy chancellor of schools, Stanley Litow, call Klein.

When Litow called Klein the next day, he had some concerns about the possibility of achieving Bloomberg's overall goal—the workforce's demands for skills and education had changed after the recession, and it would be hard to convince companies to hire high school graduates. Litow relished the idea of a corporate-school partnership, but from watching similar pairings over the years, he had strong views about the ingredients needed for a meaningful collaboration, especially given a goal to connect school not just to a job but to a career.

He envisioned a new, very different model, one that could help city public school students earn at least an associate degree and be ready for a career, while working closely with business partners who would provide meaningful assistance, including mentorships and paid internships. The model had to include community colleges because no employer would hire anyone with just a high school diploma. It had to form a pipeline that would draw students from freshman year to college and a career, providing skills employers identified. An entry-level position, he reasoned, was not a sufficient goal because if graduates had credentials for just one particular job, it could evaporate, and their skills could easily become obsolete. The partnership would aim to provide students with a wide array of skills that could help them enter and thrive in careers where people were needed now and would be needed in the future.

Litow suggested collaborating with the City University of New York (CUNY), which had seven community colleges. He was close with CUNY's chancellor, Matt Goldstein, from when they shared a mentor, Albert Bowker, an earlier CUNY chancellor.

"Let me come up with something and get back with you," Litow told Klein, and he called Goldstein that day.

On the phone with Goldstein, Litow listened to the chancellor's frustrations about how poorly prepared many of his students were and how many remedial classes they had to take, at their own expense, before they could even begin to earn credits. Graduation rates were terribly low—only 20% graduated in 3 years—and the numbers were worse for minority students and those from families living in poverty.

Maybe, they thought, if a high school worked closely with a community college and a business to prepare students to move, with support, to college and then on to the workplace, in a high school program that extended 2 years past 12th grade, the incentive of an associate degree and a job could help address what Bloomberg, Klein, and Goldstein needed.

Litow checked with IBM's human resources (HR) department to find out how many new hires had just an associate degree. The answer was zero. The company would need to make adjustments to hire such graduates, and the model school would work to make sure these applicants had the skills the company needed. Palmisano's support here was essential. He would have to direct his HR department to modify its past practices to ensure a clear path forward, and he did. Litow hoped all the players could meet the next week. He wrote an outline of a grade 9 to 14 collaboration among a high school, community college, and IBM. He emailed it to Klein.

Litow knew that for the reform to have any impact, the partners would have to work with more than one school, as one employer's pledge to hire more graduates of one school would not have a large impact. Model school plans in the past century had never spread sufficiently to make real inroads nationally, so planners would have to imagine potential barriers to this new model's success, and then eliminate them in the design phase. One school was not worth the time and the effort—the problems that needed addressing went beyond one school, district, college, employer, or city.

The model had to be scalable and sustainable. Would people get used to the idea of grades 13 and 14? Perhaps they would, given that 4-year high school for all was a relatively recent innovation, dating back only 70 years.

THE CONTEXT OF THE CONCERNS

Before World War II, American education was mandatory only through 8th grade. While public high schools had operated in the United States since the late 1600s, over the 18th and 19th centuries, they were often intended only for students with aspirations to attend college or students from families with means. Only toward the end of World War II, as companies required workers with more skills than those needed on the farm or assembly line, did it become the norm for students to stay in school until they were 18. States such as New York, Illinois, and Massachusetts instituted a grade K–12 system in the early 1940s, but some southern states did not do so until the 1950s or early 1960s.[10]

Since then, the path from public school to the workplace has developed large sinkholes. In the reforms following *The Nation at Risk* report in 1983, educators had focused on reducing high school dropout rates, which hovered at 29% in 1992.[11] By 2017, graduation rates neared 85%, up from 79% in 2011.[12] But many districts improved their graduation rates by pushing students too quickly through their courses, passing them whether or not they had absorbed the material. As more young people obtained a diploma, the value of that piece of paper fell. Completing high school, employers declared, did not make someone ready for work.

Meanwhile, community and 4-year colleges were discovering that recent high school graduates were unprepared for postsecondary coursework. At least 43% of students entering community college had to take remedial courses, which were noncredit bearing, but expensive, both for students and their colleges.

At 4-year colleges, only 45% of students finished within 6 years. Of low-income students, only 14% earn a bachelor's degree in 8 years. Completion rates are even worse at 2-year schools—only 13% graduate on time. For students of color who are poor, 10% graduate on time from the State University of New York (SUNY) 2-year schools, slightly higher than the national and CUNY rates. An IBM study of one community college in Queens showed students who needed remedial math plus one other remedial class their first semester had a 1% chance of completing that semester.[13]

Many such disappointed college students left school in debt, with college loans that would be extremely hard to repay on a high school graduate's salary. For too many young people, the high school diploma was as far as they would get.

At the same time, employers were demanding a better-prepared workforce. As the manufacturing sector shrank, jobs for high school graduates evaporated, and an increasing number of new jobs, especially those in growth industries and at higher wages, required a college degree. Such jobs grew from 28% of the workforce in 1973 to 60% in 2007.[14] By 2018, they grew to 90%.[15] Of course, with degree inflation, some of those jobs did not actually require a 4-year degree, but making that a cutoff requirement kept a number of minority job candidates in the unemployment line.

College graduates were expected to earn 83% more than people with only high school diplomas, up from 40% in 1980.[16] But such jobs with high earning potential remained out of reach for people who could not afford college, especially as state legislatures cut funding to postsecondary schools, and college costs soared. This combination led to increased income inequality among the races and classes.

Corporations began to find it difficult to fill what jobs they did have. IBM tallied 1,800 job vacancies in 2013 alone.[17] Job vacancies numbered 6 million nationally, even though 30 million Americans were unemployed, underemployed, or had stopped looking for work.[18] The shortage of qualified workers continued to grow nationally, as jobs created after the recession generally required postsecondary degrees.

To top it off, employers found that newly hired college graduates often lacked necessary "soft" skills such as writing and problem-solving. Of surveyed employers, 38% reported positions going empty for lack of skilled workers. A third said the resulting crunch damaged the quality of their work, and almost a quarter said it had resulted in lost revenue.[19] Litow figured that any program to provide employees from the city schools would have to include a community college degree at a bare minimum, plus a strong infusion of workplace skills.

If businesses, community colleges, and school districts could stop working in silos and help create a clear path from freshman year in high school to an associate degree and an entrée into a promising career, everyone would win. Students would see a clear incentive for working hard, the 2-year colleges would get well-prepared students able to graduate, students and their families could save 2 years of college tuition payments, and businesses could help both secondary and postsecondary schools understand the skills they need in their workers and then benefit from a stronger pool of applicants.

The longer-term benefits to all would include more high earners of all races, classes, and ethnicities; increased tax revenues; decreased need for and spending on the social safety net; a path to economic and social stability; and, eventually, a more equitable society.

A SUDDEN GREEN LIGHT

On Monday, September 27, 2010, as Litow was watching *Education Nation*, he heard then Mayor Bloomberg describing the new model school as if it were well underway.

"Today, I'm excited to announce a new partnership we've entered into with IBM and the City University of New York, and it's the first of the kind in the country," the mayor told a national audience. "Together, we'll create a school that runs from grades 9 to grade 14—yes, grade 14. All students will learn the traditional core subjects, but they'll also receive an education in computer science and complete 2 years of college work. When they graduate from grade 14 with an associate degree and a qualified record, they will be guaranteed a job with IBM and a ticket to the middle class, or even beyond."[20]

Litow immediately called Palmisano, saying, "This thing is happening." This thing, Litow had been thinking, was simply a plan open for discussion, not a done deal—until today. After he exhaled a few times, he figured this was both good news and bad news. Good news in that the model had approval, at least from the boss of the school boss. Here was an exciting chance to perfect a program that could bring opportunities to so many students. The bad news was, things had to move at warp speed, as incoming 9th-graders would be listing their choices for high schools in a matter of months—2 months, to be exact.

And already there was a fire to put out. Bloomberg had mentioned that graduates of the new school would be guaranteed a job at IBM. Litow warned Palmisano that the job guarantee Bloomberg mentioned had not been popular with IBM's lawyers and HR executives, who feared that if one group of graduates was guaranteed jobs, the company might be challenged by anyone with similar qualifications. After weeks of often tense in-house negotiating, during which some people questioned the entire program, IBM eventually suggested a compromise—they could comfortably promise that graduates would be "first in line" for any available job at the technology giant.

An early quandary for the planners was finding students. There would be no way for the pilot school to be listed in the high school catalogue or represented in the high school fairs, where most students learned about high school options before they submitted their list of choices in October and November. It was already October. But taking another year to plan wasn't an option—the players might change, and the moment might not be right again.

A few weeks later, Klein called a meeting at the Tweed Courthouse, the headquarters of the city's Department of Education, built under and named for the notoriously corrupt William M. "Boss" Tweed, head of Tammany Hall, the political machine that controlled New York City for nearly 2 centuries.[21] In 2001, the department had moved into the

Courthouse, right next to City Hall, as part of then Mayor Bloomberg's move for mayoral control of schools. The costs of the original courthouse were wildly inflated by political patronage—a $300,000 project ended up costing the city $13 million, almost twice the Alaska Purchase.[22] More than a century later, the building remained a money magnet—its fresh renovation cost $100 million.

Around a table in a windowless basement room, one of the few conference rooms available, sat Marc Sternberg, a deputy chancellor; the directors of vocational education and school closure; the deputy chief academic officer; Litow; Robin Willner, vice president of Global Community Initiatives, representing IBM; and Cass Conrad, then head of school support and development at CUNY. The central goal of the model was to create a direct link from high school to college to career. To succeed, the model needed a curriculum that moved progressively through skills that were important in the workplace, as identified by the employers—not simply coding, but skills that could take a graduate up the corporate ladder, or into any number of careers requiring skills in technology, IBM's wheelhouse.

The model could not require any new negotiations with the teachers unions or principals unions, as it would quickly become ungainly and hard to replicate. And it could not require any new costs other than tuition at the colleges, which, in the case of the first school, would be paid for by the city government and CUNY.

LAYING THE GROUNDWORK

First, the group agreed to create a collaborative steering committee with each partner equally represented. Everyone had to agree on the decisions made. They decided on a beginning class of 100 students, and they pledged to choose a site and pick a principal as soon as possible. No one even knew how the school's teachers and students would be selected, or which borough it would be in.

Chancellor Klein had been working aggressively to close low-performing schools, with the hopes of winning federal Race to the Top funds for the city. He also planned to continue opening smaller new schools in their place, and he had instituted letter grades for each school, a plan that the teachers union and social progressives met with skepticism. In January 2011, Klein told Litow that the Department of Education planned to close Paul Robeson High School in Brooklyn's Crown Heights neighborhood due to a history of low performance. As that school was being phased out, the department wanted the new 6-year school to move in, along with another small high school to be determined.

Litow did not love the decision to launch at Robeson. The site was more than just a school, it was named after one of the most iconic figures in African American history, a singer, actor, and political activist blacklisted during the McCarthy era. Its recent declines in graduation rates came about after another nearby school closed and sent many over-age students to Robeson, causing overcrowding.[23] The school's students and staff took to the streets and protested the closing at board meetings. Neighbors in the predominantly Black and poor neighborhood wanted their school improved, not closed.

There were concerns about attracting students to Robeson, the site of a student stabbing 3 years earlier.[24] Few neighborhoods had more densely concentrated public housing units than Crown Heights,[25] and Albany Houses, the housing project across the intersection from Robeson, appeared frequently in the police blotter. The Robeson basketball team, considered a powerhouse, had a history of brawling, and, in 2002, coaches from seven teams opted to forfeit games rather than risk playing at the school. In 2006, the team was suspended for a year following a bleachers-clearing fight at the end of a home game.[26]

When Litow reached out to people he knew in the police department from his days as deputy chancellor, they told him that young people would not choose to travel into the tough neighborhood. But it was the mayor's and chancellor's decision, and a firm one. They held that closing large schools enabled new schools to hire new staff and create new programs with higher chances of success, a process Litow had actually helped establish in the early 1990s.

Next, it was time to make sure as many factions of the education world as possible understood the model and had a chance to kick its tires and provide feedback. "We were consciously looking to get as many people who could be potential problems into the tent to be part of the process," Litow said. Every group with a stake in the school's success had to be consulted.

The school would need an innovative and gifted leader. Litow called Ernest Logan, then the head of the principals union, hoping to garner the group's support and seek help with finding a principal. Logan agreed to cohost a dinner with 20 principals at IBM's Madison Avenue headquarters. There, Litow described the new model, fielded questions about it, and explained that they were looking for a leader.

The conversation was friendly, with the principals offering positive feedback.

A principal from a small engineering high school in the Bronx, an African American man in dreadlocks, kept asking questions. Litow remembered thinking he should be one of the people interviewed for the position. After the steering committee agreed on how to find and interview candidates, sure enough, the man, Rashid Ferrod Davis, made the short list, and after a final interview in Litow's office in IBM, he was hired as the founding principal.

"It was a great homerun, getting him to lead the school," Litow said.

Next, Litow called up Al Vann, Crown Heights's representative on the New York City Council, a founder of Medgar Evers College, and a highly esteemed leader of the Black community. Litow asked for the civil rights leader's help setting up a meeting with neighborhood leaders of Vann's choosing. Vann gathered Lester Young Jr., then a member of the state Board of Regents and now its chair, who had been community school district superintendent covering nearby neighborhoods; along with local political, civic, and philanthropic leaders at the Bedford Stuyvesant Restoration Corporation, a community development nonprofit, to air and respond to local concerns about the coming changes. Litow and Davis understood that people wanted their school to excel, not close.

Robeson already had a history of working with businesses. Beginning in the late 1980s until at least 1992, Robeson had a partnership with Salomon Brothers, the investment bank, in which 73 employees mentored juniors and seniors. The bank hired 15 interns and offered 15 college scholarships that came with free computers. Eighty students received an SAT prep course, which raised their scores 95 points on average, and 20 received college advising. But P-TECH would be offering something more, as Litow explained. Its perks would be available to every student in the school, including mentoring and a free associate degree, and every class set students on pathways to college and career success.

The community members wanted to know if students in the redesigned school would be new to the neighborhood and predominantly White, if there would be special exams that would weed out neighborhood kids, if it would be a vocational school where kids of color would be warehoused and graduate with just a high school diploma into a menial job with no growth potential? Litow and Principal Davis gladly answered no to each question. In the process, they became more familiar with the level of hurt and disillusionment in the neighborhood, including how Crown Heights had been treated by the Department of Education in the past, when local students had been pushed aside so newcomers could reap new opportunities.

The planners were careful to keep in mind the criticisms leveled at earlier reform efforts. Would P-TECH cost too much? No, it was designed not to be expensive. Would it steal resources from the system to benefit a small number of young people? No, it worked within the public system. Would it benefit only the smartest kids? No, there would be open admissions, no qualifying test. Would it shunt students only toward a 2-year degree? No, many would go on immediately to 4-year colleges and universities. Litow said the model could work for the young people earlier reformers did not focus on, kids facing the most challenges—poverty, prejudice, limited English proficiency, uncertain immigration status, and special education needs.

BUILDING MORE PARTNERSHIPS

Once the site was official, CUNY identified the nearest, best community college to partner with, New York City College of Technology, known as City Tech, which already worked with high school students earning college credit through its City Polytechnic High School of Engineering, Architecture, and Technology. It was a short subway ride away from the new school.

Administrators there agreed to join the experiment, although final decisions would come slowly as to which entity would pay for the students' college tuition in the coming years. The tuition costs were quite small, as out of the original 103 students, not all would be ready to take a course or two by the spring of their sophomore year, and the cost per student per credit was very low. The tuition costs, in the early years, amounted to just several thousand dollars, which according to the mayor's direction would be split between the City and CUNY. CUNY, which used unspent state money from the Federal No Child Left Behind initiative, already had a liaison working with its early college high schools, so that person added P-TECH to the list.

The next step was to bring the teachers on board. Litow made sure that Randi Weingarten was an early visitor to the school. She was president of the city's United Federation of Teachers until 2008, when she became the president of the national teachers union, and she reached out to her successor, Michael Mulgrew, to discuss the benefits of the model.

Next, the process of picking teachers would begin. New principals of the city's new schools-within-schools would not have to choose teachers from the larger host schools being phased out, thanks to a policy Litow created when he was deputy chancellor in 1993. So, Davis would be able to interview and select new teachers based on their qualifications and enthusiasm for the new model.

Leading P-TECH would come with the chance to create what Davis later called "a new division of education."

"We had no idea that we were creating a new entity. I don't know what we thought. Model is not even the word," Davis said.

For its part, IBM hired a liaison to work in the school, to make sure its resources and needs were integrated into the school program. Temeca Simpson, a graduate of Teach for America, filled that position. IBM also helped develop a workplace skills course.

The school would not need a new curriculum, which would have required state approval and would have made it close to impossible to replicate in other states. One new workplace skills class would help students learn what they needed to know on the job, and job skills would be infused to their other courses as well, such as math and language arts.

With Palmisano's strong support, Litow and Willner consulted with HR experts at IBM to identify job categories that applicants with associate degrees could fill. None existed, but the experts identified nine that might work, and they listed the specific skills those jobs required. Many were softer skills such as problem solving, writing, and giving presentations. When Litow assured the department that the applicants would have up to 6 years of preparation combining academics with the workplace skills HR needed, the department embraced the change. As a result, the entire company's entry-level job requirements evolved to be more flexible, allowing for possible new hires from a broader, more diverse pool.

Through its employee volunteer program, IBM had already developed MentorPlace, a how-to-mentor toolkit and mentoring platform that could be used when P-TECH students were ready to be paired with employees in their field of interest. The company expanded its mentoring program, originally directed to elementary and middle school students, to include high school students interested in technology, focusing on guiding students through projects and on class-specific material. Soon, the work of recruiting 100 mentors based in the city and its suburbs would begin. With the strong and consistent support of Palmisano and later his successor, Ginni Rometty, IBMers saw that this model not only could be done, but would be done.

Meanwhile, the P-TECH steering committee worked on a "scope and sequence" for the school to ensure the following: (1) Students could take courses they needed in high school that were prerequisites for college courses, and (2) students could fit in all the required credits to earn an associate degree in either computer information systems or electromechanical engineering in 6 years, or less for accelerated students.

Qualified students would not have to wait to complete 4 years of high school to be able to start college classes; Davis was adamant that they should have the opportunity to begin college as soon as they passed their college-readiness benchmarks. For some, that meant the summer after freshman year, during summer bridge programs that extended the school year. This would help motivate them, help them acquire all the credits they needed for a degree, and, as some "dual enrollment" classes counted for both high school and college credit, enable some to finish early. For administrators, it was like fitting together a jigsaw puzzle—some early college courses required students to have mastered calculus, for example—except the pieces were adolescents, some needing remediation, some wanting to sprint.

As part of the planning, Litow kept reminding the Department of Education that the model had to spread early and often, and that the work of the steering committee needed to be widely replicable. Other participating sites needed to be found right away.

By the following September, the doors of P-TECH opened. At a first glance at their records, the students had not been stellar achievers in 8th grade. None of them had been accepted by their 12 first-choice high schools in the citywide matching process; the city encouraged many such students to consider new schools that had not yet been fully subscribed. Many of them were also rejected by their second dozen choices. And this was not a crowd of 14-year-olds who had been dreaming of STEM careers for years.

So much would depend on this group of 103 kids, all of whom were non-White and 80% of whom came from families with incomes low enough to qualify for free or discounted lunches. Some had motivated parents who were engaged in the education system enough to pick out a potentially promising model. But some looked at the school as a last resort. Half of the students were working below grade level, and, as they climbed the stairs of the 106-year-old Beaux Arts building across from the public housing project, they might not be expected to excel, let alone help solve some of the thorniest problems of American education.

PRELIMINARY RESULTS

Ten years later, the results have been encouraging. In New York State alone, 95% of the 533 eligible students had graduated as of 2019, compared to the statewide rate of 82%.[27] The first Brooklyn class had an on-time community college graduation rate four times higher than the national average and five times higher for comparable low-income students.[28] In Newburgh, NY, which opened in 2014, more than a third of P-TECH students had completed their high school diploma and associate degree in 4 years, 2 years ahead of schedule, while in Norwalk, CT, which opened in 2013, where student attendance hit 96%, almost half of the students graduated 1 year early.[29] And the Brooklyn program has produced more Black community college graduates than Guttman Community College,[30] considered one of the best in New York State.

Concerns that the model would relegate students to 2-year degrees or specific entry-level jobs were quickly proven wrong—more than 80% of those who earned an associate degree moved on to a 4-year school, compared to 55% in New York City.[31] IBM has hired more than 40 Brooklyn P-TECH graduates, and other business partners have hired many more in a variety of both technical and non-technical jobs, with more hires expected as the students in newer schools complete their diplomas and degrees.

Since 2011, the model has spread across urban, suburban, and rural communities, with at least 650 business partners. Currently an eighth of Dallas's high school students attend P-TECH schools.

How has the school model attained such milestones in less than a decade? We argue that the answer lies in its central philosophy—simply put, that all students can succeed, given proper supports—and through six aspects of its design: high expectations; elevating equity among students, staff, and the workplace; rigorous coursework designed with college and career in mind; support for learning; frequent interactions with college and business partners; and conscientious leadership. While each aspect can help students excel, even in traditional schools, we have found these factors play off each other in a way that, together, help P-TECH students soar on a smooth path from

9th grade to employment. We will address these topics by turn in the following chapters.

P-TECH AND THE PANDEMIC

While at the time of this writing, the end may be in sight for the COVID-19 pandemic, its effects on P-TECH schools are worth noting. The complexity of the grades 9 through 14 model made it especially challenging for students to schedule their high school and college classes, which they take concurrently, and to navigate separate learning systems. Many colleges use Blackboard for remote learning, while many P-TECH schools use Google Classroom. By the fall of 2020, most returning students were fluent in online classes, but incoming freshmen suffered from not having met their teachers and classmates at their schools.

In other ways, P-TECH schools were better prepared for the pandemic than regular schools were. Students had been participating in online learning before the schools closed, either through MentorPlace or OpenP-TECH, where they accessed courses and secured badges in various subjects. Their industry liaison could also refer them to people who could provide them with further support. In New Brunswick, NJ, for instance, all students in the district had Internet connections before the start of the pandemic.

In New York State, P-TECH students, already fluent in online work, had a short transition to virtual school, as they did not have to wait for contract approval, teacher professional development, or training students, according to Diallo Shabazz, director of the state P-TECH Leadership Council. But while the pandemic reduced opportunities for mentoring and internships in some schools, in others, longer-term partnerships such as with Thomson Reuters in Dallas, created online internships. IBM offered 24/7 tutoring to its partner schools, and it has been sharing with other industry partners its best practices for virtual internships. This bodes well for how the model, with its solid online presence, might fare in future national emergencies.

Principal William Smock of the P-TECH in Dunkirk, NY, felt more prepared than other principals for remote learning. "Our kids are so tech-based," he said. "We have one-to-one technology, so every student in our building has a Chromebook assigned to them. Some students have virtual welders so that we can continue on with the hands-on learning."[32]

As for the crucial question of how students fared during this extraordinary time, some school leaders and teachers found that P-TECH students were far more engaged in their online schoolwork than their peers. This was particularly important for at-risk students, who, in regular schools, were disproportionately harmed by lockdowns and the shift to virtual classrooms.

Katia Matar, the school leader of the Lycée La Tournelle located at La Garenne-Colombes, outside of Paris, remarked that students in her P-TECH school were more apt to do their work regularly and were more motivated because of their connection to future careers.

"They had one-to-one mentoring from the first month, and it's a different relationship, not like professor and student," she said. "There's no judgment. They're really there to help and guide, and it's the first time ever for some kids to have another adult, not a parent or teacher, saying 'How can I help?'" The mentors kept them from losing contact with the partner companies and helped the students cope during the pandemic.

Kevin Rothman, founding house principal of the Newburgh Free Academy P-TECH, noticed that college classes and requirements for internships helped his students stay motivated and engaged despite the challenges of virtual school. Even his freshmen, who missed out on much of the introductory mingling and icebreaker events, significantly outperformed their peers in regular school. They were also more likely to show up for live instruction.

"I attribute this to great teachers but also the extended school year," Rothman said in an email. "They spent 4 weeks with us before 9th grade in a synchronous remote environment learning about P-TECH as well as building relationships with peers and adults."

A BROADER VIEW OF REFORM

Among the 24,000 public high schools in the United States, single models of excellence are seldom replicated widely. Merely hoping that one school's success can go to scale has never been enough. So instead of running a school and waiting 6 years to evaluate its success, P-TECH's originators made a replication plan from the beginning, ensuring that the model was open to all students, requiring no new district spending, leaving out no important stakeholders, and engaging bipartisan state leaders. This led to a federal strategy with successful efforts to ensure that the nation's updated Career and Technical

Education legislation became more effective, stringent, and reflective of needs in the business world. In our final chapter, we discuss the lessons for future reform learned while developing and spreading the P-TECH model at the same time.

In many education improvement efforts over the past 50 years, division among school constituents has too often damaged chances for success and expansion. Much angry ink has been spilled over divisive issues such as charter schools, vouchers, standardized tests, teacher credentials, and test-based high school admissions. This divisiveness has hurt the forward momentum of our education system.

School leaders, business experts, politicians, parents, teachers, civic groups, unions, and students were involved in the creating and shaping of the P-TECH model, and few people have questioned the value of an educational program that leads directly from high school to college and career. Indeed, groups that rarely all agree on anything have been supportive of its early positive results. This leads us to believe that with similar efforts to create a big tent around school improvement efforts, more of them can succeed.

The new model has shown that low-income students and students of color in cities, towns, and rural areas, as well as lower performing students, can excel in learning widely applicable workplace skills in a rigorous academic program. They can enter the second half of 4-year colleges without debt, and they can find well-paying jobs, spurring economic growth and narrowing the income gap. We believe such schools can be an engine of the progressive growth that America needs to make its education system more innovative and equitable, and to compete in the technocentric global economy.

Too often, students have heard "kids like you" do not do well in school, college, or the business world. Simply put, students deserve our high expectations. They have proven that, with support in reaching their high goals, they can exceed them. Their compelling stories, which have yet to be told widely, show what is possible. We are excited to tell them.

CHAPTER 2

High Expectations

"They even told us that as P-TECH students, we're expecting more from you guys. They said you'll be college students. You know what you signed up for, and it should all be worth it. It all was worth it. They definitely told us what we were going into, and they definitely had higher expectations."

—Kelly Guillen, a 2020 graduate of P-TECH at
Skyline High School in Longmont, CO,
the first in his family to go to and graduate from college

When an educator believes students can excel, they perform at higher levels. Decades of psychological and educational studies have supported this belief, although the effect is stronger for students who have been stigmatized. The phenomenon is particularly relevant across racial lines, as studies have shown that White teachers, who make up the majority of the teaching force, are less likely to believe in the academic abilities and prospects of students of color, leading to further inequities in the quality of instruction that Black and Latinx students receive. Black teachers, in fact, have 30%–40% higher expectations for Black students than White teachers do.[1]

In this chapter, we look at research that explains how and why students thrive when the grownups in their schools hold high aspirations and expectations for them, what happens when teachers expect their students to do poorly, how the race of students and teachers affects expectations, and how to ensure high expectations are encouraged and shared. Note, as discussed in Chapter 5, backing up lofty goals with supports for students and teachers is crucial for empowering them to excel. Without those supports, high expectations become empty, dishonest taunts.

The importance of teacher beliefs is central to the success of the P-TECH model. Rashid Davis, the principal of the original Brooklyn P-TECH, wanted to be surrounded by only teachers who agreed that

100% of the school's students—including those in special education and bilingual programs—could graduate with a high school diploma and an associate degree in 6 years. Teachers without that belief need not have applied.

Davis, unlike some principals in later P-TECHs, was able to hire his own teachers, making sure that starting on the first day of school, students understand they are becoming college students and professionals in the workplace. He works to maintain a school climate that expects and honors high achievement, where students engage in friendly competition to attain college and career readiness.

Joel Duran, who graduated from City Tech in 2016, remembers how Davis would stand in front of his high school's one entrance every morning, usually in his signature tracksuit and sneakers, asking students if they were ready for a particular exam or why they scored low when he thought they could do better. You couldn't avoid him even if you took the wheelchair ramp, which Joel considered doing.

"He was definitely pretty tough on us," Joel recalls. "He'd say, 'How's it going, Joel? So, why'd you get a 75? Are you ready for the Regents?'" (the state college readiness exams).

Davis would not make much of a fuss over high scores, however. "He didn't want to get you hyped up," Joel said. "He expected more."

Davis had a history of putting faith in his students. While principal at the Bronx Engineering and Technology Academy (BETA), he read studies that showed students who attained a certain PSAT score were likely to pass the Advanced Placement (AP) exam. If even one student got a score that predicted he or she would pass an AP test, Davis opened up such a class for that student, even if it was his or her first brush with the subject. He wanted to give as many students as possible the chance to practice and pass important exams and earn college credit while in high school, and he added 12 AP classes during his tenure, when the school came to rank in the top 10%—number 143—of *Newsweek's* top 1500 high schools.[1]

Davis wants students to struggle with rigorous material and learn the habit of mastering it, as research has shown that students exposed to AP tests in high school did better in college, stayed there longer, and were more likely to graduate on time. This was particularly true for college students of color and low-income college students.[2]

Of BETA students, 90% graduated high school, compared to 64.2% citywide, at the time,[3] and most of the graduates earned challenging Regents or Advanced Regents diplomas, even though most of them had performed below grade level in middle school. From his experience running BETA and his understanding of how teenagers often model their behavior on that of their peers, Davis came to P-TECH with his foot heavy on the accelerator.

"My mantra is calculus by year 4," said the principal, even though some students could earn their associate degree without the advanced math class. "To reach a goal, you have to overreach the goal. Sometimes you have to take the express train and walk back to the local stops."

When the students proved themselves ready for college by passing their Regents Examinations in Mathematics and English/ Language Arts, the school honored them. The halls above the lockers were decorated with 6-foot-tall posters of each passing student, with a smiling picture and his or her name above the words *COLLEGE READY*. Visitors to the school, including former president Barack Obama and Tony Abbott, former prime minister of Australia, frequently commented on these posters. It was one way the principal used peer pressure to bolster the school's high standards. Teenagers respond to other teenagers more than to anyone else, and Davis knew if high school sophomores and juniors could see their peers passing calculus and going to college, they would compete to emulate them.

"They need to see their peers do it in order to know it can be done," he said. "We can't wait for grade 14 to see if the school is a success because that would not work for teenagers. For smart adults, yes, but not for teenagers."

Joel had nearly gone off the rails as a junior, after he broke his ankle in basketball practice and stopped attending classes, racking up zeros in his college classes. Under City Tech rules, his grade point average (GPA), under 2.0, would have made him ineligible to get his college degree. But Will Ehrenfeld, Joel's history teacher, showed up at Joel's apartment to give him a pep talk, and put the philosophy of high expectations into action.

Joel's NBA dreams might be as shattered as his ankle, Ehrenfeld said, but he still had time to work on the strengths he had shown in the classroom, rescue his grades, and get through his associate degree. Yes, he might have to retake classes with students a year younger, but he could still graduate. Joel had seen his neighborhood peers working dead-end retail jobs and wanted to avoid that fate. He, Davis, and Litow worked with the school to let him bend community college rules and take in one semester two computer courses that usually ran consecutively.

While before his ankle injury Joel had been on track to finish P-TECH in 4 years, he finished in 5. Despite those 0s, which had to be averaged in, he earned a 3.7 GPA for the last term, resulting in graduating with a 3.0. He had played baseball for 4 years, the last 2 years as captain. When Joel graduated from P-TECH, he crossed the stage at the Barclays Center, home of the Brooklyn Nets. His dreams had shifted from the basketball court to the college campus—with his improved GPA, he got into the SUNY at Albany.

Joel doubts other schools would boost students to try again and again after getting zeros for an entire semester. P-TECH did not encourage failure, he said, but it did not limit what students could eventually achieve, just because they failed once.

"But that's who the teachers are, and the staff," he said.

RESEARCH ON THE POWER OF HIGH EXPECTATIONS

Going back to the early 1960s, psychological studies have shown that high expectations contribute to high student performance. The most famous study,[4] published in 1968 by Robert Rosenthal, a Harvard professor, and Lenore Jacobson, a public school principal, showed that when San Francisco elementary teachers were told that certain randomly chosen students had taken IQ tests that indicated they were due for an intellectual growth spurt, those students excelled during the school year, thriving under the increased encouragement and attention of their teachers. This was dubbed the Pygmalion Effect, reminiscent of phonetics professor Henry Higgins in *My Fair Lady,* and his belief that he could shape Eliza Doolittle, a Cockney flower girl, into a high society lady by teaching her to lose her accent. His belief in her became a self-fulfilling prophecy, with a Broadway smidgeon of romance thrown in for good measure.

While critics said Rosenthal's experiment used a questionable IQ test, many later studies bolstered the study's premise that a teacher's high expectations could lead to increased student achievement.[5] Teachers have been shown to favor a student they have high hopes for in various ways—when evaluating his or her work, and by giving more praise, academic challenges, chances to answer questions, and supportive interactions.[6] One study[7] found that a preschool teacher's beliefs in a student's ability were strong predictors of that student's grades in high school. Another study[8] found that groups of 10th-graders whose teachers believed in them were three times more likely to graduate from college than students whose teachers did not, regardless of a students' race, gender, wealth, and past school performance, among other factors.

The effects of positive expectations play out internationally as well. A study of more than 7,500 Australian students found that when they reported that their math teacher believed they were competent, they performed better and had a better attitude toward the subject.[9] It is a powerful affirmation of a student's dignity to hear from a teacher, "You've got this. You're good at this."

Teachers themselves know the power of their beliefs—the 2009 MetLife survey of 1,000 teachers found 86% believed their own high expectations were connected to student achievement.[10] Yet just over a third of them reported believing all their students could succeed academically, and only 13% believed their students were motivated to succeed.

However, motivation might not even matter, according to research by the Center for American Progress, which found, after controlling for student demographics, "Teacher expectations were more predictive of college success than many major factors, including student motivation and student effort."[11] Could children be lazy and behind in assignments, yet still do well simply due to their teacher's high hopes? Could adjusting teachers' expectations contribute to a surge in student success? As in most questions regarding pedagogy, the answer is not that simple.

The first barrier to a simple fix could be the unusually low expectations some teachers have for some students. Several convincing studies have shown that students do poorly when teachers have low expectations for them, a self-fulfilling prophecy in a downward direction. Known as the Golem effect—for an often-troublesome creature in Jewish lore who is brought to life out of mud or clay—it occurs when a teacher believes the worst of a student's potential and prospects. Students are patronized and disheartened when teachers do not believe they can excel or be challenged to stretch themselves to meet academic goals. The effect harms talented students as well as regular ones, and it can be seen in the preponderance of schools where students are tracked by ability in middle- or low-level classes.[12]

EXPECTATIONS ACROSS RACE AND CLASS

Race and ethnicity play a pivotal role in these findings, as the Golem effect has been shown to be particularly damaging across racial lines. As James Baldwin wrote, "A child cannot be taught by anyone who despises him,"[13] as low expectations are clear symptoms of disdain. Former president George W. Bush called it the "soft bigotry of low expectations."[14] Low expectations also damage the prospects of students who have been previously stigmatized due to socioeconomic status.

A 2005 study of students who were evaluated by pairs of teachers of different races found that the teacher who is a different race from the young person is more likely to see the student as disruptive, inattentive, and less likely to complete homework.[15] These discrepancies were far more pronounced across genders, for Black male students, and for math teachers. There were even regional differences. In the American South, for example, having a teacher of another race "increased the odds that a student would be seen as disruptive and inattentive by 89% and 61%, respectively." That study alone would be enough to justify a national moonshot effort to make the teaching force more diverse.

Again, these effects are not limited to the United States. In a 2006 study[16] of teacher expectations and their effect on student reading achievement, teachers in Auckland, New Zealand, had low expectations of their Maori students and high expectations of students who are Pacific Islanders, Asian, and New Zealand–European. At the beginning of the year, students in all groups performed similarly, while at the end, the Maori students had made the smallest gains. "Because Maori and Pacific Island students are from the same social class and commonly perform at similar levels," the study concluded, "these results suggest that teacher expectations had more to do with ethnicity than any other factor."

Teachers found to have "implicit negative attitudes" toward non-White students had significantly higher achievement gaps in their classrooms, compared to other classes.[17] This is painfully true in STEM college classes, as we will see later in this chapter. Not surprisingly, students are quick to pick up on teacher bias. In a 2008 study called "Teacher Expectations, Classroom Context, and the Achievement Gap,"[18] two psychology professors compared classrooms where teachers had high and low levels of bias based on race and ethnicity. Biased teachers—those whom students saw giving classmates highly differential treatment based on ethnicity—ranked White and Asian students at least 7 points higher on a 30-point scale than Black and Latinx students. Even when diverse students had begun the year with similar achievement levels, teacher bias had a statistically significant effect on the overall year-end achievement gap by ethnicity.

Researchers have even been able to measure the power of teacher expectations. A 2016 study[19] by the IZA Institute of Labor Economics found if you ask a pair of teachers, one Black, one White, they will agree on their level of expectations for White students, but the Black teacher will have higher expectations for Black students. The study found "if a student is randomly assigned to a teacher whose expectations are 40% higher, which is the average difference in expectations faced by Black and White students in the sample, the student becomes 7% more likely to complete a 4-year college degree."

Beyond putting a number on faith, researchers have gone so far as to study the magical power of a single sentence, particularly for students who have previously been stigmatized. High school English teachers wrote feedback on hundreds of essays, but put the following sentence at the bottom of half the papers: "I am giving you this feedback because I believe in you." The students' teachers next year did not know who received that positive feedback, but those students earned higher grades.[20] "This effect was significant for students of color, who often feel less valued by their teachers," the study concluded.

HOW TO ENSURE HIGH EXPECTATIONS ARE ENCOURAGED AND SHARED

Short of writing "I am giving you this feedback because I believe in you" on every student assignment—not the worst school reform idea, if one considers its effectiveness, cost, and ease of implementation, but the kids will catch on—there are a variety of ways to ensure that teachers recognize their students' innate promise.

One is to ensure that teachers have a growth mindset, meaning they know—and can teach their students—that their minds are constantly growing, and that their abilities are not set in stone but evolve with hard work. The differences between growth and fixed mindsets were first described in the 2006 book *Mindset: The New Psychology of Success*, by Stanford psychology professor Carol Dweck.

Teachers with a fixed mindset believe that a student's talents are innate and inflexible. That does not make them bad people; they are simply unaware of a useful piece of research and missing a tool from their kit that could help them help their students greatly.

Stanford math education professor Jo Boaler found that low participation and achievement, particularly of minority and female STEM students, could be attributed to their fixed mindsets and those of their teachers. Students do far better in schools that have adopted a growth mindset and pulled back from grouping students by ability, which can cause those in all but the most advanced classes to believe they are "not smart."[21]

The fixed mindset has been damaging to students of color, and—a focus of our model's efforts—students of color in the STEM field. The issue extends beyond secondary school to college, where the stakes are even higher. Elizabeth Canning of Indiana University rated 150 STEM professors, teaching more than 15,000 students, as to whether they had a fixed or growth mindset, and found racial achievement gaps were twice as large in the classrooms of professors with fixed mindsets.[22] Students in those classrooms were understandably less motivated and reported negative experiences with those professors.

"Faculty mindset beliefs predicted student achievement and motivation above and beyond any other faculty characteristic, including their gender, race/ethnicity, age, teaching experience, or tenure status," the researchers concluded.[23] Such professors can and must change their own mindsets. Student success depends on it.

Studies on the differences between a fixed mindset and a growth mindset can shed light on possible solutions. By simply informing students that their minds are still growing and can learn new skills, teachers have seen significant leaps of growth in classroom-wide achievement, especially for students who were convinced they were not good in a particular subject.

In addition, to address the way stigmatized students too often lose out on the proven benefits of high expectations, the racial makeup of school staff must be addressed. Black students have been shown to score higher on tests, attend school more regularly, be less likely to be suspended from school, and be more likely to be recommended for gifted classes if they have Black teachers, who have been shown to have not just higher expectations for them, but higher likelihood of advocating for them.

For example, in 2016, researchers from Vanderbilt University discovered a "giftedness gap" among Black students and White students with the same scores in math and reading tests, in which White students were twice as likely to be assigned to gifted programs. For

Black high achievers with Black teachers, the gap disappeared. (White students with Black teachers did not experience similar gaps.) How many children of color miss out each year on challenging, enriched programs solely because of their skin color or that of their teacher?

The researchers noted a simple solution—rather than factoring in parent and teacher recommendations, just screen every student for giftedness. When Broward County, Florida, schools did so, Hispanic student enrollment in gifted programs jumped by 130%, and low-income student enrollment jumped by 180%. The students who benefited most from this, it turns out, were not those who tested extremely high. If there was just one student who qualified for a gifted class, a full class would be chosen. Those extra students were, like the district, predominantly Black and Hispanic, and it was they who experienced the most and longest-lasting gains in such classes, which cost the district no additional funds and did not harm students in regular classes.[24]

When the process of screening all students was later discontinued, deemed too expensive after the Great Recession, disparities resurfaced, with White students entering gifted programs at twice the rate of Black and Hispanic students. Nationally, the Education Trust estimates that 76,000 more Black students and 103,000 more Latinx students would be enrolled in gifted and talented programs each year if they were enrolled equitably.[25]

The benefits of same-race teachers affect typically performing students as well as gifted ones. Low-income Black boys who have had one Black teacher in elementary school have a 40% lower risk of dropping out of high school.[26] But in the United States, only 22% of Black students have a Black teacher,[27] and only 2% of the teaching force is Black and male.[28]

In light of such findings, the demographics of the teaching force must be addressed. If White teachers are less likely to recognize and nurture the potential of students of color, it is crucial to adjust the racial imbalance between teachers and students—a student population that is only 48% White[29] is currently learning from a teaching force that is 79% White.[30] (See discuss of minority teacher recruitment in Chapter 3.)

Hiring minority teachers is one way to address increasing educational expectations for students of color, which can in turn increase their achievements and their enthusiasm for school. But this must happen concurrently with addressing the ambivalence or negativity some White teachers express when teaching students of color. A 2016 study by Papageorge and others noted that for Black students who were objectively unlikely to complete college, hiring more Black teachers was most helpful, whereas for Black students objectively expected to finish college, both solutions worked equally well.[31]

And while there is currently a shortage of minority teachers in the United States, it is possible to ensure more students of color are more likely to have teachers of color: "This isn't a situation where students need two, three or four Black teachers to make a difference," according to Papageorge in an interview.[32]"This could be implementable tomorrow. You could literally go into a school right now and switch around the rosters so that every Black child gets to face a Black teacher."

Again, it is never that simple in the classroom. Putting all the Black kids in the Black teacher's room might be statistically helpful for the students, but it has echoes of segregation, and Black teachers would need to think an all-Black class is a good idea. Many rightly object to the unofficial but common practice of giving students seen as "discipline problems" to Black teachers, who are perceived as being very skilled in working with them. This often comes at the expense of the Black teacher's career growth, and it is a factor behind the disheartening loss of Black teachers when they are needed most—a 2014 study found that 22% of Black teachers left the profession or changed schools in a year's time.[33]

So, what is the best way to increase expectations among the teaching force? Robert Pianta, dean of the School of Education and Human Development at the University of Virginia, writes about one way for teachers to develop high expectations for their students: through ongoing professional development coaching that targets their classroom behaviors, not their beliefs. Teachers given an intensive course that used a wide range of video-based resources on ways to get to know their students' interests, to practice how to respond to their problems, and to engage with them in non-academic activities, ended up with higher expectations for their students than those who were exposed only to antibias awareness-focused training. Changing behavior is time-consuming work, best started at the beginning of the school year, and it has been shown to be far more effective than attitude- or awareness-focused training.

Other research Pianta directed showed that teachers who had received ongoing coaching sessions, each based on watching three short video clips of their interactions with different kinds of students—male, attentive, White, distracted, Black, female, Hispanic, disruptive—were able to fine-tune and adapt their behavior toward their students and improve the quality of their relationships. Researchers followed these teachers into the next year and found the academic performance of those new students rose 10 percentage points, compared to students with teachers who had not received the coaching. One group of predominantly White teachers in predominantly Black classrooms showed negligible rates of harsh discipline practices after the coaching, whereas a control group of uncoached teachers showed standard (disproportionate) rates.

This research grew into an online program that is aimed at raising expectations and reducing bias, without ever using that word. "It focused entirely on relationships between you the teacher and your students," Pianta said. "We're helping a teacher focus on understanding an individual kid."

Too often, antibias trainings focus on teachers' biased attitudes as a problem in cognition, curable by more information delivered during inservice days. "Once you call it bias, forget it, you just shut down that individual's receptivity to the very information and skills you want to develop," Pianta added.

When teachers can see their own behavior and how it may differ based on the characteristics of the learner in front of them, they ask for more coaching. Researchers at the University of Virginia have begun to address these issues by developing a simulation of a small classroom with a handful of avatar children for teachers-in-training to work with and then receive immediate feedback.

Of course, it is possible that teachers who did not believe their students could make it to college were not necessarily gloomy or bigoted, but simply realistic. As the Center for American Progress put it, "one cannot rule out the possibility that teacher accuracy, rather than influence, can explain the predictive nature of teacher expectations for students' academic outcomes."[34] If a teacher sees that very few students from his or her high school go on to complete college, they may just be speaking truthfully when they rate their students' college prospects as low.

In the Center for American Progress study, "Secondary teachers predicted that high-poverty students were 53% less likely to earn a college diploma than their more affluent peers. They also believed that African American students were 47% less likely to graduate from college than their White peers. Finally, they believed that Hispanic students were 42% less likely to earn a college diploma than their White peers."

Those predictions were distressingly accurate. One study[35] showed 14% of low-income students receiving a 4-year degree within 8 years of high school graduation, less than half the rate of middle-income students. A 2010 study[36] by the National Student Clearinghouse Research Center found 6-year completion rates in 4-year public colleges of 45.9% for Black students, 55% for Hispanic students, and 67.2% for White students.

Those accurate predictions, however, do not make low expectations any less damaging and painful to children. Lee Jussim[37] and Kent D. Harber of Rutgers University concluded that accuracy accounted for 75% of the overall predictive validity of teacher expectations, and self-fulfilling prophecy accounted for 25% of it. That 25% is worth trying to address.

In schools that offer high expectations and high support for students who have struggled in middle school and are of low socioeconomic status—schools such as P-TECH and many successful public and charter schools—students have been able to excel. A study of Boston's charter schools found that students in the city's charters that offered high expectations plus support saw the gap in test scores by race drop a third to a half in a single year,[38] compared to a control group of students who had applied for charter schools but not gotten in. Nationally and internationally, P-TECH's entering freshmen classes have significant rates of minority students, those with low socioeconomic status, and those performing below grade level, yet their graduation rates from high school and community college far exceed the norms for those groups and, in many instances, exceed rates for well-off White students entering high school at grade level as well.

WHEN PRINCIPALS AIM HIGH

Ideally, high expectations start at the top and reach principals, teachers, students, and parents. For example, in New Brunswick, NJ, Superintendent Aubrey Johnson's first message to the second class of P-TECH students set the bar high, long before school started. "You can do it in 4, 5, or 6 years, but I expect each and every one of you to graduate with a high school diploma, an associate degree, and connections with industry partners," he said via Zoom to the students and their parents in May 2020, preparing them for their summer school. Failure was not an option, and the school would provide all students with comprehensive support (see Chapter 5).

Principals, too, can set the tone. Armando Rodriguez, the principal at Chicago's first P-TECH, the Sarah E. Goode STEM Academy, works to convince parents and students that everyone can thrive in the program.

"It's always in my mind, that all the students can learn, regardless," Rodriguez said. "My goal is to support all students regardless of their academic performance, socioeconomic status, sexual orientation, language, or race."

Like Davis, Principal Karen Amaker expresses her high expectations for the occupants of P-TECH Norwalk by calling them scholars instead of students, and, if she forgets, they call her on it. "The expectations we have for and of them is of a scholar. We discuss what that means, at the very outset," she said. "It means we don't willingly allow someone to fail, we try everything to prevent that, and if and when it does happen, we ask what lessons are to be learned."

Greg Stephens, administrator of the P-TECH at Skyline High School in Longmont, CO, wants students there to think and work like college students. "In every lesson we give, we're always talking about doing things great," he said. "That culture is in our conversations with families, our marketing, and our recruitment. We constantly expect greatness out of our kids." And when students or staff fall short, he said, the school uses a family approach, and he or other staff members will preface difficult conversations by saying "this is coming from a place of love."

Dr. Charla Holder, principal of P-TECH at PANTHER Academy in Paterson, NJ, believes in expressing high expectations for the students immediately.

"When you start low, the only way is up," she said. She tells students, "Make sure you use the resources that are there for you. You want to make sure your expectations of yourself are high, so you're not just relying on other people to do so."

The school's guidance counselors help the students reach high by having small group conversations with them. Some do not yet know about credit accumulation and GPAs, and they need assistance preparing for college.

Holder, a proud Patersonian, does not want teachers who are "bleeding hearts" because they're not helping students.

"You challenge them," she said. "Push students to rise above the challenges they are faced with in their community. For example, gangs, drug, and alcohol abuse, not having the support network in their homes." She figures the earlier students learn those lessons, which her parents infused in her, the better. "You can go beyond what your circumstances are."

While staff of the Newburgh Free Academy P-TECH believes all students can succeed, sometimes success is getting that high school diploma for students who have been held back 2 years, for example.

"We have students who shouldn't have been in 9th grade, but we advocated to have them come to us because the data on them repeating 8th grade doesn't bode well," said Kevin Rothman, the founding house principal.

While many principals point with pride to the students who graduate with both high school and college diplomas in 4 years, "our 6-year students are the ones that we're proud of," he said. "Those are the ones, if not for this, they wouldn't be earning a high school diploma and college degree. It wouldn't have happened outside a program like this." The ones who graduate in 6 years are the ones who prove the program works, he said.

For instance, no one could consider Irann Martinez, who suffered a brain aneurysm and required two surgeries her senior year at Chicago's Goode STEM Academy, anything but a success. In Chicago, P-TECH students have to take entrance exams to get into college, and Irann had to take her math test twice and her reading test four times, but she prevailed. She completed two semesters of community college her senior year and another semester her fifth year, but she was unable to finish her associate degree because of her late start. She then won a scholarship to attend two more semesters of community college, won a full-ride to the University of Illinois at Chicago's pre-med program, and is now interested in pursuing a career as a neurosurgeon.

"I have to keep my hopes up," she said, feeling the need to finish a degree now, or never. "What's the purpose of my parents killing themselves so much, and I not take advantage of it?"

Irann grew up in Mexico, in a house made of mud. When she was 6 and her little brother was 4, they and their family spent a month walking in the desert to Texas. She does not remember it well, but when she has dreams about that time, her mother says they are accurate. Her parents did not speak English, and she taught herself the language by copying her bilingual books word for word, and then translating for her parents and helping them find jobs.

She chose the school because it was near her house, and she wanted to stay close by, as her mother was often sick, and Irann sometimes needed to pick up her younger siblings from school on short notice. She was also excited about the free college.

"It's a good opportunity, especially if you don't have a lot of funds or anything like that, or money just laying around. We don't have anything, not even savings," she said, adding that she and her brother work to help out their parents—her brother in cleaning out old buildings, Irann in restaurants. Their father works two jobs, in a factory and a bank, and her mother makes pinatas. Her brother now attends the Goode STEM Academy as well, and her teacher's sister, a lawyer, is helping her figure out their immigration status, as she is a Dreamer, under the Deferred Action for Childhood Arrivals (DACA) immigration policy. Fearing Immigration and Customs Enforcement raids and the prospect of having to take care of herself and her three younger siblings without her parents, she hopes to move to Canada.

THE BENEFITS OF DEDICATED TEACHERS

Teacher Joan "Mama" Casey, who retired in 2017 as the world history teacher at Brooklyn P-TECH, believed fiercely in her students, hosting weekend study sessions for Regents Exams in her Brooklyn home.

Here's how she describes her approach: "You have to say, 'Angel, are you aware how talented you are? Do you know it's a joy to hear you express yourself? You need some work—you need to be consistent, you need to read some more, you need to know where your strengths are.' Don't say 'You're weak here,' but 'It's important to work in this area, strengthen you more here, so you see the whole flower bloom.'"

She had her own way of working with P-TECH students in special education. "I said to my angels with special needs, 'The only thing special about you, I have to find a special way to teach you to get this work.' I always believe that if children come my way and don't succeed, I have to go home and look myself in the mirror. I have to say what it is I did not do. I can't blame either them or their parents. Did you give your best shot? If I did, I should've been able to see a different kid."

Students notice these high hopes and can be inspired by them. For Amalik Morille, a 2018 graduate, Mama Casey's dedication to the classroom and her belief in her students became contagious. He recalled how she came to teach 3 days after being in a car accident, wearing a boot on her foot: "Someone that dedicated? It becomes symbiotic. It's the energy you put out there, and the energy people receive—she kept just being positive, determined and steadfast in what she believes, and preaching that belief for everybody. After hearing it for the 50th time, you actually start to believe it, thanks to her positive influence."

In Chicago's Goode STEM Academy, Aleexis Sahagun said high expectations made him more passionate about his work and made him care more about school. "If they said, 'calculus whenever,' I think it would've been more difficult, because if it was just 'whenever,' I might just forget most of the math I had before," he said.

There are several ways to build a teaching staff who believes 100% that each child can succeed. One is to make sure all teachers start their jobs with that mindset, as Davis did, but that is an opportunity available only in new schools, to principals who have full discretion in hiring.

A 2018 meta-analysis[39] of ways to raise teacher expectations in the United States and in New Zealand looked at 12 earlier studies and found it is possible to raise teacher expectations and, in turn, student achievement. To do so most effectively, however, teachers must collaborate in designing programs to raise their expectations, as they are more likely to support such programs rather than those imposed from outside.

The authors found three ways to raise teacher expectations: (1) teach teachers behaviors that high-expectation teachers used, (2) teach teachers about the effects of their expectations on students and how their expectations can be inaccurate or biased, and (3) address the beliefs of teachers about underlying "biased expectations toward student achievement."

Dr. Pianta of the University of Virginia told NPR[40] that it is hard for teachers to change their own expectations, and traditional efforts to convince teachers to do so have not had stellar results. No one takes well to being told they may be biased or have blind spots around race. Most White people, who make up the vast majority of the teaching force, have preconceptions about children of other races worth questioning and resisting, and all have benefited, often unwittingly, from societal structures that give them disproportionate power. In antibias trainings, White people often spend more mental calories defending themselves than listening to ways to recognize and work against bias. This defensiveness is a human reaction, but it can close one's ears to ways to reduce a phenomenon that can cause great harm to students.

Young people understand the power of the expectations of the adults around them. They may rebel against them, but they are honored by them. Kelly Guillen, quoted at the beginning of this chapter, remembers Kathleen King's particularly hard college class, History 121, that a lot of students disliked because of its workload—lists of 20 vocabulary words, lots of annotations assigned for every chapter, student-led Socratic seminars to discuss the readings. But he knows the class prepared students well for further college courses.

"There are some P-TECH students I know in college who are a little more ready," said Kelly, who does not think he would've pursued college any further if P-TECH had not been available. "They're still struggling like any other student, but they're more prepared, because of the high expectations at P-TECH."

TAKEAWAYS

People working in traditional schools, as well as P-TECH schools, can serve their students best by giving them high expectations, plus the support to meet those expectations. In districts where student graduation and college completion rates have been historically low, or where students have been stigmatized, this is particularly important. The same holds for all job titles, from the statehouse to the district office to the principal's office to the classroom.

States

State policy can help students of all races, ethnicities, and family income levels to take the most challenging coursework possible, leading to a free college degree, through the P-TECH program, which should be implemented more broadly. Students deserve the best preparation, starting in prekindergarten and elementary school. Students of color and low-income students should be encouraged to participate in gifted programs and enroll in 8th-grade algebra whenever possible, as an entrée to college-level high school courses.

Districts

In Paterson, NJ, rising 9th-graders who had committed to P-TECH were feted at a Signing Day at the school, featuring local Super Bowl champion Victor Cruz. "You students made a decision and have taken direction for the challenge to become a champion," Paterson Public Schools Superintendent Eileen Shafer told them.[41] "You have taken up the challenge of becoming academic athletes, and you will get an education and experience you need to become champions in the technology sector of our nation's economy."

New York City should be applauded for its AP for All effort, aiming to offer students at its 548 high schools a minimum of five AP courses,[42] as should Richmond, VA, another district aiming for AP for All.[43] The city saw a 25% increase in the number of students taking AP classes. As Superintendent Jason Kamras put it, "We can't expect greatness of our students if we don't ask greatness of them." (See Chapter 4 for a longer discussion of the need for broader participation in advanced courses.)

Principals

One of the biggest steps a principal can take in bolstering student success is to gather a talented staff dedicated to the belief students can excel. Young people benefit from a school climate that honors and expects student achievement.

In a school based on high expectations, teachers thrive as well. Davis's strong faith in his students' abilities extends naturally to his teachers, who are more likely to thrive (and return year after year) when given permission to experiment, feel trusted, and grow professionally (and, on occasion, to leave to lead other schools).

Guidance Counselors

It is important to encourage students—particularly those who may not see themselves as advanced—to take the most challenging courses possible, as well as to support them wherever possible, with thoughtful planning about course sequences and referrals to tutoring and other supports. This is particularly important for students whose parents are not up to date on the workings of the school system. An adult who understands a student and encourages his or her ambitions is priceless.

Teachers

Gina Bruno, who teaches social studies at the P-TECH in New Brunswick, NJ, summed up the model's philosophy well: "I think, in general, if you have low expectations of your students, you probably shouldn't be the person standing in the room."

High expectations need to be central to any successful educational effort, particularly for students who have been stigmatized in the past. But expectations form merely the foundation, not the walls and roof, of an excellent school. We will discuss the fundamental requirements of the P-TECH model—elevating equity, rigorous coursework designed with college and career in mind, support for learning, frequent interactions with college and business partners, and conscientious leadership—in the following chapters. Only when all these components are working together, like gears in an engine, can students experience optimal acceleration.

CHAPTER 3

Elevating Equity

The United States has rarely, if ever, been so divided politically, racially, and socioeconomically. The public school, as the institution most Americans participate in during their most formative years, is the likeliest spot for healing to take place, yet the goal of equity in education has eluded us for centuries, and certainly for the more than 60 years it has been the law of the land. Education is a civil right, a service provided by the government that must be available to all in equal measure and quality. Full stop.

Yet there are many clues showing that our system fails to treat each student equally: the achievement or opportunity gap; segregation by race and socioeconomic status; the funding gap; and teacher quality. In addition, children of color are far less likely than White students to be taught by someone of the same race, another less commonly discussed form of inequity.

The COVID-19 pandemic exposed and deepened these structural divides, as poor children and children of color fared worse academically than their rich, White counterparts due to lack of access to the devices and connectivity needed for online learning and lack of quiet, supervised places to study. Students of color and poor students were less likely to be engaged in online learning and less likely to receive quality instruction than their White and wealthier peers. As students of color were already disproportionately behind academically and overrepresented in English Language Learners (ELLs) and special needs classes, the pandemic's problems exacerbated those inequities. And, in the fall of 2020, when some districts opened their doors for in-person or hybrid learning, more students of color remained at home, even though online learning was less effective.

The achievement gap between races appears early in the lives of students, with Black and Hispanic children scoring lower on the National Assessment of Educational Progress (NAEP) in elementary school,[1] less likely to take AP and International Baccalaureate (IB) classes, and less likely to graduate from high school. While 89% of White students graduate from high school on time, only 81% of Hispanic students and 79% of Black students do.[2] Racial disparities grow starker after high school, with fewer graduates of color continuing to higher education and less than half of them finishing 4-year degrees in 6 years. Given the wage disparities between high school and college graduates, income disparities by race continue to grow. P-TECH, with its goal of college completion for all, aims to tackle these inequities.

It is far more just to address these concerns by looking at the opportunity gap—students should not be judged by what they have been able to achieve in an inequitable system. Instead, we as a society must address the enormous discrepancies in each child's opportunities to succeed. Students of color have fewer chances to excel when they are sent to segregated schools, when their schools receive less funding, and when their teachers are less qualified and experienced. The deaths of Breonna Taylor in March 2020 and George Floyd 2 months later, as well as the ensuing and enduring protests against police brutality, led many to conclude that, as one protest sign read, "The system isn't broken. It's supposed to work this way."

Indeed, despite hopes that the moral arc of the universe bends toward justice, school segregation by race and socioeconomic status in the United States has grown markedly worse since the early 1970s due to gentrification and other real estate trends, school-funding formulas on the state level that rely on property taxes, and systemic racism. Many schools are just as segregated now as they were in the 1960s. Nearly 70% of Black children in the United States attended majority-Black schools in 2017. Only 31% of White students attend schools where students are predominantly poor, while 72% of Black students do.[3] Still today, 15% of Black students attend "apartheid schools," where 99% of the students are Black,[4] and the percentage of hyper-segregated schools rose from 5.7 in 1988 to 18.4 in 2016.[5] In the process, the opportunities of children of color have been greatly diminished.

Educational research tells us that when schools are integrated according to race and socioeconomic status, opportunity gaps shrink and students thrive. Integrated classrooms not only promote critical thinking, problem-solving, and creativity, but also reduce stress[6] for all students. Studies have shown that attending integrated schools does not hurt White students academically—they perform the same in schools with lots of Black students as in schools with only a few.[7] But schools segregated by race (aside from all-Black charter schools, where students' families choose a segregated setting) have been shown to be harmful to Black students' achievement as early as 1st grade, and they reduce overall achievement regardless of their students' family income. Attending integrated schools has been shown to help increase Black students' graduation rates, income, and health.[8]

School integration peaked in 1988, the year 9th-grade NAEP scores for Black students were only 18 points below those of White students, a gap that had shrunk from 39 points in 1971.[9] The news has not been good since—high school reading scores in 2019 showed a gap of 32 points.[10] If the achievement gap had continued to close at the same rate as from 1971 to 1988, the height of integration, it would be less than 3 points today.[11]

Schools can be integrated through rezoning, busing, building affordable housing near existing schools, or employing controlled choice, a strategy where families list their preferences for a variety of schools, which are taken into account along with racial and socioeconomic balance, to create school rosters.

Integration of schools based on socioeconomic status is also necessary, as the concentration of poverty in schools has increased. From 2000 to 2014, the percent of schools with 75% poor and minority students grew from 9% to 16%.[12] And, of course, race and socioeconomic status are linked. Black and Latinx students are five times more likely than White students to attend a high-poverty school.[13]

As a nation, we have too often reserved high-quality, well-funded schools for already privileged students. School districts serving White and well-off students receive far more funding than districts serving kids of color—an average of $1,800 more per student per year, or $9 million for a district of 5,000 students.[14] High-poverty districts, on average, spend $1,000 less per student per year. Across the country in 2016, districts serving mostly White students received $23 billion more in funding than those educating predominantly students of color.[15]

The quality of classroom teachers is considered the biggest factor in student success,[16] and wealthy schools with a higher percentage of White students tend to employ more experienced instructors who are more likely to be certified, to be better paid, and to stay in their positions longer. As might be anticipated, a larger percentage of them are White, compared to the general teacher population.[17]

THE BENEFITS OF SAME-RACE TEACHERS

Many studies have shown that children of color can benefit greatly from having teachers who look like them. Teachers of color may also help keep poorly integrated schools more stable, as they "appear to be more committed to teaching students of color, more drawn to teaching in difficult-to-staff urban schools, and are more apt to persist in those settings," according to a report on teacher diversity by the National Education Association.[18] They are also better informed about their students' heritage, and they help students feel more confident and more like they belong in academia.[19]

Overall, Black students with at least one Black teacher do better on standardized tests, have higher attendance rates, and have lower suspension rates.[20] Studies on same-race teachers have shown higher rates of gifted program recommendation for Black and Hispanic students.[21]

Black teachers have been shown to have higher expectations (as seen in the previous chapter) for Black students, especially math teachers and male students.[22] Black teachers are more likely than White teachers to believe that a given Black student will earn a bachelor's degree.[23] White teacher biases were stronger against Black boys than against Black girls.

Another study found the effects of same-race teachers to be particularly strong and helpful for lower-performing students.[24] This extends to behavior issues as well—students with teachers of a different race are 46% more likely to be labeled as disruptive, compared to students with same-race teachers.[25]

"The Power of Teacher Expectations" study[26] from 2018 concluded that "to raise student attainment, particularly among students of color, elevating teacher expectations, eliminating racial bias, and hiring a more diverse teaching force are worthy goals."

THE SHORTAGE OF TEACHERS OF COLOR

While Blacks make up 13% of the population today, the percentage of Black teachers has fallen from 8.1% in 1971 to 6.9% in 1986, to 6.7% currently.[27] By raw numbers, the Black teaching force has increased less than that of any other racial group except for Native Americans.[28] Overall, Black males account for less than 2% of the teaching force.[29] According to research from the Education Trust, in a third of the states that provided information, a third of students went to a school with an entirely White teaching staff.[30]

Especially given the current shortage, the story of Black educators throughout the civil rights era and beyond is particularly heartbreaking. Efforts to integrate the schools in the middle of the previous century had disastrous results for Black educators. The 1954 *Brown v. Board of Education* Supreme Court decision, which ruled that "separate but equal" segregated schools were unconstitutional, had the unintended effect of disrupting and even ending the careers of tens of thousands of Black teachers and principals from all-Black schools.

From 1954 to 1964, the ruling's effects were minimal. During that decade, the 11 states that had joined the Confederacy effectively ignored the ruling—fewer than 5% of Black students went to school with White students. Then came the Civil Rights Act of 1964, which gave the federal government powers to enforce desegregation. By 1970, more than 90% of Black students attended integrated schools.

But in those 6 years, tens of thousands of Black teachers and principals lost their jobs. Owen Thompson, an economics professor at Williams College, studied the employment of Black teachers in 781 school districts from 1964 to 1972, and saw a 32% drop as a result of integration. Half of all college-educated Blacks at the time worked in teaching. After integration, half left the profession for lower-paying jobs, and half moved out of the South to teach elsewhere. In just eight states, Thompson calculated that more than 15,800 Black teachers left their schools.[31]

They did not have much choice. When districts were integrated, many White administrators refused to hire Black teachers and principals. Black teachers were often replaced by White teachers who had less experience and fewer and less prestigious credentials, according to research by Leslie Fenwick, a professor and former dean at the Howard University School of Education.[32] Black educators who worked in integrated schools were frequently mistreated by White staff and students. By 1972, the number of Black principals had declined by 30%, with White principals outnumbering them nine to one.[33]

Black teachers had shown their Black students a path to succeed academically, often by traveling to integrated northern universities for their training. By example, they showed it was crucial to return home to serve and inspire their communities. Their loss spread into the future, for children of teachers are twice as likely to become teachers as children of non-teachers, an effect that is particularly strong for daughters.[34] With one generation of Black mothers gone from southern classrooms, there were fewer daughters moving up to take their place.

The loss of Black educators hit hard on the psychic level. They were "the teachers who showed Black children that they could believe in themselves . . . who taught civics curriculum where they participated in democracy . . . who, in the midst of oppression, taught children to aspire," said Vanessa Siddle Walker, Samuel Candler Dobbs Professor of African American Educational Studies at Emory University.[35] They also advocated for Black children, challenged them, and shared with them their thirst for knowledge. While segregating Black students in substandard schools had been one of the biggest crimes of the post-Civil War era, one of integration's biggest unintended transgressions was splitting Black students from educators who could inspire them from the history and community they shared.

The decline of the Black teaching force continued. When North Carolina raised the minimum scores for new teachers taking the National Teacher Exam in the late 1970s, it saw a 73% drop in new Black teachers over 7 years.[36] From 1984 to 1989 alone, new requirements for teacher education and certification resulted in the displacement of another 21,500 Black teachers, according to former professor Linda Tillman of the School of Education at the University of North Carolina at Chapel Hill, who found that states were using standardized test scores as a yardstick for Black teachers, firing them when they did not earn certain scores.[37]

From 1993 to 2008, the number and percentage of non-White teachers continued to decrease, while the number and percentage of non-White students increased.[38] And from 2002 to 2012, Black teaching staff decreased by 15% in New York City and by 62% in New Orleans. It fell in seven other cities as well.[39]

REBUILDING A DIVERSE TEACHING FORCE

Traditional recruiting methods have proved challenging when every public school concerned with equity is trying hard to recruit from a relatively small pool of candidates: teachers wanting to change schools or towns, second career teachers, and the approximately 7,700 new education school graduates each year, a group that in 2017 grew by only 1.4% over the previous year.[40] Only a quarter of the students in education schools are non-White.[41]

Sponsoring hiring fairs and developing relationships with historically Black colleges and universities (HBCU) or public universities with large percentages of minority graduates can get a district only so far. Some well-organized districts jockey for position by figuring out their vacancies early in the spring and hiring teachers then,[42] but other districts are unable to plan and budget that far ahead. In the end, all the districts are competing to attract a small number of people.

Clearly, we need many more teachers of color to build a teaching force that represents our students. Currently the stream of future teachers, moving from high school through graduation from a teacher preparation program, gets less diverse at each level. While 52% of public school students are non-White,[43] as are 43% of high school graduates, only 38% of students in 4-year colleges are. There are even more White students in teacher preparation programs (75%) than the broader college population,[44] and there are even more graduates—73% of White students finish their degree in 6 years, compared to 42% of Black students and 49% of Hispanic students.[45]

Kevin Rothman, principal of the Newburgh P-TECH, sees local evidence of a new-teacher pipeline lacking in diversity.

"I teach at a local college here, an education course, and it's not representative of our community," said Rothman, who is White. "They look like me, the students in my class."

Widening this pipeline is possible, and nonprofits, school districts, and states have found ways to do so by helping future teachers while they are in high school or community college, providing paid internships to student teachers, encouraging paraprofessionals and day care workers to become classroom teachers, creating alternate routes to teaching from other professions, providing tuition assistance and residencies, forgiving student loans, directing efforts specifically to men of color, and increasing teacher salaries (as of 2017, teachers earned 23% less per week than other college-educated workers, and the gap between them was growing).[46] The following descriptions of a sampling of such programs can be useful to districts everywhere, as they aim to build a teaching force that more closely resembles their students.

Starting in High School

Boston Public Schools, where 85% of the students are non-White,[47] employ a teaching force that is 37% non-White, and the district is trying to address the discrepancy. In 2015–2016, a quarter of new teachers were Black. The district's High School to Teacher program gives mentors, college prep courses, and 50% of college tuition to students

identified as potentially great future teachers. Of the young partici-
pants, 87% are Black or Latinx. If they succeed in their college work,
they are offered teaching jobs.[48]

Colorado has a similar Pathways2Teaching[49] program, a collaboration among several urban districts and the University of Colorado
Denver. It encourages non-White high school students to see teaching
as social justice work and a way to fight inequities in the schools. It offers up to nine college credits and school-based fieldwork to students,
60% of whom are Latinx, 35% of whom are Black, and 42% of whom
are male. Three rural districts in eastern Oregon have also adopted the
program.

It is worth noting that while P-TECH centers on the STEM fields,
there are two similar programs devoted to future educators: a P-TECH
in Dallas, and P-TEACH in the St. Vrain Valley Schools in Longmont,
CO.

In Dallas, the Bryan Adams P-TECH has a pathway to an early
childhood education degree that gives students the skills to be education leaders, partnering with Dallas College Eastfield Campus and the
Dallas Independent School District.[50] In Longmont, students can learn
about special education, early childhood, and cultural awareness in
the classroom; get field experience for college credit in district schools;
work with teacher mentors; and earn up to 21 college credits from
the University of Colorado Denver.[51] It hopes to inspire graduates to
return from college to teach locally.

In fact, many of P-TECH's STEM graduates have expressed interest in pursuing careers in teaching and school administration; most
of them are non-White and would be welcome in districts trying to
create a more diverse teaching staff. For similar programs to thrive,
a community college and a partner—such as a state government or
large school district—would need to provide mentoring, internships,
and a path to full-time employment, perhaps as paraprofessionals or
teaching aides, on a pathway to a 4-year teaching degree.

Working With College Students

Certificate programs and associate degrees in teacher education can
help address the shortages of teachers of color. One community college[52] saw its Black and Hispanic graduates completing their 4-year
degrees at the same rate as all students who had attended a 4-year
school for all 4 years, and at a higher rate than community college
students of the same races in all majors.[53]

In Illinois, where 1,800 teaching jobs went unfilled in 2019, enrollment in colleges of education fell by half in a decade.[54] Half the state's students were non-White, while only 15% of the teachers were. Golden Apple, a nonprofit organization, mentors and recruits high school seniors and college freshmen and sophomores to residency and licensure programs with tuition assistance, paid classroom experiences, job placement, and academic and social-emotional support. After the program's graduates get licensed, they commit to living and working in targeted school districts for 4 years. Half the program's alums are the first in their families to go to college, and more than half are non-White. The group also reaches out to college graduates without teacher education preparation who live in communities with teacher shortages.[55]

Virginia passed legislation allowing teachers to be licensed after earning a 4-year degree from an education school. As a result, the University of Virginia has accepted a number of racially diverse graduates of Tidewater Community College in Virginia Beach to earn their teaching degree at its Curry School. The superintendent of schools in Virginia Beach guarantees them jobs if they return there to teach.

It does not always take a large investment to help make the teaching staff more reflective of the community. In Hopkins, Minnesota, a state where only 5% of teachers are Black,[56] the district is hiring three student teachers from the public Metropolitan State University, the alma mater of the largest number of teachers of color in the state. Such funding would be helpful for the many students in teaching programs who find unpaid student teaching a hardship.

Elevating Aides and Workers From Nonprofits

School leaders can encourage and give incentives to teacher aides or paraprofessionals to pursue teaching credentials, and they can reach out to day care and after-school child-care providers as well, helping them get certified. In some districts, a high percentage of these workers are Black or Hispanic, and they are already familiar with the district's culture and students. For example, New Mexico's Grow Your Own Teachers Act set aside $6,000 scholarships per semester for paras who studied to become teachers while working.[57]

Education officials in South Dakota created a scholarship program for paras at schools with large Native American populations to help them finish college and get certified as teachers. This was part of an education package that included a half-cent sales tax increase that lifted the average teacher salary by $8,000, paid for a mentor program for new teachers, and created ways to make it easier for out-of-state teachers to work in South Dakota.[58]

Another potential pool of teacher recruits includes people working in nonprofit organizations, especially social services, mental health, and health care, who would consider a second career in teaching or guidance. Many nonprofit organizations are already engaged with schools in their communities, providing after-school, weekend, and summer programs. Other nonprofit organizations contract with municipal and state agencies to provide youth services, day care, and Head Start programs. To the extent that these workers are diverse, they can have the background and skills to become effective and more representative teachers.

Incentives such as tuition, pay for student teaching, relocation costs, and tax breaks could help increase the pipeline of potential school staff. They, like all new teachers, would require mentoring and support.

Second Career Teachers/Alternate Route

The Georgia Teacher Alternative Preparation Program has been able to attract a wide variety of applicants, including minorities.[59] It was created in response to a teacher shortage when, in the late 1990s, half of all new teachers were hired from out of state. The alternate program offers a summer course in teaching essentials and best practices, and then pays full teacher salaries to new teachers moving through the program, which offers additional supervision, support from mentors, and monthly seminars.

A national study published by Harvard Education Press found that alternate routes were particularly effective; the states that showed double-digit increases of minority teachers between 1993 and 2008 had used such programs.[60]

Near Retirees

Districts can find second-career teachers among qualified workers in the community who are near retirement age. IBM, for example, created a Transition to Teaching program for employees and executives with at least 10 years' experience, giving them up to $15,000 to obtain their teaching credentials and do student teaching. When they left the company, they could become public school teachers in the STEM fields, an area where teacher shortages have been common. Some had been enamored of a teaching career but had been unable to make the financial sacrifice to enter the profession earlier. They also received mentoring, support, and help from IBM in working with the HR departments of school districts. Since the program began in 2005, 100 IBM alums entered teaching.

Other businesses could follow suit, as could local governments and health systems. If information technology firms adopted this model, they could contribute expanded technology skills to the teaching force, for example. And they may find, as IBM did, a side benefit to the bottom line, in that such a program helps employees who are nearing retirement—often at the top of the pay scale—be more productive in their last year at the corporation, as they do not have to spend a great deal of time and energy planning what comes next. The pathway to teaching is a smooth one for them.

State Programs

States need to keep data, by race, about the number of teachers recruited, hired, and retained, with clear, attainable goals and timelines for improving educator diversity. States can use student loan forgiveness plans to attract minority teachers, as noted in Milwaukee, where undergraduates are offered up to $30,000 in loans to pursue teaching, with a quarter of the loan forgiven for each year the borrower teaches in a qualifying school district.[61] Nevada gives up to $24,000 in tuition assistance to future teachers who agree to teach for 3 years in a needy school, with preferences available to veterans, people experiencing poverty, and those studying subjects experiencing teacher shortages, such as special education.[62] The Education Trust and Teach Plus also recommend relocation incentives for new teachers.[63]

Men of Color

Some nonprofits are working specifically to encourage more men of color to become teachers. Man Up, a small Memphis-based organization, uses grants to pay for full-ride scholarships to master of education programs for Black and Hispanic men who commit to teaching for 5 years. The group also has plans to reverse the school-to-prison pipeline by providing training, teaching labs, and summer courses to men who have expungable misdemeanor offenses on their criminal

records and want to become teachers. The group cites research showing men are less likely to pursue teaching because of its low status as
a profession, low pay, and concern that they will be falsely accused of
wrongdoing while on the job.[64]

Retention

To be sure, hiring a diverse group of educators does not solve
everything. A school must have a culture of equity and inclusion to
help teachers feel welcome, valued, engaged, and therefore more in-
clined to stay for a long time. A qualitative study by the Education
Trust and Teach Plus found teachers of color often felt undervalued,
deprived of autonomy, and unwelcome in the cultures of the schools
where they worked.[65] Unfortunately, it often falls to teachers of color
to educate not just their students but their coworkers, principals, and
school parents.[66]

Currently Black teachers are more likely to change schools or
leave the teaching profession.[67] According to federal data from the
2012–2013 school year, about 22% of Black teachers, compared to
15% of White, non-Hispanic teachers, moved from their school or
from the profession.[68]

Researchers who focused on North Carolina schools surmised
that this could be because Black teachers tend to work in schools
with weaker principals and lower-quality mentoring and professional
development. When they stayed in the profession, they tended to
move to schools with better working conditions and more White
students.[69]

Black educators are more likely than White teachers to work in
challenging classrooms: 70% work in schools with a high percentage
of poor students,[70] while 30% of teachers of color work in charter
schools.[71] Some figures indicate Black teachers are a bit more likely to
stay in their classrooms in hard-to-staff schools[72] and those with more
Black students,[73] perhaps due to loyalty to them.

In any case, districts must create school cultures where teachers of
color want to stay and, if they wish, move up the career ladder to lead
schools. High teacher turnover rates are harmful to students, affect at-
risk students disproportionately, and are highest in schools where the
students are disproportionately low-income and non-White.[74] In fact,
students of color and ELLs are more likely than White students and
those whose first language is English to be taught by inexperienced,
uncertified, and underpaid teachers.[75]

Finally, it is important to note that if teaching staffs become more diverse in districts around the country, a proportionate number of people of color will likely rise into leadership roles on the school and district level, making schools even more welcoming to diverse staff members, and more likely to have a school culture that values them, benefiting students of all races and ethnicities.

LIFE AFTER SCHOOL

Beyond the doors of public schools, evidence of inequality is everywhere, with unemployment[76] at 12% for Whites and 16% for Blacks. Twenty-two percent of Blacks and 19% of Hispanics are poor, compared to 9% of Whites, according to 2018 figures.[77] As of 2017, the U.S. prison population was 33% Black, even though Blacks made up only 13% of the population. Hispanics made up 23% of the prison population, but only 16% of the general population.[78]

The pandemic has disproportionately affected workers with only high school diplomas, and workers of color, while it is widening the income gap based on race. These problems will likely intensify during the economic recovery, which is predicted to be lengthy.

That's wrong. Our institutions need to recognize racism for the cancer that it is and work to excise it. And our education system must be triaged first, as it is the institution with the greatest and earliest impact on children.

P-TECH AS A STEP TOWARD EQUITY

When creating the P-TECH model, we believed that a smooth, supported, and barrier-free path from 9th grade to career could begin to tackle the racial inequalities in high schools, community colleges, and workplaces. It is our greatest hope that by providing any student—not just those who pass certain tests—the option of an affordable, rigorous high school program leading directly to college and career, with high expectations and wraparound supports, we (or rather, they) can prove that every student can succeed. As school supporter Jeff Livingston wrote on the P-TECH Facebook page, "After seeing what P-TECH is able to do with its tough student body, continuing business as usual at the rest of the high schools in the city has moved from neglect to assault."[79]

P-TECH hardwired the goal of equity into its design and into its expansion efforts. In the following list, we describe some of the aspects of P-TECH that fight against inequity. The model works against the biases inherent in the education system by

- actively recruiting applicants,
- removing barriers to entry to its classes,
- providing rigorous and challenging coursework (see next chapter),
- recognizing the benefits of same-race teachers,
- recruiting and hiring teachers and leaders of color,
- working to retain them,
- removing roadblocks to college, and
- easing entry to the workplace.

The end results are schools that aim to fight the effects of racism as soon as they open. Mike Dardaris, former chief learning officer of the Hamilton Fulton Montgomery P-TECH in Johnstown, NY, had witnessed blatant prejudice in nearby Amsterdam, NY, against Latinx students, who were marginalized and subjected to stereotyping he found hard to believe.

"The kids came to us from that area, feeling that way about themselves, you could see the burden of it," he said. He was amazed to watch their transformation at P-TECH.

"Those kids outperformed, once they understood they could shake off that when they came in the doors," he said. "It was pretty amazing to watch."

Early results have shown that the model can help counter segregation in a public school system. Because students do not need to achieve a certain test score to enroll in P-TECH, their chances for future success do not hinge on entrance exams that tend to put impoverished students and students of color at a disadvantage.[80] Given its success with low-income students and students of color, the model could be directed purposefully for these students to reduce the achievement gap, or it could, by admitting students via a lottery, improve the prospects for whichever students express interest in it.

In 2019 in New York City, Stuyvesant High School, where admission is based solely on an exam, admitted only seven Black students to a freshman class of 895.[81] Keep in mind that 70% of the city's students are non-White. Conversely, in the first Brooklyn P-TECH, all the students were Black, Asian, or Hispanic, and 27% came from the lower third of their classes in 8th grade, were learning English, or had disabilities. Yet they completed community college on time at far higher rates than their peers did.[82]

Clearly, the city (and nation) can do well to examine entrance requirements that result in a population that does not reflect that of the students.

STUDENT RECRUITING AT P-TECH SCHOOLS

Because of its speedy ramp-up, the first P-TECH school had time to recruit its first class only at high school fairs for kids who had not been accepted in their first dozen high school choices, but its students were still able to thrive in the program. After the first cohort of students signed up, Principal Rashid Davis went door to door at the nearby housing project, encouraging residents to send their children to P-TECH, as the new school, with its innovative offerings, welcomed them.

Other schools in their start-up year may find themselves pressed for time in recruiting, but principals have managed to give presentations, sometimes offered in Spanish as well as in English, to their feeder middle schools. In Baltimore, Lori Bush, head of P-TECH at Carver Vocational-Technical High School, speaks to the parents or guardians of each student entering her program to be sure they are on board with the school's requirements, including occasional limits on participation in team sports and after-school activities. (Many coaches and advisors are able to work with P-TECH students to accommodate their schedules.)

Early on in her recruitment process, Bush lets prospective students know anything is possible. She asks the 8th-graders she visits, "Are you the same person you were in 6th grade?" When they say no, she says, "Who you are today is not who you are in 4 years. . . . You have the opportunity to change your story, to write your story and tell us who you want to be. This is your opportunity to do whatever it is you want to do."

In doing so, she hammers home the school's growth mindset, its credo that brains can grow, skills can be honed, and telling your own story is not only empowering, but actually enhances your achievement levels. Studies have indicated that simply having students write short exercises about their self-affirming values "invites students to acknowledge their self-worth, combating the corrosive effects of racial stereotypes," and "invites them to situate themselves on the path to belonging." In one study, such exercises had no effect on White students but helped Black and Latinx students excel, reducing the achievement gap by 40%.[83]

When P-TECH Norwalk had 6 months to launch, and, given the timing of summer break, even less time to recruit students, Principal Amaker scrambled to fill her classrooms, as she was beginning her recruitment efforts after many 8th-graders had already chosen their high schools. She held six conveniently located evening information sessions at the middle schools, City Hall, a church, a community center in a Spanish-speaking neighborhood where she had a translator, and, perhaps most important, the partnering Norwalk Community College. Representatives from the high school, college, and business partner (IBM) attended each session, and there were daytime sessions for students at their middle schools as well. The school passed out paper applications, which were also available online.

The session at the college had the largest turnout.

"It may have had to do with parents thinking that it wasn't just talk about students having access to college classes and accessing the resources at NCC," Amaker said.[84] "Being on the campus helped them to see their children as NCC students as well."

NO BARRIERS

Open enrollment is a central feature of the 6-year model. P-TECH students earn slots in the program by having the luck of being chosen in a lottery, not by having high grades, test scores, teacher recommendations, or vocal parent advocates—perks that often correlate with Whiteness and wealth. Much consideration went into this unbending rule.

We believe giving 8th-graders access to an innovative college and career program through any method other than by chance would be wrong, for reasons involving equity and justice, and for practical reasons that advance the development of broader school reforms.

Assigning spots in P-TECH to students based on their future promise, as measured in traditional ways, would give unfair advantage to well-supported students who are already well on their way to school success. That would not be just in a country where 8th-graders in the richest tenth of the population consistently perform 3 or 4 years ahead of those in the poorest tenth.[85]

Rising-star students as traditionally defined are more likely to have grown up in homes with two college-educated parents, lots of books, and access to tutors to help them do well in standardized tests, which often have inherent bias against at-risk students. Successful 8th-graders are also more likely to succeed in any high school setting, pre-prepped as they are for achievement. Inviting large numbers of them into innovative programs would be merely offering them a fourth or fifth potential path to college. We believe reserving rigorous, high-quality schools only for those who test well or have achieved earlier success merely continues decades of inequity.

More importantly, we see that kids considered "less than" readily meet these challenges and succeed on a par with their better-prepared peers. It is a waste of human potential to horde rigorous and supported schooling for the traditionally more privileged. Operating without a screening process provides broader opportunities more equitably across the population. Why keep such opportunities from students who, due to their circumstances, may not excel on entrance exams?

Students whom the system considers unsuccessful or mediocre are much more likely, statistically, to be in segregated, underfunded schools with high teacher turnover and lower-quality school leadership. These structural inequities have persisted for generations, through decades of generally ineffective efforts at integrating classrooms and improving low-performing schools. The students in such schools are more likely to be students of color, of low socioeconomic status, and doing poorly in middle school, and they are more likely to have single parents, parents who did not complete college, or parents whose first language is not English. The current system reinforces racial and ethnic barriers to high school success, college completion, and career preparedness.

At-risk students, we argue, should be the first to receive the benefits of innovative school improvement efforts. It is right to do so not only to address inequality but also to give important insights into the effectiveness of reforms.

What can we learn from a school improvement effort that garners high success rates among high-performing, handpicked students? How can we learn what aspects of that reform work when all cherry-picked students are likely to succeed in any classroom anyway? There would be scant evidence of the benefits of expanding the reform to a broader population —what could be learned about how it may or may not work for a wider variety of young people?

We concluded that a model that helped only those who did not need help would not be worth replicating. But if students are chosen randomly to be part of an innovative model, they can be compared to the instant control group of the rest of their district, and their success can more clearly be attributed to the unique aspects of their school. Soon after, education leaders expanding the program to other cities and towns have data backing up their odds of success, as well as clear reasons to believe it could work for their own students.

Few young people illustrate this point better than Oscar Tendilla, a graduate of the second cohort of students at the original P-TECH. Oscar, the son of Mexican immigrants with uncertain immigration status, had been earning grades of 55 out of 100—the lowest you could get and still pass—in his middle school, where he was bored and saw no connection between his classes and his future. He doubted his ability to succeed in high school, let alone college.

But during the first week of school, in geometry class, Oscar was the first to finish a problem set, and the teacher acted surprised he had finished so soon. After the teacher looked at Oscar's work, he recommended that he move over to the harder math class, Algebra 2 and Trigonometry.

"It made me realize I wasn't lacking in intelligence, like I thought I was," Oscar said. He graduated with his associate degree in a record 3½ years, was his class's valedictorian, and earned a full scholarship to Cornell. His mother earned her high school equivalency diploma the same month Oscar graduated.

Early on, Davis had thought P-TECH would set entry requirements for students, and when he mentioned that to Oscar at one point, the student's response intrigued him.

"Well, you wouldn't have students like me," he recalls Oscar saying. "I was a horrible middle school student."

It was an a-ha! moment for Davis.

"We created a culture to allow him to believe in himself, and see the value of access for all," he said.

Davis found it interesting that only half of his students had put P-TECH in their top choices. Many ended up at the school thanks to the city's school assignment algorithm, which weighs the student's top choices, location, and availability of seats. Still, they were able to do well and to benefit from the focus on technology, which can be applied to careers in a variety of fields. Oscar, for example, first planned on studying to be a vet in college, a STEM career, but now wants to go into teaching; in both professions, he could use his technical skills and degree. Throughout the P-TECH network, many students are not committed to joining the specific field the model schools offer degrees in, but they still benefit from the rigorous preparation and free degree.

Another Brooklyn student, Amalik Morille, used to make fun of the lottery admission process, and he told Davis he could have saved himself from having to deal with some misbehavior if he had just screened students for admission.

"He didn't, and I respect him for that," Amalik said. "His philosophy is everyone should have this chance. He knew he was offering a specialized high school level of education, even beyond that, and he did not put a stigma on anybody," he said, referring to specialized city schools filled via competitive entrance exams. "He didn't care what type grades people have beforehand. Everybody was welcome."

Around the country, other P-TECHs have embraced open enrollment. In Dallas, the 18 fully subscribed P-TECH schools, as well as other early college programs, are designed for students who would be first-generation college students "and have been historically underrepresented in higher education."[86]

Students are selected by lottery at the Goode STEM Academy in Chicago, and any students on the waiting list are likewise chosen that way if spots free up.

"It's very transparent," said Rodriguez.

Similarly, at the P-TECH at Skyline High School in Longmont, CO, where 110 students applied for 55 seats in 2019–2020, the entering class was chosen with equity in mind. Student applications got extra points if neither parent had attended college, if the students had good attendance ("we want kids that show up," said P-TECH Administrator Greg Stephens), and if recommendations were received from teachers and counselors about a student's motivations, ability to collaborate, and other factors. The incoming class was exactly who the administrators were hoping for—at least three quarters of the students had been failing middle school.

"What we see in 9th grade, when they feel part of a community, all that stuff kind of goes away," Stephens said. "They kind of have a new life, a new beginning. We don't look before 9th grade. We live in the present here. We start new. As long as you put in the right effort and work, we will be there for you, to help you be successful."

Nationally, research has shown that many worries about lowering barriers to school entry are unfounded. Studies of very selective schools in Boston and New York found a "precisely zero effect of the exam schools on college attendance, college selectivity, and college graduation."[87]

Chicago is one of the few cities that has created a more equitable weighing of factors, including socioeconomic status, in choosing students for its selective schools.[88] But overall, selective high schools perpetuate segregation.

In the Brooklyn P-TECH, all the students have been Black, Hispanic, or Asian. It has one of the highest percentages of Black male students of any school in the city. In Chicago, the Goode STEM Academy is 61% Hispanic, 38% Black, and 88% low-income, and it has a 97% graduation rate.[89] Other P-TECH schools have included more students of color than their districts' overall population.

In addition, immigration status is not a barrier to entry into the 6-year program. A significant number of U.S. students have Dreamer status, under the DACA program, and they have fared well in the coursework, even winning college scholarships. Some schools have been welcoming to their families as well—the first Brooklyn P-TECH held workshops with IBM lawyers to help family members complete their immigration paperwork, and IBM held career workshops for parents there as well, where the corporate partner helped parents find jobs.

TEACHER RECRUITING AT P-TECH

Many P-TECH schools are led by principals of color, and they and their peers have worked to build a diverse staff. But they need help from all levels of education, including the pipeline of new teachers.

Almost all P-TECH schools are schools within schools. Some principals employ teachers already working in the parent school, some are able to hire their own teachers and support staff, and some use the guidance counselors and support staff of the parent school. They understand the value of teachers, staff, business liaisons, and mentors who resemble their students.

In Norwalk, Karen Amaker said nine of her 24 teachers are non-White, and all her science department teachers are women, including a Black engineering teacher with a master's degree. She has found that the school's innovations make recruiting easier.

"The folks coming to us are choosing us," she said, and are therefore self-selecting as people attracted to innovation, with ambitions to build out a new school. "We're so fortunate to have these amazing people, 10 new teachers who are tech savvy, hungry, thirsty, new to the field, not jaded, and working so well, collaboratively, with the old guard really pushing for the new agenda we have."

P-TECH principals have other ways to ensure that their students have diverse adults in their school lives. Stephens of the school-within-a-school P-TECH at Skyline High School, said, "One place we can control is with mentorships, and being strategic in how we set up those, and the opportunities those mentors can open up for our students." The students are primarily Latinx, and it is helpful to have Latinx mentors to describe their own paths through school and into the working world.

P-TECH TEACHER RETENTION

Rothman of the Newburgh P-TECH is delighted that his teaching staff of 10 has remained constant, with only one teacher leaving in its first 7 years. His teachers all had 5 to 10 years of experience, and they relish having the chance to innovate.

"I think this is a way to motivate mid-career teachers, and I say it to anyone who will listen," he said. "This is more agile than traditional educational models, and it's motivating." Staff members there have also enjoyed having the same students as freshmen and again as upperclassmen, which helps them know their students better.

"They're having consistent conversations from 9th grade through freshman college English," he added. "We're a team. We talk a lot."

In Brooklyn, the original P-TECH's teachers logged the second-best attendance rate of any city school, and Cheree Macdonald, the lead teacher at the P-TECH in Ballarat, Australia, called her work "addictive," saying it helped her stay engaged with teaching. "I thought I would be shifting careers right now," she said.

REMOVING ROADBLOCKS TO COLLEGE

Students of color have, more than their White counterparts, faced the challenge of needing noncredit-bearing but expensive remedial courses in college, which harms their chances of graduating on time, if at all. By preparing P-TECH students for and supporting them in their college studies, these model schools have helped remove a barrier to college that has cost other new college students a great deal of time, effort, heartache, and expense.

Most P-TECH students are either non-White, the first in their families to attend college, or economically disadvantaged, and their successes in college classes while still in high school shows they can overcome some of the inequities in the transition from secondary school to college. If we as a society agree that the income gaps among the races are unacceptable, one way to begin to erase them is to make sure Black and Latinx college students graduate from high school *and* college. One way to do that, central to P-TECH's mission, is to ensure that no incoming community college students require remedial courses. P-TECH has promised its college partners that none of its students would need remedial classes, and it meets that pledge through supporting students conscientiously throughout high school with tutoring, mentoring, and monitoring (see Chapter 5).

Sending only certain students to remedial classes is demoralizing and labels them in front of their peers as "not good enough." We believe a more general summer bridge program for rising community college students would be more effective, equipping them with college study skills and providing review sessions and tutoring to prepare them for credit-bearing coursework. We discuss this and other possible solutions in the next chapter.

TEARING DOWN WALLS AROUND THE WORKPLACE

Racial inequity also infects the highest levels of the business world. As noted above, the senior leadership at technology giants Facebook, Google, and Microsoft is less than 4% Black.[90] In addition, the pipeline of employees on various levels, from new hires to the C-suite, needs to reflect the country's population better.

"Coming from the perspective of a Black male, I look around the table and do not always see a lot of people that look like me in corporate America," said Jason Mudd, an IBM director who has overseen P-TECH interns. He enjoys working with them in part because he sees them both as talented future coworkers and as part of a solution to segregation in the workplace.

"The future talent, the diverse talent, the skills set, that's a very, very powerful value proposition," he said, adding, "From the human perspective, it's just the right thing to do."

Other companies are also trying to do the right thing. To address inequalities in the New York City workforce in 2020, 27 technology and banking firms, led by Jamie Dimon, the head of JPMorgan Chase, vowed to hire 100,000 low-income workers of color in a decade.[91]

Their work would be far easier if more schools worked with businesses and higher education to ensure that they could provide students with the skills needed in jobs available now. Hiring 100,000 underprivileged New Yorkers into low-wage jobs without room for advancement might be a benevolent gesture, but bringing on employees of color who are mentored, supported, trained, and promoted is far better. And onboarding 100,000 graduates of public high schools prepared with 2-year degrees and relevant work skills and experience could boost the chances that these companies and, eventually, their leaders, could fully represent the city they call home.

Nationally, IBM's former CEO Ginni Rometty and former Merck CEO Kenneth Frazier have helped launch OneTen, a group of 37 CEOs promising to hire, train, and promote 1 million Black workers in the next decade.[92] While CEO, Rometty spoke frequently at international tech conferences and national gatherings about the school model with students at her side; her leadership in OneTen will likely spread the lessons learned from P-TECH, which she considers one of her most meaningful legacies.

We hope the talented graduates of P-TECH can play a significant role in making firms in STEM fields and elsewhere more diverse. The more than 100 P-TECH graduates who have been hired by IBM and other partners in Brooklyn, Chicago, Newburgh, Dallas, and Syracuse are overwhelmingly young men and women of color. Some of these new employees, often with just 2 years of college, are already rising through the ranks of their firms into management positions, as they were prepared with the exact hard and soft skills the companies needed.

Looking at corporate America more broadly, we see how the P-TECH model can address the injustices of degree inflation, when an employer requires a higher degree for a job than it really needs. Because members of minority groups are less likely to attain higher degrees than White people are, this contributes to inequity in hiring and, by default, in income.

A Harvard Business School study showed that two-thirds of the postings for jobs as production supervisors, for example, called for a

4-year degree, while only 16% of people with that title actually held a bachelor's degree.[93] When just over a quarter of Black workers 25 and older have such degrees, such hiring prerequisites discriminate against them, reducing their chances of employment needlessly.[94]

The National Bureau of Economic Research (NBER) studied people who had high school diplomas but no bachelor's degrees and found 71 million—60% of the workforce—fit that description.[95] Many African Americans had gained the skills for high-paid work, either on the job or by completing some college, but were held back by employers requiring a 4-year degree. P-TECH's focus on jobs requiring only 2-year degrees can help its minority graduates gain toeholds in the business world that might otherwise be unavailable to them while making it easier for companies to become more representative of the country.

TAKEAWAYS

For States

In its reports on teacher diversity, the Education Trust urges states to provide data to districts and principals about how staff diversity reflects (or doesn't reflect) the student body, why, and how this affects students. States should set specific goals, with deadlines, for enhancing staff diversity.[96] States should also ensure that districts with a preponderance of students of color and those whose families are less wealthy should have access to strong teachers.[97] For example, Mississippi gave itself 5 years to send 25% more teachers of color to districts with critical shortages.

States should also require their educator preparation programs to have their students and graduates reflect the general population, as well as to prepare teachers to educate all groups of students.[98] For example, Rhode Island's strategic plan for public schools for 2015–2020 focuses on "recruiting educators who are culturally diverse" and keeping track of the number of diverse graduates of educator preparation programs.[99]

Creating additional P-TECH schools can be particularly valuable for students of color and students of lower socioeconomic status, and other states should be encouraged to open such schools for their students. This can be done strategically to reach populations that would benefit most. In New York State, for instance, where Governor Andrew

Cuomo made replicating P-TECH a priority, participating districts were required to serve low-income, non-White students. Maryland, Rhode Island, and Colorado, and several countries, used New York's request for proposal as a basis for theirs. The model has by no means been reserved just for students of color, as there are White students in some P-TECHs in a variety of regions, but directing model schools to low-income districts, as several governors have done, has resulted in a large percentage of non-White graduates.

For Districts

School boards and district leaders need to prioritize equity, inclusion, and hiring of diverse staff. They should keep and publicize records of the race and ethnicity of the people they interview, hire, retain, and promote in their schools.

District human relations staff should forge relationships with HBCU and with public universities with large populations of minority students potentially interested in teaching.

Districts should work with principals to strengthen their managerial skills, to help retain teachers of color.

Districts should use student selection models that work to promote equity—by pure lottery, as used in most P-TECHs as well as in many thoughtfully designed, inner-city charter schools—or by taking a number of students from each catchment district for geographic and socioeconomic diversity.

In addition, paying teachers more competitive wages could draw more diverse people into the profession. Resources should be invested strategically in schools with the most urgent needs for prepared, supported, and diverse teachers.[100] A failed 2018 California bill proposed tax credits to help new teachers pay for the costs of getting certified; it would have provided income tax breaks to teachers working at least a decade in high-poverty schools.[101] And raises across the board could help attract more people to the teaching profession.

For Principals

School leaders have a variety of steps they can take to ensure that their staff and students reflect the socioeconomic and racial makeup of their communities, much of which can be done without additional expense.

- Determine openings early—start hiring in March instead of June.
- When recruiting diverse students to promising programs, make sure all eligible students know what the school offers and how to apply by giving presentations to all middle schools in convenient locations at a variety of times to accommodate working parents and in commonly used languages or with translators available.
- Mentor new teachers and provide high-quality staff development to reduce turnover, particularly among new teachers of color.

CHAPTER 4

Rigorous Coursework Designed With College and Career in Mind

I've been at Skyline a long time, and we've tried so many alternative programs for at-risk, underrepresented populations. The thing we always missed—and P-TECH helped me believe this—is we never tied a high-level curriculum to it. We never had the expectations of being great, of doing really difficult work and doing a good job at that. We cared a lot, we loved those kids a lot, but I'm not sure how much good we did for those kids to prepare them for the real world. What P-TECH taught me was that the component we were missing was a high-level curriculum and high-level expectations, where we expect the kids to meet them every day.

—Greg Stephens, P-TECH administrator,
Skyline High School, Longmont, CO

The need for high school graduates to be ready both to start and complete college *and* to join the work world was the central catalyst for the creation of the P-TECH model. The schools offer engaging, challenging courses and impart important workplace skills for a course of study that guides and prepare students from high school to college degree to career. Academic courses and workplace skills are not mutually exclusive; in fact, they are most effective when intertwined. Unlike other Career and Technical Education programs, P-TECH places college completion as a primary goal with academics center stage.

When students are challenged and they see their work as relevant and building toward an engaging future, they are more likely to take school seriously and excel, in any setting. We dismiss their dignity and their futures if we fail to engage them in the classroom, if we patronize them with dull and overly simple work, and if we neglect to inform them of the wide range of opportunities they can reap if they gain specific skills and credentials.

In the United States, students' inability to finish college is one of the most pressing challenges to our education system. When less than two-thirds of all students entering 4-year degree programs graduate in 6 years, and just over one-third aiming for 2-year degrees get them in that time,[1] it appears our elementary and secondary schools are poorly preparing their students and setting them up for failure that is expensive, demoralizing, and life-limiting. We must keep in mind that the quality of high school curriculum has more impact than any other factor on a student's chances of finishing college.[2]

Currently, 60% of 2-year college students[3] and 20% of 4-year college students[4] require remedial classes, which do not count toward their degrees and are expensive both for the students and the schools. Spending for remediation for students on the college registers exceeded $7 billion as of 2012.[5] Less than half of remedial students ever earn college credits, and less than a tenth finish their degrees on time.[6]

"Remedial courses are a challenge for students," said Cass Conrad, the former dean of K–16 initiatives at CUNY, who was part of the Brooklyn school's planning committee. "They have to spend the money and time, the coursework itself is often not what the student is interested in, and it's a huge barrier for students. In general, we as a university are working on a whole strategy to reduce the number who start in remediation."

In New York City, at least 43% of students entering community college had to take remedial courses. Students whose families are poor and/or non-White take more remedial courses, which severely limits their college completion rates.

Our high schools, clearly, are failing our students. If parents were paying for test-preparation courses that failed at such a rate, you can be sure they would find better ones. Unfortunately, many high school students are not able to shop around for a course that prepares them to enter and complete college. P-TECH's premise is that all students will graduate with a 2-year degree, ready to succeed in a specific, available job or a 4-year college.

In this chapter, we discuss how challenging and relevant coursework, combined with workplace skills, helps students succeed and progress to the next stages of their lives and careers. We discuss how the P-TECH model does this, and we explore the strengths of other tough programs, such as Advanced Placement (AP) classes, the International Baccalaureate (IB), and early college dual enrollment programs, where some, usually not all, students take individual college courses in high school. We explore how many advanced programs do not yet reach non-White and poor students in an equitable manner and how to address that. And we describe P-TECH's rigor and results, plus the specific ways P-TECH educators make the model work. Altogether, 6-year high school allows for a more seamless transition to the college classroom, college diploma, and workplace. Of course, as we will discuss in the following chapter, such rigor is only fair and effective when coupled with support for the students as they travel the pathway.

THE PERILS OF REMEDIAL COLLEGE WORK

It is unfair and damaging to students to let them graduate from high school unprepared for college. Looking at the racial breakdown of students in remedial classes, we see an all-too-familiar pattern with 64% of White students taking such classes, 75% of Latinx students, and 78% of Black students, and completion rates are far worse for non-White and poor students.[7]

Research is beginning to show that remedial education in college is counterproductive, in that it stigmatizes and discourages students who feel labeled as not good enough for college. The methods for assigning students to their first college courses have been unscientific and harmful. A 2012 NBER study found that when colleges use entrance tests to determine placement, a quarter of math students and a third of English students were sent to the wrong first college course, more often to too-easy remediation than to too-difficult, credit-bearing courses. When colleges use high school grades and tests, placement errors went down significantly, fewer students were sent to remedial courses, yet they succeeded nonetheless. The study also found some entrance tests resulted in classes that were imbalanced according to race and gender.[8]

Encouraging alternative approaches to traditional remediation are emerging. SUNY, for example, under the leadership of Senior Vice Chancellor Johanna Duncan-Poitier, has adopted a suite of innovative math courses known as Quantway and Statway in all 30 of its community colleges. Developed by the Carnegie Foundation for the Advancement of Teaching, Quantway, a one- or two-term class, provides algebraic reasoning skills for students moving into college-level algebra or transferring into a STEM field, while Statway provides statistical reasoning skills used for decisionmaking in uncertainty.[9] They are often presented as "corequisite" courses, taken for credit by students who might not otherwise be considered ready for college math. Students in such classes have fared significantly better than students in traditional remedial math classes.

Other community colleges have stopped offering remedial classes, instead providing tutoring, summer programs, and other supports to incoming students who need an academic boost before tackling college-level work.

To address student preparedness, more advanced coursework must be made available to high school students, particularly those who are poor and non-White. In fact, for Black and Latinx students aiming to graduate from college, a "high school curriculum of high academic intensity and quality" has more positive impact than anything else, and it has a far higher impact on them than on White students.[10]

The U.S. Department of Education found that of high schools serving the highest percentage of non-White students, about a quarter do not even offer Algebra 2, even though most college-level courses require it.[11] No wonder students languish in remedial college courses, as they lack the high school preparation they needed.

OTHER OPPORTUNITIES FOR ADVANCED WORK

While we believe P-TECH has many advantages over AP and other advanced courses, as it leads directly to a college degree instead of just a few college credits for individual classes, we also urge the expansion of more rigorous courses for all. AP courses are required to be offered in eight states and the District of Columbia,[12] and more states should follow suit. The New York State Education Department, for example, is investing in online AP courses for students in schools without enough AP teachers or smaller schools that have limited access to the courses.[13]

While 87% of school districts offer some form of these courses,[14] according to research by the Education Trust, more than 500,000 poor and non-White students are missing from U.S. IB Programme and AP courses.[15] If schools successfully encouraged all those students to participate in these rigorous classes, it could close the racial participation gap completely and close 90% of the socioeconomic gap, according to those findings.

States, districts, and individual schools can work toward this goal, and they can start by collecting and publishing data on which groups of students take advanced courses, then, if necessary, create and work toward public goals for a more equitable mix. In Federal Way, WA, for instance, the board, superintendent, and teachers worked together to offer open access to AP and IB classes, and then automatically enrolled students in them who had scored as proficient on common exams.

Under the earlier system, when students had to apply and collect their own teacher recommendations, fewer participated. Principals worked with teachers and parents to address their concerns about the possibility that students would need much more help, and school leaders provided instructional coaching to help teachers with the new challenge. One student reported feeling "like I had a special glow, and I could do anything, even AP." In other schools trying to open up the AP program, teachers expressed confidence in students who had mild doubts about taking an AP course. The teachers showed the students they were willing to support them in more challenging work.

Advanced Placement Courses

Currently, Black and Latinx students are underrepresented in AP courses—nationally, only 9% of Black students took AP classes.[16] Of students who signed up to take at least one AP class, 54.9% were White, 21.4% were Latinx, 10.7% were Asian, and 9.4% were Black, as of 2015–2016,[17] with non-White students underrepresented compared to their portion of the whole student body. If their share of AP enrollment reflected their school enrollment, there would be 157,513 more Black AP students and 68,102 more Latinx AP students.[18] This could stem in part from their inequitable representation in 8th-grade Algebra I classes, although one study found non-White students pass that course at the same rates as White students.[19] Taking that class in middle school has traditionally been a near-requirement for reaching calculus in high school, a prerequisite for many higher-level STEM classes. Yet schools that serve mostly non-White students offer fewer advanced classes,[20] and even in schools where there are plentiful offerings, non-White students are not well represented.

As of 2016, only Arkansas, Connecticut, the District of Columbia, Indiana, Iowa, Louisiana, Mississippi, South Carolina, and West Virginia required schools to provide AP courses.[21] Of all AP tests, only 5.8% were taken by Black students. Of students becoming eligible for college credit through their AP scores, only 2.6% were Black, as were only 1.2% of students scoring a 5 out of 5.[22]

In New York City, the AP for All initiative aimed to convince each city high school to offer at least five AP courses, and between 2017 and 2018, the number of students taking AP exams rose 11.4%.[23] In 2016, Washington, D.C., began requiring each high school to provide at least eight such courses. In Baltimore, where nine high schools offered no AP courses in 2018, the goal is six in each city high school.[24] And after the White Plains School District in New York removed the application process for AP courses, more students and more non-White students took the classes.

In New Jersey, one district created a summer AP preparation program for first-time AP students, one simply eliminated an honors course in a subject and made the AP course the only option, and another built a new science lab to accommodate more AP students.[25]

While such district- or citywide programs are laudable and need to spread further, it is just as critical for each school to work hard to recruit the students who have too long been missing from AP classes. Facing declining enrollment, Corbett High School, in a rural area near Portland, OR, decided to require every student to take six AP courses.[26] Most now take 10. The rigorous curriculum attracted out-of-district students from great distances, 65% of graduating seniors passed at least one AP test, and suspensions fell from 200 to 6 in a few years.[27] But the reform did not meet with universal approval, as some parents felt it left students without time to do extracurricular activities.

St. Vrain Valley School District in Longmont, CO, home of four P-TECHs, has worked hard to increase participation in its AP classes. At Skyline High School, an AP coordinator visits each classroom early in the year to recruit students for next year's AP classes, with the goal of each taking at least one such course before graduation.[28] At the high school, where 64% of the students are non-White, primarily Hispanic,[29] any student who wants to take an AP class can, as there are no prerequisites. The district supports its AP students with Saturday study sessions and opportunities to take practice AP exams to be better prepared. That is a laudable start. AP enrollment went up by 50% since 2004, and enrollment by non-White students went up by 80%. Skyline High School boasted 797 AP enrollments, which is 55% more than in 2014.

The College Board, which administers AP tests, sells Pre-AP Program course curriculum and offers a useful free timeline for any school to organize steps toward greater student participation.[30] It includes a summer Equity Audit by the counseling staff of how

AP and honors enrollment compares to the overall school enrollment by race, gender, and ethnicity; a fall faculty meeting to discuss the results; shared autumn reading by the Parent Teacher Student Association about equity issues; winter focus groups for pre-AP students; and then active marketing by counseling staff in the winter to encourage students to enroll in the more difficult classes for the following year.

Students themselves have also taken the lead in fighting for rigorous coursework of interest to them. For example, students and staff of the Brooklyn Preparatory High School created a national petition[31] that has garnered more than 29,000 signatures so far asking for two new AP classes in African Civilizations and African American History.

Of course, advocating only for more students of color to take AP tests is meaningless—even damaging—without supporting students to succeed. As of 2016, only 30% of Black students and 43% of Hispanic students passed their AP tests.[32] Relevant to the population generally served by P-TECH, of everyone who took the AP Computer Science exam in 2007, only 2% were Black, and they scored the equivalent of a letter grade and a half lower than White students.[33] The education and support students of color receive leading up to high school and advanced testing must be of higher caliber, or we risk setting them up for failure.

International Baccalaureate Programmes

About 1,500 public schools in the United States offer an International Baccalaureate (IB) programme.[34] For high schools, the IB Diploma Programme is a rigorous 2-year course emphasizing critical thinking, global study, multilingualism, writing, and community service. Some colleges recognize an IB diploma for credit.

In 2005, the programme acknowledged that students enrolling tended to be White and were wealthier as compared to the broader population.[35] By 2015, however, the organization reported that 60% of schools offering the IB programme were Title I schools (serving low-income students) as are 68% of all schools.[36]

The IB programme has shown great success with its Black students, 87% of whom go on to enroll in college, a higher rate than any other racial or socioeconomic cohort in the program, and far higher than the 57% rate for Black students in regular high school programs.[37] And 84% of low-income IB graduates enroll in college, the same rate as well-off White students from regular high schools. While these figures

reinforce our argument that rigorous coursework is helpful to traditionally underserved students, schools using the IB curriculum choose
independently how to enroll students, either enrolling everyone or
requiring them to pass a test. Statistics are not available for compar-
ing schools that use tests with those that don't, so it is not possible
to compare the IB's results with P-TECH's. To the extent IB students
enter the programme without barriers, it can have encouraging results
with students of color, and it should be expanded to far more schools
in order to reach more students.

Other Early College High Schools

Of the 24,000 public high schools in the United States,[38] about 300
are early college high schools, offering students enrollment both in
their high school and in an affiliated college, where they can take
courses for credit. More than a fifth of these students earn enough
credit for an associate degree.[39] In 2013, a study by the American
Institutes for Research found that after 6 years, 29% of early college
students earned such a degree, compared to 11% of a control group.[40]
Students of color and students who are economically disadvantaged
have been shown to benefit even more from dual enrollment programs
than White and well-off students,[41] but a study[42] by Wheelhouse, the
Center for Community College Leadership and Research, found that
of the 13% of high school students participating in dual enrollment
programs, 19% are Asian, 14% are White, 11% are socioeconomically
disadvantaged, 11% are Latinx, and only 9% are Black.

The Bill and Melinda Gates Foundation invested heavily in the
early college model and later found that, compared to a control group,
students in the program were more likely to graduate from high school
(86% vs. 81%) and enroll in college (80% vs. 71%).[43] The impacts
were stronger for minority students, female students, and students
achieving well in middle school. A study by the Community College
Research Center at Teachers College found that 88% of students in
dual enrollment programs went on to 2- or 4-year colleges.[44] And, as
we have seen at P-TECH schools, where the goal for every student is
an associate degree, students who were also enrolled in college had
better high school attendance, lower suspension rates, and higher
levels of engagement.[45] Early college programs, like other advanced
opportunities, would do well to work harder in recruiting and supporting underserved student groups in order to open these opportunities more broadly.[46]

CLASS SCHEDULING THAT ENHANCES RIGOR

P-TECH schools use various techniques to help students thrive in a challenging curriculum. Many model schools use block programming to fit in as many requirements as possible early in high school. In Chicago, for example, the Goode STEM Academy students would take only four classes a semester, each worth double credit. This allowed them to earn eight credits, while their peers in other high schools were earning seven. It allowed them to reach junior status in the second half of their sophomore year, helping them qualify for college early. Such front-loaded schedules leave room for students to retake classes if necessary and still graduate on time.

Joel Duran, from the Brooklyn P-TECH, learned early on that the work was hard, but failure was not the end of the road. He had to take the math Regents three times to qualify for college coursework, missing the passing score by 1 point the second time. He took advantage of tutoring, and he had to retake one math class. He hated seeing freshmen in his class when he was a sophomore, but he qualified for City Tech math that year. His color photo, with "College Ready" under it, went up on a poster over the lockers in the halls of P-TECH, joining dozens of others.

Such rigor at the flagship P-TECH school started to show results early. A study of the program by the MDRC, the nonprofit education and anti-poverty research firm, showed that 42% of the Brooklyn school's students had qualified to take college courses by passing Regents exams, compared to 25% of their peers in other schools.[47] They were also more likely to earn job-related credits than their peers, but not at the expense of core academic credits.

In P-TECH schools such as those in New Brunswick, NJ, and Norwalk, CT, students can begin earning community college credits as early as the summer bridge program before 9th grade or during freshman year, while most P-TECH students can take college courses as high school sophomores.

At P-TECH, we have seen how young people enjoy prestige among their peers when they can attend college classes early on. In New Brunswick, rising freshmen get their own Middlesex County College email addresses almost immediately, and they have college instructors in their summer school. In Chicago, on the first day of class at Sarah E. Goode STEM Academy, when entering students were told they were already in college, their faces reflected a mixture of shock and joy.

PEDAGOGY AT P-TECH

To perfect this new model, educators at P-TECH schools have had to create their own philosophies and practices. Beyond adopting the universal premise that every child can succeed and graduate with a high school diploma and 2-year degree in 6 years, P-TECH teachers have developed ways to impart workplace skills, encourage project-based learning, create bridges across subject areas, and make lessons relevant to each other and to college courses and the world of work. A great P-TECH teacher has different goals from other secondary school teachers, as the lens is longer—what's important is not just this class, but the longer pathway that moves through high school to college to the workplace.

In addition, because many students in the program may not have been fully prepared for or accustomed to advanced classes, teachers in all subject areas have to find a balance between toughness and understanding. "All in all, it takes somebody extremely empathetic and compassionate, and willing to hold the line to hold kids accountable," said Greg Stephens, of Skyline High School. "Especially if you're a newer teacher and err on the side of too much caring, you might let things slide a little. But that accountability has to go hand in hand with expectations."

P-TECH students follow the same curriculum as regular high school students, and they take the same state tests and meet the basic diploma requirements for arts classes, foreign languages, and science. If the model had required a different curriculum, it would never have gone to scale, as any changes to established courses outside state standards could take decades. Instead, teachers approach each class with an eye toward what workplace skills they can share, be it clear writing, critical thinking, teamwork, problem solving, or giving presentations. In some schools, a workplace skills teacher delivers an elective class on such issues, but even in those cases, each subject matter teacher aims to touch on such skills in every lesson. This in-school teaching is reinforced when a student interacts with mentors, visits workplaces, and holds internships (see Chapter 6), where he or she can see workplace skills in action.

"We constantly remind them how important each day is to their future goals," said Eric Waliszewski, the math and workplace learning teacher at the Newburgh P-TECH. "We emphasize setting weekly goals and weekly reflection on those goals to hammer home the point that they are working toward a fulfilling career each and every day.

But it can be a slow process. For many, this is the first time they've thought about it."

Dardaris, formerly of the Johnstown, NY, P-TECH, has thought about what the model's teachers need for success:

> You have to be extremely flexible. At our school you had to believe in project-based learning and honestly believe in the model. If you don't believe in the students, the students that New York has deemed at-risk, they're like bees and dogs who can smell fear. They can smell disbelief; they can smell when you're patronizing. If you're that, you can't be here. You've got to believe every kid is a Rhodes Scholar, the next president, or finding a cure for cancer. If you don't really believe it, you've got to go isolate yourself in a classroom somewhere else. We start every faculty meeting that way.
>
> You have to be coachable, open to new ideas, and willing to practice. You've got to be resilient, because projects will fail. You'll have to look at it and say, that's ok, we'll keep two things and start over, or start from scratch next year. You have to be that kind of person who has love for kids and willingness to work with a population that's underrepresented. These aren't kids who come in always ready to learn. But they have so much potential that they typically outperform everybody else.

Gina Bruno, who teaches social studies at the P-TECH in New Brunswick, NJ, has learned that working with the new model requires patience, and the secret superpower of helping kids be patient as well. While each student is expected to excel, he or she does not have to ace everything on the first attempt. Success is cumulative. Bruno explained that when a school accepts students by lottery, success at first may mean getting a student who had failed history last year to pass it. A P-TECH educator will often tell students they are starting with a clean slate.

"I don't know what teachers they had, what their life situation was and why that impacted them," she said. "Maybe they had history first period, but now they're getting their lives together. There are so many factors that go into adolescents and how they learn. Flexibility is the key, and the understanding that it might take one student longer to get them where you need them to get." So, if a student needs to retake a quiz or come in for extra help four times a week, that is expected and fine.

"Rigor doesn't always mean the same thing for every kid," she said. It might mean writing five paragraphs, or 10 pages, or just getting homework in on time. "Offering that flexibility," she said, "that's a game changer for a lot of kids. It allows them to feel human. They make a mistake, and that's when their learning can really take off."

TRYING NEW METHODS

The ability to pivot is required of any teacher in a new program, and new methods often spring up when established ones fail, especially with accelerated coursework.

Jamilah Seifullah, for instance, remembers how Davis at the Brooklyn P-TECH wanted as many students as possible to start college math in 10th grade. To achieve this, they agreed she would teach her students who had passed Algebra 1 in 8th grade 90 minutes of Geometry, followed by 90 minutes of Algebra 2 and Trigonometry.

"I started realizing no matter how engaging and interesting I thought I was, 3 hours of math for 13- and 14-year-olds was not that interesting. . . . We had to be creative in different things," she said, noting how another staff member would get permission to take students off-campus briefly for snacks in between sessions. Seifullah would rearrange the furniture every day for variety, and she would have half the students working on computers on their own, and give more support to the other half, where students were teaching each other. That was her way of getting students to learn the concepts better, while getting practice in the workplace skill of giving presentations and communicating clearly. As a variation of the "see one, do one, teach one" method used in training new surgeons, having students teach a lesson ensured that they gained a deeper understanding of their material.

"I assigned them standards," she said. "I would work with them and make sure they were being accurate. I served as moral support, and they completely respected each other, and they still listened to me," she said. In such exercises, the stronger students can advance faster than they would have otherwise, as, in some views, you really do not know something until you teach it to someone else. And the weaker students learn the material more thoroughly because they had to learn the information as well as prepare to share it.

"I think that when people walked in, they wouldn't see me, they would always see students teaching each other, in every class. It freed me up to do so much more. Teachers are always very wary of trying it," she said.

The students welcomed the chance to teach, as well. "I think students need to be challenged," she said. "They want to be challenged, knowing there's something they're fighting towards."

All of her students passed their Geometry Regents exams, and most passed the Algebra 2 and Trigonometry exam.

One visitor to Seifullah's class, then president Barack Obama, saw her interdisciplinary teaching methods at work. When he visited the school in 2013, she set up three workstations and let her students lead the lessons. At one, in collaboration with the physics teacher, the students demonstrated three-dimensional simulations of two earthquake-proof structures, assigning the commander in chief the weaker one, and seeing which collapsed first when shaken.

"I don't know if they planned it this way," she said with a laugh, "but knowing them, they probably did. He tested the weaker one, and it kind of fell apart."

MAKING LESSONS RELEVANT

It makes sense that students will care more about school and do better there if they feel what they are learning is relevant to their futures. As the Commission on the Future of Undergraduate Education noted, in designating P-TECH as a promising practice, collaborations among colleges and businesses "serve to incentivize students to earn and to stay in school by giving them added confidence that the academic work they are doing will prepare them for actual jobs when they graduate, as many students see no clear link between what they learn and productive employment afterward."[48]

Some research in dropout prevention has noted that pathways to careers matter to high school students, particularly to young males of color and those whose families struggle financially. They have especially benefited from relationships with career counselors and teachers who help them build leadership skills, confidence, and connections.[49]

P-TECH teachers within all disciplines work to make their material relevant to the associate degrees their students will pursue. Interdisciplinary work is a hallmark of the model, so Bruno instructs her students about the challenges ancient civilizations faced in terms of engineering problems: How did the Mayans build their pyramids with the technology of their time? How did the Aztecs make floating gardens to feed residents of what became Mexico City?

"When you look at this, don't look at this as ancient history and dead people who lived in the past," Bruno tells her students, who will be pursuing associate degrees in electrical or mechanical engineering technology. "You have to remember these people in history were presented with problems and had to engineer solutions. You might be studying one kind of engineering today, but it will be different 15 years from now. You're studying for a job, but you have no idea what your engineering problems are going to be. I really focus on that critical thinking aspect, and how civilizations move forward and progress."

Seifullah integrated problem solving, teamwork, presenting, and writing skills into her algebra class, asking students to work in groups to create a business plan for a fictional company to compete with Nike. Visitors to her class, including the president of Johns Hopkins University, were struck by the student work she posted on the classroom walls, and by how she proved that strong writing and collaboration skills can be reinforced in any academic class.

PROJECT-BASED LEARNING

While every school operates slightly differently within the model, for the Johnstown P-TECH in New York, professional development took center stage, with a full-time instructional coach for a staff of six or seven teachers. They met 3 to 5 days a week, while students had their non-P-TECH classes, such as Chinese and chorus, because they needed to create multidisciplinary project-based learning challenges for the students to tackle during the long blocks of class time that allowed for deeper learning and collaboration.

Regarding his former chief learning officer role, Dardaris said, "I wish I could take credit, but my main role was carving out time for teachers to plan, and get great trainers, and get out of the way." Teachers learned to teach everything through projects. And any project that could be completed in one period, the educators figured, without struggles with group interactions and ambiguity, would not reflect projects in the business world.

The social studies teacher, for example, covered the Cold War by assigning every student a role in a weeklong game of Clue.

"Nobody knew what everyone else's role was, and it took over the entire school during the week," he said. "The kids got really into it."

The school used flexible block scheduling, so teachers could spend up to 3 hours with classes of students ranging from 25 to 50. At other times, teachers could go back to small, shorter classes and teach traditional subjects, as scaffolding for the larger projects, say during a crime scene investigation project, when they needed to discuss DNA, genetics, or the geometry of blood splatters.

"Sometimes it looked like a regular math classroom, where they'd be plotting points on a graph, because the Regents were coming up," Dardaris said. "Other times, they'd be wearing suits and ties, and the kids were ready to present, because the business partner was there, and they were pitching ideas they had around marketing."

KNOW THY STUDENTS

At times, P-TECH teachers give lectures, but overall, they are more like coaches. "It's a sports and music model we all try to emulate in the classroom, where the responsibility is on the student," Dardaris said. The result was teacher as coach and caring adult.

Really knowing one's students, as shown in the previous chapters, can remove harmful stereotypes and biases, as well as enable a teacher to train students to ask for help.

"When you really know your students, that's when you understand what the standards should be," Bruno said. "They should be advocating for themselves, that's something they have to learn early on." She recalls standing near students she knew well enough to see they were stuck on a problem, but they would not admit it. She wished they would tell her they were confused, and she worked to get them to ask for the help they deserved.

"If you don't understand this, I can't read your mind, you have to tell me," she said. "It will make you successful in school, in the workforce. Asking for help is something many people don't know how to do. They're afraid to look weak or unintelligent or not capable of the task put in front of them. That self-advocacy is something we're working on, and other schools should be working on."

P-TECH students develop this skill throughout high school and into college. David Vazquez, a recent graduate of the P-TECH at Skyline High School in Colorado, remembers how hard he found his Advanced Java course at Front Range Community College, particularly because it was online during the pandemic. His teacher reinforced what David had been learning from his mentor—to learn, a student has to ask for help. This is a central P-TECH lesson, missing in other schools. When students ask for assistance, they are not considered failures; rather, they are proving themselves to be learners and demonstrating their trust in their partnership with their teachers.

"I was struggling a lot, so I talked to my teacher, and he said I just needed to not rely on what I know, but go further out, look for answers, ask for help," he said. "Now I feel a lot better about that class. Asking for help kept me going."

Dardaris found that teachers and students built strong and necessary relationships through working on projects together.

"We found that the project-based learning was the conduit to relationship building," said Dardaris, who has since gone on to work at Stride, the national online school venture.

"Before I left, we asked the students what's important to them about P-TECH, and we thought they'd say the laptops or the free college," he said. "They never reported that. They said, 'the teachers.'"

Close collaboration with teachers on projects was particularly beneficial to special education students, some of whom would have spent their whole school day in a resource room with an aide, a teacher, and only five other students if they had stayed in a regular school. When classes worked on projects, it was difficult to see who was the regular teacher, who required an aide, and who was the special education teacher, in a school where up to half of the students had some sort of special need, and all were eligible for free or reduced-price lunches.

"These kids outperformed all the general education students in New York State, not only in schooling, but in the Regents and on the college campus," he said, in every area except language arts.

INDUSTRY CHALLENGES

One notable project the school took on, at the request of a business partner, was designing the website and helping create a sales PowerPoint presentation for one of its business partners, Frozen Parts, which had relied on brochures and catalogs to sell its ice cream freezers and parts. Through leading the project, teachers were able to meet their school's goal that each lesson is "applicable and interconnected."[50]

P-TECH schools often present such "industry challenges" to students, a project that lets them attack real-world problems while working in collaborative teams. Examples include creating product packaging, organizing material, making processes more efficient, and dealing with ergonomics, safety, sustainability, office layout, or product innovations, according to descriptions[51] by the P-TECH OHM in Oneida, Herkimer, and Madison counties in New York. Industry challenges last 6 to 12 weeks, are developed by teachers and business partners working together, involve visits from business partners to the classroom and from students to the workplace, and include feedback from business partners and reflections from students.

It might seem to be harder to make a social studies class on the 14th century feel as real-world relevant as a class on building a website, but Bruno figured out a way to tie the Renaissance to an issue close to home for her future engineers in New Brunswick. Some critics have suggested a P-TECH education prepares a student only to fit into a particular job in a narrow field, and while the decision to join P-TECH is voluntary, some families strongly urge their children to do so. Bruno asks her kids to address that tension.

"For many families, the idea of a free associate degree is probably something they never dreamt of," Bruno said. "Whether a kid wants to be an engineer or not, the parents want that opportunity, and we know that's going to break a cycle of poverty or get them closer." Are they at risk of feeling too much pressure, and being less than well-rounded scholars?

"This is a classic Renaissance question," she said. "Do you want to be a Renaissance man or woman, or a specialized person? I make our kids write about this when they study the Renaissance." They write Document-Based Question (DBQ) essays, which they answer using primary sources.

"Most people study things and don't work in those fields anyway," she said. "It's not that they're just fed math and science all day and released into a job. They study languages, literature, and history. They're still getting exposures kids in normal high schools would get. They're just getting a supplement." Ideally, she said, all the classes would be connected, and students should be able to draw connections through all their classes as they move through their day. "To me, that's the definition of being well-rounded—learning, and learning that all is connected as well."

Some P-TECHs have adopted different grading methods. In Johnstown, for example, Dardaris explained that the traditional grading system was punitive and had treated grades as motivating factors. "We wanted them to start thinking of learning skills as a fun experience, as a motivating factor, compared to 120 years of 'we beat this into your head, to get a good grade,'" he said.

Realizing that students were likely to score poorly on early assessments of unfamiliar material, the school weighted later assessments more heavily, though adjustments were needed for more advanced students who gamed the system and coasted early in the term. If students needed to retake a test or redo an assignment, it was their responsibility to design a way to do so, which teachers would have to approve. Some made videos, took oral quizzes, taught a lesson, drew illustrations, demonstrated the use of robots, or any variety of ways to prove that they had mastered the material. Dardaris noted that when employees of Apple visited the school, they said the grading system looked like their quarterly performance assessments.

SEAMLESS TRANSITION TO COLLEGE

Students have the highest chance of being ready for and succeeding in college when high schools and colleges work together, subject by subject, to create a curriculum that progresses seamlessly. If high schools and community colleges communicate, secondary school courses can be designed to prepare students well for college credit courses. When high school students are challenged and see their work as a relevant stepping-stone to college, they are more likely to take school seriously and excel.

Akhtar, a student at the first Brooklyn school who prefers to go by her last name, appreciated the structure. "Honestly, P-TECH aligns its curriculum in a way that actually paved the pathway for you. As a first-generation college student, without the system of P-TECH, I probably would not have gone to college," she said. "The curriculum is always standing there and pushing students without them actually asking to be pushed."

At the Newburgh Free Academy P-TECH in New York, founding principal Kevin Rothman arranged the math curriculum so that students can take Calculus as juniors, even if they are not honors students as freshmen. They can take a college placement exam after taking Algebra, and if they pass it, they can place into Precalculus. Ninth-graders may not believe this is possible, but he convinces them otherwise, showing them the buses full of students heading from high school to their college classes at 8:45 A.M.

"You can point to the students getting on the buses and say, 'Look, if you bring those 9th-grade grades up, these kids were sitting in your seat in 9th grade, and you can be there too,'" Rothman said. "It makes our job easy. It's very, very tangible for our students to see those things."

TAKEAWAYS

For too long, students in traditional high schools—poor kids and kids of color in particular—have struggled with scant opportunities to be challenged and with boring instruction that is irrelevant to their futures. Schools have focused too assiduously on standardized tests and on hidebound ways of teaching, at the expense of making classrooms exciting, engaging, and nurturing of creativity. As a result, students have been poorly prepared for college and the workplace.

By watching the P-TECH model expand, we have learned that students rise to the level of expectation and rigor set for them. We have learned, through research around the country, that students can excel in a variety of rigorous programs, if only given the chance. We have to give more students the chance to challenge themselves with advanced coursework, and we have to ensure those opportunities serve all students, reflecting the racial, ethnic, and socioeconomic diversity of their districts.

As a nation, we need to measure how many students have access to rigorous coursework and educational challenges, and how diverse those students are, and we need to set and meet goals to address any inequities, along with timelines for fixing them. This can be at the state level, as Washington State legislated that students scoring at or above grade level on state exams be placed automatically in the next higher level courses in high school.[52] Likewise, the New York State Education Department recommended that each of the state's districts be wary of using teacher recommendations or GPAs as rigid criteria for taking advanced coursework and to be wary of considering unrelated tasks or exams, all of which can result in classes that don't reflect the student body.[53]

This can be done at the district level, requiring students who show promise to be automatically enrolled in advanced courses, unless they or their families choose otherwise.[54] And it requires wider course offerings, including making Algebra 2 available in every high school.

While we believe one of the strengths of P-TECH is the synergy among the public school, the community college, and the business partners, aspects of the model can also be beneficial separately. Superintendents can develop relationships with colleges, ensure their curricula mesh well together, and arrange for high school students to take their courses for credit. In formal partnerships, curriculum experts can collaborate on how to prepare high school students for specific college courses, particularly in math, where most remediation is needed.

We also urge principals and teachers to inspire students with guest speakers, visits to local colleges and workplaces, and options for enrichment courses to pursue locally or online. Developing partnerships between high schools, colleges, and businesses helps students understand what will be expected from them in the future, and it can guide them in decisions about what degrees and summer jobs to pursue. Students, families, and eventually entire communities benefit as more students gain more skills, degrees, and employment in growing fields.

CHAPTER 5

Support for Learning

High expectations and rigorous coursework are crucial, but they are worthless, even damaging, if students are not buoyed up in their efforts to succeed. Support for students—including tutoring, mentoring, and after-school programs; close monitoring of progress; and comprehensive guidance counseling—is crucial to the success of the new model. Many P-TECH schools provide a summer bridge program to ease the transition from middle to high school as well as extended day or after-school programs. Some students will need English language help, while some need academic and other forms of guidance counseling. Often, supports focus particularly on the transition to college.

A supportive school culture is a central feature of a P-TECH school, as evidenced in the various ways students are welcomed into the program, the social events that help make it feel like a regular high school, guidance during the often-perilous transition from high school to college, and parental involvement. The school climate benefits from the approach some P-TECHs take to discipline and to the schools' community service projects. Through these efforts, staff and students come to know each other, almost like family.

As the model has spread, students speak about how their classmates provide them with an additional and significant support system, as well as friendly peer pressure to succeed, with informal competitions in accumulating credits (and LinkedIn connections). Likewise, teachers have benefited from working together in teams, learning from college and business partners, and being part of an innovation movement.

In the following discussion of ways to shore up student effort and bolster success, we see again how all the ingredients of the model depend on each other for students to progress on a navigable path from the summer before 9th grade to the start of their careers. Individual aspects of the model could be used separately and are in place in many successful traditional schools today, but we believe they work best all together, under the firm and often-repeated guiding principle that *every* student in the building can graduate with both a high school diploma and college degree.

EXTENDED SCHOOL YEAR

Many P-TECH programs meet during the summer and/or have shorter vacations to help incoming students start to earn credits and to allow for more instructional time. The instructional lags many students experience over long vacations are less common in the P-TECH model. The costs for such programs are budgeted at the district level or funded by city or county governments. Summer bridge programs, such as the ones offered at P-TECH, have been shown to lead to community college success for students of color and economically disadvantaged students in California.[1] Other colleges and universities also offer bridge programs for incoming students, but they usually focus solely on remedial work. P-TECH's summer bridge programs are particularly effective because they prepare students for what to expect when school begins, and students learn specifics about how the program will prepare them for college and career. Even though they must get up early for weeks during the summer, students are engaged by these programs—New Brunswick's program had a 98% attendance rate.

Sometimes students need not just an extended school year, but an extended number of years to complete the program. Seifullah, the former math teacher, admired one particular aspect of Davis's philosophy at the Brooklyn P-TECH, one she shared.

"His vision and approach of how to support students was, you don't give up on them," she said. "If you don't succeed in the first 3, 4, or 6 years, some students might need 7 or 8 years." Supporting students means believing in them for the long haul.

EXTENDED SCHOOL DAY OR WEEK

"It's 24/7, 365, the support we can give to students," said Rothman, of the Newburgh P-TECH. "It doesn't stop when the school day stops." Students there can reach staff at all hours using different forms of communication, which continues over the summer and during other breaks from school.

P-TECH staff often reach out to students to ask what they need. "You may just need more time, so you're not focusing on going from one class to the next," Rothman said. "You may need a block of time here. Very often they don't even need an adult to support them, they just need space to be separate from their home environment on a Saturday, where they know they can have an uninterrupted focus on schoolwork."

Before the pandemic hit, one of the most important supports the school could offer was a variety of quiet settings with connectivity for students to study, do their homework, or talk to their mentors. When Rothman opened up the school building for Saturday study sessions, he did not require the staff come, but most did. He models that behavior himself, attending with his family for company, so he can balance work with his home life. Likewise, in Chicago, Rodriguez asked all the teachers to meet with students who were behind for a "catch up" day at the library near the school on a day school was closed. The mother of one chronically behind student brought him, and he stayed for the whole day, to the staff's surprise. Afterward, his schoolwork improved steadily.

In New Brunswick, NJ, many first-year P-TECH students were failing classes in the first months, so the school created an after-school program for everyone (see Chapter 8). The program allowed students needing help to have more one-on-one time with teachers, keeping them from making excuses or pretending they understood difficult concepts.

"Even if they're desperate for help, they will sit there and look you in the eye and tell you they don't need help," social studies teacher Gina Bruno said. "I'll say I'm getting paid to help you, *please* let me help you." That can happen better after school, she said. "Now kids who really need the help, find the time on their own time, and pace themselves. Sometimes it takes a little bit more time to build up courage to ask for help."

In Baltimore, a number of 10th-grade students did poorly in their first summer college English class with a professor who had not fully recognized that they were high school students without strong foundations. "It's no fault on either person's side, it's just not a match," said Lori Bush, the head of the Carver P-TECH in Baltimore. "We didn't get the right professor for our learning style."

Bush arranged for her students to get an extension through winter break, and assigned a high school English teacher to be the conduit for their makeup assignments and rewrites. "She's going to teach them what the college teacher didn't teach them this summer, so they don't have that F and have to retake the class," she said, showing her students by example that flexibility and an ability to solve problems are valuable skills in both the classroom and in the workplace.

P-TECH at PANTHER Academy in Paterson, NJ, had a school day that ended at 1:30 P.M. during the pandemic, so Principal Charla Holder made sure programming continued until 3:00 P.M. On Mondays, students meet with tutors; even if they are doing well, they can benefit from skipping ahead. On Tuesdays, everyone signs in to Open P-TECH, a platform IBM launched during the pandemic, that any student or teacher can access for free. Students take short courses in artificial intelligence (AI), cybersecurity, blockchain, cloud and quantum computing, and workplace skills; can take tests that feel like videogames; and can earn badges showing they have attained valued professional skills. A dashboard helps teachers keep track of student progress. On Wednesday, the English teacher has office hours for those not working in Open P-TECH, Thursday is for math help, and Friday is for getting schoolwork done early to keep weekends free for social time.

TUTORING

Many P-TECH after-school programs—funded by their cities, towns, or districts—include tutoring, food, fun, and opportunities to accelerate. Tutors can be school staff or mentors from the business partner. In the words of the students, these programs can make the difference between passing and failing.

When she arrived at P-TECH and heard her 9th-grade math teacher telling students that they probably learned certain principles in 8th grade, Akhtar, a graduate of the Brooklyn P-TECH, realized how far behind she was.

She signed up for tutoring on Mondays, Wednesdays, and Fridays with Frantz Carty, a math teacher, and started staying at school till 7:00 P.M., which her parents, who are South Asian immigrants, did not like. They had given her a 5:00 P.M. curfew, which had kept her off the robotics team. While in Bangladesh 59%[2] of girls are married by 18, even in the United States, as a firstborn daughter, Akhtar would be expected to get through an all-girls' high school at the most and marry young.

"Their main concern is that I'm getting older and I'm a woman," she said. "There's a stigma that women don't have the same qualities as a man, like it's the 1500s," she said. When a family trip to Bangladesh kept her out of school for 4 months, Akhtar spent the next year and a half catching up, getting up at 6:00 A.M., staying at school until 8:00 P.M., and coming back on weekends to study for Regents exams she had missed.

She found herself with only 18 of the 33 credits she needed to be a junior. Her guidance counselor, Jefferson Jean, encouraged her to fill up her schedule as much as possible, including working for extra credit during lunch.

"Looking at my transcript, I don't know how I did it," she said. "He helped me plan it out. I was lost, but he showed me. . . . He said it will be hard on you, but it will be worth it in the end." It made her more determined than ever to graduate and to continue her volunteer tutoring, which she had started at 14, working with other Bangladeshi immigrants.

"I see them struggling, and I'm seeing that their parents had to work two jobs left and right just to pay the bills," she said. One of her students graduated from the very competitive Stuyvesant High School, and Akhtar was able to help another student get help when she suspected, rightly, that he had dyslexia. At times when she sees herself in a student who is struggling financially, she tutors him or her for free.

Akhtar has recommended P-TECH to many other students to help counter the bias she sees in Asian culture toward prestigious public high schools such as Stuyvesant and Bronx Science, which have a large percentage of Asian students but require entrance exams, leaving many others out. She believes P-TECH is better for low-income, racially or ethnically diverse students whose families might have trouble affording college. The connections young people can make in such a school are invaluable for them, she said.

She is now completing a bachelor's degree at City Tech and has a full-time job at IBM, where she wants to volunteer with UNICEF, an IBM client, to help women experiencing domestic abuse and to empower girls forced to marry young.

"I'm doing this not for me, but for future generations," she said. "I don't think I'd be in college if I were in a different school," she said. "It all narrows down to one decision, that I came to P-TECH." The tutoring program was one of the first supports that launched her on her way.

Joan Casey, who taught history and several other courses at the Brooklyn school, tutored Akhtar and would host study sessions at her home in East Flatbush, which she called The Villa. She would serve them tea and work with them for as long as they needed, sometimes driving them home, a safer option than public transportation late at night.

"I'm not putting them on a bus at midnight and then open the paper the next day and read about them," she said. So strong was her belief that they had to pass their exams, she added, "Whatever it takes to make the magic happen."

Akhtar remembers Casey with great fondness. "She made me take the Regents twice," she said. "She said, 'Why are you settling for an 80? Go for a 90,' and I did it just for her."

In Paterson and Baltimore, school leaders were grateful for IBM's offer of 24/7 tutoring during the pandemic. "I said to the students, you can't get this through Princeton Review on your own," Charla Holder, the Paterson principal, said. "It would be $150 a session, but here it is offered to you for free."

MONITORING STUDENT PROGRESS

P-TECH staff have found it crucial to monitor all aspects of student progress carefully. For example, when the first cohort of Brooklyn P-TECH students began their college courses, about a fifth were receiving Ds or Fs and risking their ability to stay enrolled. P-TECH added extra tutoring hours. Davis insisted that every teacher take responsibility for a handful of students, finding them in class or in the halls daily, to ask how they were doing and what help, if any, they needed.

In 2014, 100 of 250 10th-graders at the Goode STEM Academy became college ready, having passed their placement exams, maintained a GPA of 2.5, and logged at least a 90% attendance rate. When 15 started struggling in college precalculus, their high school and college instructors started meeting biweekly to monitor their progress and support them.

"When students first started college courses, we had the impression that students weren't getting enough support from the college," said Goode math teacher Kyle Birch.[3] "But after we began meeting with the professor and the Dean of Instruction, we understood that they were holding very high expectations for students and were willing to help them, but they also needed our support as well." Students, they found, needed to get in the habit of asking for help when they did not understand lessons.

Likewise, staff members at Skyline High School were flummoxed when, in the first week in October, an unexpectedly high number of the first P-TECH students were failing every class. For the second semester, the staff created a guided study period, and the following year, they hired a guided study teacher who works with the program manager from the school's business partner, IBM, prepping students for their internships and setting aside 45-minute periods for students to work on classes they were behind in. The school also ran Saturday sessions, serving breakfast and lunch with food donated by a local restaurant, which attracted 100 students. They extended the school day on Monday, Wednesday, and Friday, which was mandated for anyone who was failing. Mentors from IBM offered support, as did teachers from each core area, who were compensated for their time. At times, students were on Webex calls with their teachers at 8:00 P.M.

"It's about people, about getting people on board that won't give up on kids, that believe in the model, in what we're trying to do, and that believe in each other," Greg Stephens, the P-TECH administrator there said.

In Chicago, Mr. Rodriguez, principal of the Goode STEM Academy, said he learned a great deal on monthly Zoom calls with other P-TECH leaders, one of them being Davis of the Brooklyn school, which focuses passionately on trends in student data; Rodriguez learned from him how data could help teachers and administrators make informed instructional decisions to support students' needs.

"It makes me more intentional in analyzing my school data, to see how each student is performing, and break it down based on race, ethnicity, gender, etc.," he said. "It's part of the process of growing."

COMPREHENSIVE COUNSELING

An effective guidance staff is crucial for helping students through the program, which can be challenging and stressful.

"This is hard. We never sugarcoat that with our students. There are going to be difficult things, but sometimes things that are worth it are difficult," Rothman said of his school in Newburgh, NY. "We talk about good stress and bad stress. If it's shutting you down, it's bad. Very often some stress can help you achieve, to meet deadlines."

Mariana Rivas, a graduate of Stephens' school in Colorado, struggled with the stress. "Some of us wanted to leave because it was hard," she said. "But P-TECH had such a great support system." The IBM mentors who tutored after school, the teachers, the guidance counselors, all helped students master the classwork.

"I decided to stay because I got the right support sophomore year of high school," when the work was particularly challenging, she recalled. Louise March, her counselor, said to give it another semester and see what happened. Mariana is glad she stayed, as she got her associate degree in 4 years, becoming the first in her family to graduate from college. She and her father, who works for the water department, and her stay-at-home mother are proud that at 19 she is working at IBM. "They look at it as a big thing," she said.

Keira Downes, a P-TECH freshman in the University of Newcastle Food Science & Nutrition program, considered quitting the program multiple times, as the coursework was stressful and difficult, especially in light of her ADHD, which she received medication for only in 11th grade.

"At some points, I was very close to dropping it, then I kind of weighed out the pros and cons if I did drop it, and the cons outweighed the pros," she said. It helped her to talk to two women she saw as mentors, Jade Moffat, head of Corporate Social Responsibility for IBM in Australia and New Zealand, and Jillian Williams, the liaison between IBM and the school. Keira doesn't see herself as a tech person at all, and she was the only girl in her difficult Information and Digital Technology course. (It didn't feel too strange, as she was friends with half her class. "I felt like one of the boys," she said.) She felt her male teacher was one of the best in the school, and she also knew she could always go to the female head of the IT faculty for help.

While at P-TECH, Keira struggled with the death of her grandfather and the murder of her aunt, who left three children behind. Her mentors understood when she needed more than academic help.

"They were still willing to listen," she said. "I have my moments where I just can't do work because I'm remembering them, and I can get very emotional." Jill, Jade, or her teachers would tell her to take a moment and breathe.

"I was able to get back on track, and got where I got mainly because of P-TECH," she said. "It was a major contributing factor in my life, helping me overcome all these struggles."

Jade admires Keira for never shying away from the opportunities the school offered. "She took it all on with gusto and enthusiasm," she said. "She definitely has a huge future ahead of her, and to be honest, one day I feel like I may be working for Keira."

At Skyline High School in Colorado, Xavier Gutierrez also benefited from P-TECH supports. When he was in 8th grade, Xavier felt he was giving up on everything, and he did not expect to be able to handle high school. He figured he would drop out by sophomore year, and he was making plans to find work without a diploma.

He was struggling with his mental health, but P-TECH gave him a boost, providing opportunities for him to talk in front of big groups. "I started feeling confident, like 'oh, I can actually do this,'" he said. "I started making really good grades in my college classes. They were set up so we had quite a lot of support." Freshman year, there was a study group after school every Monday for anyone who needed help with anything. Sophomore year, when he came out as transgender, the group supported him.

Xavier, 18, is doing a yearlong apprenticeship in cybersecurity at IBM, and he has set his sights on veterinary school, as he has built up a small zoo in his room, including fish, a snake, and a tarantula. He never felt pushed to enter a tech job, but instead sees his associate degree as a fallback to keep him secure.

"It's going to take me a while to get to vet school and have that money," he said. "For now, I have a degree, and I've already started a career, so I'm making a living for myself." If he decides against veterinary school, he has options.

"For my family, personally, we really wouldn't have this chance otherwise. College is a very rare thing in my family. . . . My mom was honestly amazed about it." His father had never gone to school, and his mother had dropped out of high school when she started having children, but she graduated from college when Xavier was in elementary school, and she is now a special education teacher.

"P-TECH was almost like my escape from my personal problems," he said. "I would hit dark spots and really want to drop out, and I'd go talk with Ms. March. She'd remind me I was loved, and could do this, supported." Now he is glad he did not give up. "I'm realizing how my work has paid off, not only just with my classes, but I wouldn't have ever gotten this job I have without P-TECH."

Sometimes the counseling students receive revolves around how they can pursue their varied dreams within the school's structure. Karen Amaker, the founding principal of P-TECH in Norwalk, has tried to work with students who have entered the school, perhaps at their family's urging, but do not want to pursue the three college degrees the school offers. She hopes to add a fourth option—P-TECH schools have asked colleges to add new courses of interest to students, say in design, to computer degree programs—but in the meantime, she asks students what kinds of experiences they want to pursue.

"What does it look like for you if you're interested in being a veterinarian?" she said. "It requires a certain level of commitment and expectations. It doesn't mean you can't shadow a vet, or take courses out of sequence, so we can challenge you to be college ready earlier."

It is important to capture the interest of such students early and to encourage them to advocate for themselves. She likes to get students thinking about how they learn best and what experiences they want to have, and encourages them by inviting, for example, a videogamer/physicist into a class, to talk about how he had earned a master's in a year and followed his passions.

Amaker looks forward to future years when she may have even more options to offer students. "At 14, you don't know what you want to be when you grow up, but I would love to ask them, if you could build your own program for the next 4 years, what would it include? What do you want to know; where do you want to study?"

SCHOOL CULTURE

P-TECH schools have worked hard to develop school climates that can help every student thrive. At the P-TECH in Joppatowne High School in Maryland, which partners with Harford Community College and the U.S. Army, assistant principals visited new students' homes to welcome them, and gave them yard signs and T-shirts to help boost school spirit, especially during the pandemic.[4]

Dardaris, formerly of the P-TECH in Johnstown, NY, made sure students had their own prom, which he described as a little unconventional, with pizza, rather than a sit-down meal, in the decorated gym. The school had Halloween dances and a year-end picnic and awards ceremonies, with families in attendance. It also hosted families for holiday celebrations, even though it was a challenge to shop for a halal turkey. When some of the students experienced homelessness, the teachers often provided them with food or clothes.

Bush, head of the Carver P-TECH in Baltimore, made sure college classes never met on Fridays, so students could attend football games and dances.

In Chicago, Rodriguez supports his students by empowering them whenever possible. Teachers applying to work at the school give a sample lesson to Goode students, who then provide their feedback on the candidates' abilities (as do students at P-TECH New Brunswick).

At Goode STEM Academy, students also take "learning walks," touring the building to sit in on other classes to see how other teachers teach.

"Students' voices are an important component of how the school functions and makes decisions," Rodriguez said. When a group of students was upset about a new fence installed around the school, feeling it was expensive and not as needed as other school improvements, Rodriguez explained it was part of the school design and didn't affect any actual school funding, but he also pressed them for their ideas on other improvements they felt the school needed.

"It's your building, you have the right to know what we spend on it," he recalls telling them. "It's not my money, it's your money, and if you have ideas on how to spend it (doable or not), I'll let you know." When African American students asked him for support to create a group called Black Organization of Successful Students, to express their needs and concerns, he agreed. The student-led group meets weekly and brings its issues and suggestions to him.

Dr. Holder, of PANTHER Academy in Paterson, who welcomed her students with a "signing day" starring a Super Bowl champion, notes that she has only 4 years with her students before she sends them out into the world.

"That's a short period of time to have, to change the students' mindsets," she said, noting that she asks them not to wear hoodies or sagging pants in her building. "I treat them like I treat my own children. They know that. I tell them right from the beginning, welcome to the family. I run our school so we're like a family. It's small enough to do that. I won't ask your children to do anything more than I would've asked my own children."

That kind of care matters to students. For Joel Duran, with his broken ankle, the visit from his history teacher, Ehrenfeld, was a very simple action, just a check-in, but it meant a great deal.

"At that time, I wasn't the focus of anyone's attention," he said. "To have someone give me that attention, it meant a lot."

MOVING ON TO COLLEGE

Studies show the transition to college can be perilous for students, especially those who are underserved. Many students who are the first in their families to go to college, as well as non-White or low-income students, have no interaction with higher education until they walk through the gates of college. We have found that when they engage with college staff starting in 9th grade and are supported by high school staff as they try their first college courses—with guidance counselors helping with the adjustment, and teachers and tutors able to shore up understanding of new topics—students are more likely to thrive.

Before students at the Goode STEM Academy in Chicago start their college courses, the school schedules meetings with their parents.

"We are always trying to innovate in our school, to be able to serve all of our students," Rodriguez said. "How can we teach our students if we don't know them? We need to build strong relationships with them." If any student starts to fail a college course, the guidance counselors and principal can meet with him or her to see the root causes and offer assistance.

"We fight to the last effort to try to support students, and make sure students finish," he said, by using constant communication (multiple reminders, by text as well as email), providing academic support, and meeting with parents and students at the same time.

"We work with parents to build the college-going culture, through our Local School Council, Parent Advisory Committee, and Bilingual Advisory Committee," he said. "We offer training and workshops. We need to support parents, on how they can support their children in having that college mentality, beginning in their freshman year."

Kyle Birch, a math teacher at Goode STEM Academy, thinks the system works well. "We have the advantage of teaching students how to succeed in college while they are still in high school," he said. "The risk is lower, and the safety net is bigger."[5] Students there get tutoring from Richard J. Daley College students during a required College Support class. They can also attend office hours with Professor Abolhassan Taghavy, who teaches precalculus at the college. He has given them practice quizzes and helps the College Support class reinforce the concepts needed in college. The majority of the initial college classes are taught at the high school by Goode teachers who are also adjunct professors at Daley. Some other P-TECH schools have high school teachers who become accredited at their partner community colleges, making the transition to college less jarring for students.

PARENTAL INVOLVEMENT

The families of many first-generation college students understand the model's importance, and they are, on average, very supportive of and involved in their children's education. This can be crucial to the success of those young people.

Bush, head of the Carver P-TECH in Baltimore, begins investing in relationships with students' families early, starting with the application process, trying to meet with each new student's family.

"Having that relationship with families is everything," she said, describing how she explains the school's expectations for its students—year-round school, up to 10 hours a day, so they can get associate degrees in cybersecurity or computer information systems in just 4 years, not the usual 6. "It's so we can feel we're all partners in the child's education."

Rothman, the head of the P-TECH in Newburgh, meets with the family of each new student before school starts.

"The reality is that we are asking families to make a decision about their child's future in 9th grade," Rothman points out. "Many parents I met with struggled with the fact that their children wouldn't have the same high school experience that they had."[6] He assures them that the program is flexible, offering students a great deal of choice. "Ultimately, every student will earn an associate degree at no cost that will put them ahead—whether they choose to continue their education, move directly into the working world, or pursue a combination of both."

STUDENT BEHAVIOR

Principals report that certain aspects of the school culture have helped keep incidents requiring discipline to a low level. It helps, they say, for the staff to know the students very well. For example, Akhtar, in the Brooklyn P-TECH, saw an immediate improvement over her middle school, where she was the only Asian girl and was bullied for having different eyes and lighter skin, although by any standard her thick, long hair and symmetrical, cheerful face are striking. She started wearing eyeliner to make her eyes look bigger, and she started tanning. She did not know how to open up to her parents about what was happening at school, as they did not understand peer pressure. Kids would pull off her hijab, so she stopped wearing it, even though she was quite religious at the time and felt the head scarf was an important part of her.

"I was a little sad puppy, and I wouldn't make eye contact with anyone," she said. "I wish the person I am now was there for myself, so I could've told myself, 'It's ok, you'll do fine.'"

At P-TECH, the principal, dean, and guidance counselors enforced the anti-bullying policy and shut down any students who made comments against someone's race, religion, or ethnicity.

"That's how the administration would deal with it, before the domino could drop," she said. "They'd say, 'Why are you doing that?'"

In Chicago, Rodriguez encourages teachers to check in with their students every morning before class, as it is important to see how they're doing every day. "The first week of the semester for us is essential to get to know the students, who they are, what their goals are, etc.," he said.

The better they know their students, the better they can de-escalate conflicts. For example, if a teacher doesn't know a student well, and the student is persistently late, it could lead to false assumptions. The teacher could think the student wasn't interested in the class, when the real problem was that the student had a tiring night shift.

"We need empathy, we need to be in the student's shoes, so we can understand the why," he said. "Building relationships is a key component in a successful student's career." Empathy, he said, is crucial for breaking down the barriers of racism.

Zaretta Hammond, author of *Culturally Responsive Teaching & the Brain: Promoting Authentic Engagement and Rigor Among Culturally and Linguistically Diverse Students,*[7] calls the ideal educator a "warm demander" who builds strong relationships, and then uses the resulting trust to engage young people in their coursework and hold them to high standards.

Such efforts have worked well in both Brooklyn and New Brunswick, where teachers or administrators, respectively, take responsibility for a handful of students to check in on them regularly, see if they need any help with current classes or advancement to more challenging ones, and reinforce the idea that the adults support their success. In the Brooklyn P-TECH, teachers are given professional development periods to gather in groups of three to review the progress of specific students and compare notes about what teaching or support methods work best for each young person. The teachers welcome the time to collaborate with and learn from each other, and the students receive the extra benefits of their combined attention and wisdom.

In Norwalk, Amaker's teachers follow restorative practices. "We don't believe we have the right as educators to give up on any child," she said. "Relationship building is at the forefront of everything we do. The students feel it and know it."

Seifullah, the former Brooklyn P-TECH math teacher, is a proponent of restorative justice, the philosophy that punishments are less just, equitable, and effective than solutions that grow out of community conversations and shared values, and she saw it work well at the school.

She remembers when Davis had to figure out what to do with Gabriel Rosa, a freshman in the P-TECH's inaugural class, who had hacked into the school's computer system, installing remote software. When Gabriel owned up to his mischief, Davis did not suspend him or kick him out of school. He told Gabriel how the act had harmed the community, then gave him a MacBook, the student's first laptop. It was a message to use this opportunity, and his skills, to create and learn. Gabriel immediately used it to make iPhone apps. (Gabriel graduated with his associate degree in just 4 years, and he has been promoted twice at IBM, where he is a software developer.)

Seifullah has instituted attention periods, a variation on detention periods, when teachers volunteer to have lunch with students who have late or missing homework assignments. She found the conversations they had were more effective in transforming student behavior than having them sit, wasting time, as punishment.

The P-TECH in Johnstown, NY, unlike its feeder schools, did not experience violent incidents, Dardaris, the former chief learning officer, recalls. Students would say to him, "It's not anything special about the school, Mr. D, it's just that we didn't want to get kicked out." Dardaris said, "They're consciously making the choice to not engage, because they didn't want to lose something."

Casey, who was known for her well-behaved classes, wanted other teachers to come in and critique her lessons. On the first day of school, she tells her classes she has a one-word rule: respect. She would assign disrespectful students to write essays, giving her an insight to their thought processes, as well as to their writing skills.

"Teaching is theatre at its best," she said. "I would go to my desk, to a folder of documentation of situations in my room. I choose the words I use, not a *problem*, a *situation* we have to address. When I choose those words, I'm already putting them in a place where I'm building expectations. We don't have problems, we have situations, and we should be able to address them."

If she catches a student daydreaming, unable to answer one of her questions, she gives him or her the option for her to come back in a few minutes.

"I'll wait," she said. "I tend to encourage them—remember, if you don't speak to me, I don't know what's going on in there. You can't put kids down, you cannot. You can't even let them think you're going at them." Empower them instead, she added.

She wants her students to feel free to say what they are thinking, without feeling stupid or judged. "I let them know it's a family, it's not entertainment, and when your colleagues are talking, you are supposed to listen." With the help of such language, she prepares them for success both in school and in the workplace.

"As long as kids are aware there's a structure and expectations, and they test the care, that you're doing this really for them, half the battle is won, right there," she said.

COMMUNITY SERVICE

Several P-TECHs have worked on community service projects, an additional way to strengthen student solidarity and enhance the school climate. At Skyline High School, Greg Stephens pointed with pride to Tech Thursday, at first a social time, with food, board games, and other fun activities for students. It evolved into including more tech activities, such as a yearlong coding project, and a group of P-TECH students became experts on Sphero robots, programmable robotic cars. At times, younger grades would come to visit for Tech Thursdays and learn from P-TECH students.

"To see kids teaching kids, that was really powerful," Stephens said.

Rothman, in Newburgh, NY, said his students volunteered—along with school staff and Rothman's mother—to plant trees and do cleanup work in nearby parks, counting eels for the Department of Environmental Conservation, and helping build homes with Habitat for Humanity. Students have also volunteered by tutoring younger students.

"If students are involved in the community from an earlier age and feel like they can be service providers and change agents, instead of receivers of services—which very often they have been—they can see what it is like to be in control of situations," he said. "I think it makes them more likely to stay in the community."

Even though these events happen on the weekend, staff turnout has been strong.

"It never seems like something extra. It's what we do," he said. "We like our students and enjoy their company. We get involved in the community. I surrounded myself with really smart people, and they're involved in the community, and that translates into the students being more involved in the community than they would be otherwise."

Students at the Goode STEM Academy in Chicago tested local water for safety; at the Norwalk P-TECH, a group of students started a club that ran a clothing drive and other service projects; and at the Brooklyn P-TECH, Selah Bah remembers making 48 websites in 48 hours, when she and other students helped an organization that ran after-school programs.

"Not only did we meet new people and build our web design skills, we made some friendships," she said. "Since there are not a lot of us at P-TECH, we form tight bonds with each other."

PEER SUPPORT AMONG STUDENTS

Numerous students speak of the importance of their peer group as a vital lifeline. For example, Mariana Rivas, who had struggled at Skyline High School before graduating with an associate degree in just 4 years, said that her classmates pulled together strongly, forming a safety net for each other.

"The expectations really helped us grow over the 4 years and pushed us to become better," she said. "A lot of us struggled, but definitely we had each other. We tried to motivate one another because we were all in the same boat. If one of us said, 'I can't do this anymore,' someone would say 'Come on, I'll help you, I know what you're feeling. We're all in this together.'"

From the Brooklyn school, Selah Bah explained that unlike her classmates, her friends from outside P-TECH had trouble relating to what she was going through. "Someone finally understands me more, and how I'm having to balance everything, like college, and having to leave school late," she said. "They were like family to me."

Like all teenagers, P-TECH students are susceptible to peer pressure, but in a school that values college readiness, that pressure veers in a productive direction.

P-TECH's competitive culture certainly motivated Joel Duran, who saw his classmates claiming bragging rights for finishing school in 4 years instead of 6. In middle school, kids had felt intimated if they were too smart or accused of being a teacher's pet, he said, but P-TECH students valued intelligence. "You learn early on that failing is not cool. You don't want to be left behind, with new upcoming classmates, when all your friends are moving on."

P-TECH graduates are beginning to create ways to stay connected after attaining their diplomas and degrees, joining alumni networks through which they maintain their connection. They often visit with current P-TECH students to encourage them and talk about their experiences, widening the net of support.

TAKEAWAYS

Strong support for students and a positive school climate are certainly not unique to P-TECH schools, and many of these elements are present in effective schools. Many districts use volunteer and peer tutors when formal after-school programs are cost-prohibitive, and industry mentors are unavailable. We urge schools to consider adopting all the support measures discussed in this chapter to help their students succeed in school and beyond. We strongly believe engaged college and business partners can provide priceless support and connections among kids, college diplomas, and careers.

CHAPTER 6

Frequent Interactions With College and Business Partners

What makes for successful collaborations among public high schools, community colleges, and businesses that want to help students enter the world of college and work? When simmered together, a few relatively modest ingredients create a stew that is more nourishing than the sum of its components. From their college and industry partners, the schools receive the carrots, if you will, that inspire students to higher rates of attendance and achievement, at no cost. From the partnership, the colleges gain well-prepared students (usually from the demographic groups they have struggled to serve) who can skip remedial courses and graduate at high rates. The industry partner also wins, gaining relationships with engaged adults and talented students who can form a pipeline of well-prepared future employees whose demographics reflect those of society.

So, for example, a summer youth employment program helps students, but if it is disconnected from their education and skills, it is less valuable. Mentors are great, but again, if they are not engaged with a student's schoolwork, their returns are smaller. Fieldtrips can be fun, but they increase significantly in value when they are connected to an academic goal. The synergy among each of P-TECH's separate ingredients—skills maps, course progressions, workplace visits, mentors, paid internships, apprenticeships—helps students reach their goal of a rigorous, equitable, relevant education leading to a free college degree and, ultimately, employment.

In the P-TECH model, the community college agrees to provide access to credit-bearing courses to students as soon as they are deemed ready, to modify any earlier dual-enrollment programs to allow for attaining a full degree, and to provide faculty for the courses. Frequently, they give qualified high school teachers credentials as adjunct professors, so they can teach courses either on campus or, more often, at the high school. The college ideally will designate a liaison to resolve any issues with course registrations, communications, or other challenges, although some university systems may assign more than one high school to one community college liaison.

In Newburgh, for example, the college liaison is an adjunct professor in the program and connects with the students as early as 10th grade. "He has daily access to them in an academic setting, and knows exactly where they need academic support early, and can help advocate in that level," Rothman said.

Most businesses designate a full- or part-time liaison to their P-TECH school, an in-kind contribution. Contributions by all three partners build on each other year to year, with refinements as needed.

States creating P-TECH schools often offer planning grants of anywhere from $50,000 to several hundred thousand dollars, issuing a request for proposals through their education departments. During this planning period, high schools find business and college partners. All three partners can then inform parents, students, and the community about the program; identify school leaders and faculty; make sure the courses mesh between high school and college into the degree the employer is looking for; and agree on how the partners will work together. Successful collaborations include all three partners in all major decisions and many minor ones. Regular meetings are crucial as schools open with one 9th-grade class, adding an additional grade per year.

In states with multiple P-TECHs, a similar steering committee at the state level oversees the collaborations. For example, in New York, that committee includes the chancellor of SUNY, the state education commissioner, and representatives from the Business Council and IBM, with the committee's staff funded by grants from foundations and corporations. On each level, the collaborative planning and decisionmaking process helps resolve issues early on, smoothing the way to success.

THE ROLE OF THE COLLEGES

Public higher education systems have an enormous amount to gain from their partnerships with secondary schools and their business partners. Community colleges are very concerned about declining enrollments, the significant cost in remedial courses, and disturbingly stagnant college completion rates, particularly for low-income and non-White students, the population P-TECH serves. And yet, effective collaboration between higher education and the K–12 systems has been relatively rare.

Cass Conrad, the former CUNY dean of K–16 initiatives, said P-TECH and other early college programs have made for a great partnership in the work of reducing the number of students in remedial classes.

"We think about this broad set of models as helping us understand how to improve education at the high school level and college and career-readiness level," she said. "It really is a way to help rethink education so it can help the most students."

Direct engagement between high school teachers and college professors can help shrink the gap between expectations students have about college, and the realities, said Ian Rosenblum (former executive director of Education Trust—New York, now deputy assistant secretary for policy and programs in the U.S. Department of Education).

The Goode STEM Academy, one of the first P-TECHs to open in Chicago, certified the maximum number of its teachers allowed by the district to be adjuncts at its partner, Daley College. Students can take 28 credits of English, biology, math, and computer science from their high school teachers, making it easier to fit in the classes they need without changing campuses, especially in grades 10 and 11. Plus, the high school teachers, with their familiarity with that age group, can help ease the transition to more difficult coursework and call in extra supports if necessary.

Of course, growth comes with growing pains, and colleges had to be flexible in permitting students to take their courses as soon as possible in their high school experience, often as early as the summer between 9th and 10th grade.

Sometimes college rules can nearly thwart student progress, as when, early in the planning stages, the former president of Orange County Community College in New York told Newburgh P-TECH and IBM that students would not be able to take college courses until grade 11 at the earliest, even if they passed the state Regents exams. Both the district and IBM pushed back, and after a face-to-face meeting, the college relented, letting 10th-graders enroll. The students' success impressed the college's current leader, Kristine Young, who has been a strong supporter of the model. At the SUNY Orange graduation in 2019, at the end of year 4 of the 6-year program, Newburgh P-TECH students represented two-thirds of the school's cybersecurity graduates.

Rodriguez, the head of the Goode STEM Academy in Chicago, focuses on understanding the relationships among his students and their college professors, and keeping communication channels open: How are the students adapting to college? Are the professors sensitive to their needs?

"We have to put it on ourselves to meet the professors," he said, "and explain what we have done, invite them to come into our building, so they can get to know us. We need to continue collaborating with the college professors, to find, together, ways to support our students, for everyone to understand the stress an individual P-TECH high school student may be experiencing. Like I told my teachers and liaisons at IBM, we need to build positive relationships with the professors, so we can communicate better with them, and build strong partnerships to support our students." It is important to see the partnership as a family, he said.

From the colleges' perspective, P-TECH has some unexpected benefits. Conrad said CUNY's partnership with IBM has helped create structures that assist a broad range of employers to become more involved at the high school level, and she envisions the model expanding. "What I've talked about in New York City is having enough early college and/or P-TECH type schools that every neighborhood in the city has access to one," she said. "To have enough so students who are interested have relatively easy access is possible."

WHAT BUSINESS PARTNERS DO

Identifying Business Skills

Most large companies require their new workers to have mastered skills such as problem solving, writing, collaborating, and giving presentations, and P-TECH graduates joining the workforce at 18 to 20 years old needed to have a lot of early practice in such skills.

When designing the model, Litow worked closely with the IBM HR department to find nine entry-level jobs that had previously required a bachelor's degree but could be filled by someone with an associate degree in computer science or engineering. He incorporated the skills HR required for those jobs into a skills map, for the standalone workplace skills class, and for incorporation into all courses. (Sample skills maps are available at ptech.org.)

Using the map, industry partners work with high school and college faculty to determine when these skills will be taught. Ideally, the skills map is a graphic view of how students will be prepared, year by year and class by class, with the skills they need for the career pathways ahead.

For instance, at the Northern Borders Academy in Malone, NY, an Adirondack town 12 miles south of the Canadian border, students can earn associate degrees in human services, health sciences, and chemical dependency counseling, leading to entry-level jobs as activities leaders, dental assistants, care coordinators, and resident counselors.[1] Students who pursue further education and accreditation can go on to become social workers, case managers, substance abuse counselors, clinical dieticians, medical coders, massage therapists, and EMTs, among other options.

The skills map for care coordinator, for example, includes "Active Listening/Empathy—Giving full attention to what other people are saying, taking time to understand the points being made, asking open-ended questions as appropriate, and not interrupting at inappropriate times" and "Social Perceptiveness—Being aware of others' reactions and understanding why they react as they do."[2]

At the Greater Southern Tier Stem Academy, the P-TECH in Corning, NY, one skills map[3] shows how the job of robot technician requires proficiencies in reading blueprints, wiring, tearing down and rebuilding equipment, and using forklifts, shop equipment, and hand and machine tools. As for softer skills, new hires are expected to be team players, give attention to detail, embrace and anticipate change, multitask, resolve conflicts, and be self-directed and punctual.

One way for companies to come up with a complete skills map is to ask staff to write want-ads for entry-level employees and search out what other companies require for similar jobs. Skills maps will evolve over time, just as available jobs will.

"We looked at what workforce deficiencies were going to be projected over the next 10 years," Smock, of Career P-TECH Academy in Dunkirk, NY, told his local newspaper.[4] "These pathways align to exactly where those deficiencies are going to be, so we are creating the pipeline for backfilling. So when Baby Boomers and folks are looking to retire, we can fill those job vacancies as they open up."

Contrary to early concerns about the model, industry is not dictating what a student will learn at the expense of the freedom to pursue his or her dreams. P-TECH schools, which students volunteer to join, are not producing cogs to fit specific gears in the STEM world—the students are too talented, and those gears change too rapidly. Instead, P-TECH aims to give students a quiver full of skills and credentials, along with more choice and preparation as they progress through the program and learn of new opportunities.

The model does not lock students in to one future; rather, it prepares them for many. Four out of five recent P-TECH graduates have headed off to 4-year colleges with 2 years already completed for free, without debt, and some are in fields unrelated to their associate degree. The rest have gone to work, usually with the business partner affiliated with their program. They have had a great deal of freedom in forging their paths, with some working in marketing, communications, or HR, while others continue in the jobs corresponding to their degrees.

Mariana Rivas, a graduate of the P-TECH in Longmont, CO, which offers an associate degree in computer information systems, had struggled when committing to P-TECH, because she wanted to pursue the arts as well as technology in high school.

"I started realizing we still had that freedom," she said. "Even if I wanted to do more art classes, our schedule could be adjusted. P-TECH is 6 years, so if you really wanted to do more art stuff, you could push some college classes back if you wish. I had those options, but I didn't take them because I wanted to finish in 4 years. The schedule was very flexible, and I still got to do stuff I really like."

Mariana said she was glad she recommended that her sister, Stephanie, join the program. "She's such a free spirit person, and does her own thing," Mariana said. "Anyone can do it, the most techie person, or a free spirit like my sister. . . . She's learning, because she's being challenged."

Gina Bruno, the social studies teacher at P-TECH New Brunswick, notes that not every student there wants to be an engineer—some are artists at heart.

"It's about finding that sweet spot. If you want to be an artist, maybe you could be a graphic designer and work for one of these companies, or an architect," she said. "You can find a way to let your engineering job support your artwork." School staff needs to have such conversations early on with students, she said.

Of P-TECH graduates in 4-year colleges, many have chosen routes unrelated to their associate degrees, aiming to be lawyers, doctors, teachers, or veterinarians, but the workplace skills and degrees they gained in the model will be useful in any educational and business ventures after they leave the program.

At the end of their time with P-TECH, graduates are readier than most 18- to 20-year-olds for whatever comes next. They can meet the kind of need identified by Pavel Krsička, Head of Personnel Department, Bosch Diesel, the first P-TECH industry partner for IBM in the Czech Republic.[5]

"Students and graduates in [the] Czech Republic have a high level of theoretical knowledge but not practical experiences," he said. "P-TECH will help us bridge this gap. . . . It creates a pipeline of skilled employees for us. Ones that we help develop."

Liaisons

In most collaborations, the business liaison helps coordinate the workplace-related activities in the model school. Many liaisons have worked as teachers, often with Teach for America, so they can engage well with school staff as well as with employers when recruiting mentors, determining skills students need, and arranging events. At the Goode STEM Academy in Chicago, Calvin Chu, the IBM program manager, is involved at every opportunity, Rodriguez said, including in meetings with parents, in starting to make connections between students and employees during site visits, in matching students to internships, and in developing projects for IBM's STEM Fest, which every student participates in.

In Connecticut, industry liaison Austin Hutchinson, a former teacher, came up with a program called P-TECH Norwalk Studios, where students can televise segments about their projects.

"He just brings another element to the whole plan," Amaker, the head of the school, said. "It comes together so nicely and is so integral to the academic program." The students are learning how to interview, edit video, and market their work. The school would never have had the funding for such a program without the help of IBM, she said.

Dr. Charla Holder, the principal in Paterson, NJ, said her school's industry liaison comes up with his own enrichment activities and anticipates the needs of the class. When PANTHER students expressed interest in coding and videogaming, IBM paid for a class for 25 of them.

"He's a part of the team," she said of the liaison, Jarad Ford. At the Brooklyn P-TECH, Jennifer Lucia, the former IBM liaison, not only assisted all students with their college applications but frequently led trips to colleges to ease the transition to 4-year degrees, functioning as a college counselor.

Structured Workplace Visits

Students, some of whom have never ridden in an elevator, benefit from visiting partner businesses and learning about professional life, especially from younger workers who look like them. Visits and presentations reward students for their hard work and help business partners get to know the students. Young people who may not have friends or relatives in STEM careers come to see themselves in such positions.

Some workplace visits have had themes, such as International Space Day, when students from Brooklyn traveled to IBM's offices in the East Village to learn about a personal assistant for astronauts named Crew Interactive MObile companioN (CIMON), programmed using AI. They then heard from a marketing expert and research psychologist, and they designed a companion for a fictional space traveler. On a visit around the theme of #SheCanSTEM, Newburgh students heard panel discussions, including one on a day in the life of an engineer. Students have toured a Cloud Object Storage Data Center, learned about how the hardware of a server works, heard conversations on Python and Java computer languages, and then tackled coding challenges. One visit included a workshop in breaking down postgraduation career goals into achievable steps. Teachers and mentors are involved, so they can reinforce lessons from the workplace back in the classroom or in mentoring sessions.

Sometimes, interactions with business are more like a *Shark Tank* show. Kelly Guillen, who graduated from the Skyline P-TECH in Colorado, is now running his own custom sneaker company, after his Business and Entrepreneurship class pitched ideas at the high school's Innovation Center, which offers industry work experience and research opportunities. With a seed loan from the Young Americans Bank in Denver, CO, created for people age 21 and younger, he ordered paints, airbrushes, and a printer.

"It's good money, something fun, and I'm painting whatever the customers desire," he said, adding that he is making a profit while he plans his next steps regarding college or career.

Mentorships

According to Strada, the nonprofit college-to-employment network, eight out of 10 college students say work-based mentors would be more valuable than any other mentor relationship, yet only two out of 10 college students have access to such mentors from business.[6] That is a lost opportunity. P-TECH ensures students have high-quality mentoring from professionals in their field. Such advisors are particularly helpful for first-generation college students, students of color, and low-income students, who may not have adults in their social circles who can give advice on college and career. Mentors can show them the ropes of the specific professions they may want to enter.

At IBM, thousands of employees serve as mentors to P-TECH students, with almost 150 in Colorado alone. The company recruits, trains, and supports mentors through a free electronic portal called MentorPlace, which connects directly to high school and college curriculum and project-based learning activities. An online-only effort even before the pandemic, it is an enclosed system, allowing mentors and students to interact securely, saving mentors from having to meet in person and reducing concerns schools have about adults interacting with students. Mentors, who often must first be fingerprinted as a security precaution, are matched with mentees, usually meeting at an event at the school or workplace that features team projects and advice on how to benefit from mentoring. Students and their mentors then start what is hoped to be a long-lasting relationship, beyond mere homework help, including guidance about workplace skills and careers.

Mentors bring their own value to the P-TECH collaboration. When one of the mentors at the P-TECH at Carver Vocational-Technical High School in Baltimore heard that a student loved sneakers, he arranged a tour of a secret Under Armour facility, where students could learn how materials were developed.

"They told the students, 'We're looking for people like you,'" said Lori Bush, who runs the Carver P-TECH. "Who would ever think of it, if I had a degree in cybersecurity, that I could go work at Under Armour?"

Xavier Gutierrez in Longmont, CO, had one mentor for 4 years, and he keeps in touch with her through LinkedIn. She went to a lot of his school ceremonies and has been "a huge support in my life, personal and educational," he said. "Sometimes when I was having my mental health days, I had a comfort level with her that I'd be able to talk about it." She also helped him build his résumé and navigate the corporate world. "I learned how to be an adult," he said, and she assured him of IBM's antidiscrimination policies, which he might not otherwise have known to ask about.

Xavier's schoolmate, David Vazquez, 18, graduated with an associate degree in Computer Information Systems—Programming from the Skyline P-TECH in 4 years, and he was hired by IBM for a yearlong apprenticeship. Throughout, he found his mentors taught him a great deal.

"I knew nothing about being a professional, what it meant to be a professional, having a real job, fulfilling all the requirements," he said. But his mentor, Tory Liesenfelt, was available whenever David had questions. "Coming from him, and him being so available and willing to help, reinforced the fact that yeah, I'm not alone in this, I can ask, I can learn."

Liesenfelt helped David with what he was learning beyond his schoolwork: "Being a professional is not just about what you know, but about what you bring to a team, if you're a good person, if you're willing to help, if you can receive help as well," David said. "I struggled with that."

He learned about asking for help in a mock job interview with his mentor.

"I was getting interviewed but didn't really know what the interviewer was talking about, and I didn't want to look like I was not knowledgeable because it was an interview, and I want to get this job," David said. "That was hard, for me to ask a question there, because of the impact on the job you get, but I just kept thinking, you know what? I'm going to do it. I'm going to show that I'm willing to ask."

Turns out, that was what the interviewer was looking for. If David *hadn't* asked for help, Liesenfelt explained, he would've been a weaker candidate for the job. That helped David moving forward, in class and in internships.

Keira Downes a P-TECH freshman at the University of Newcastle Food Science & Nutrition program, said access to her mentor was perhaps the best support for her educational progress.

"For the majority of my life I was someone who tried to figure things out on my own," she said, remembering how she would spend five periods confused in a class, for fear of looking dumb and being judged. Now she spends less time in that limbo.

"Having those mentors definitely helped me realize there's so much more I'm able to be capable of," she said. "I'd been restricting myself, because I wasn't reaching out, getting that help as needed."

Her mentor, Veronica Maszke, the group IT manager at P-TECH's partner, Sanitarium Health Food Company, helped Keira work through her issues with diabetes and gain perspective about it.

"I had put myself in a position where I thought I could not achieve what I wanted to achieve," Keira said. "Veronica helped me understand that just because I had this medical condition, it wasn't going to stop me from being whoever I please . . . and do whatever I wanted to do, if I had the right connections in the industry."

Paid Internships

In internships, students come to imagine themselves in careers they might not otherwise have considered. Higher-income students often get internships through family connections, and they can afford to work for free. P-TECH provides a path to paid internships for students of color and those from lower-income families, opportunities that serve them well when they apply to universities or jobs later. Paychecks for their summer work form another incentive for them to stay in school, and the businesses sponsoring the internships can come to know diverse potential job candidates.

Arranging internships can be time consuming, as in Brooklyn, when 61 students qualified for a position the first year. I took almost 9 months for IBM, which previously had only worked with upperclassmen college interns or those in graduate school, to develop positions for 41 high school juniors, with the rest working at Brooklyn Navy Yard, CUNY, City Tech, Grand Central Tech, and a city law firm. Some New York City students were able to do their internships on IBM's Global Technology Services team, working with cloud services, on a management system used to support the U.S. Open, which they attended, to see their work in action.

Before students start such placements, P-TECH staff spend several months coaching them on learning the specific technical skills they will need, plus soft skills such as dressing appropriately, interviewing, and creating online portfolios of their work from school and from extracurricular activities such as hackathons, where software developers, designers, and others work on software challenges on a deadline.

The workplaces prepare as well, to be sure managers and staff offer students the most useful and engaging experiences. Business liaisons often plan an event at the end of the internship to review the students' work and progress. At IBM, teams of interns often present their work at summer's end, with awards given for excellence.

Rothman, the principal at the Newburgh P-TECH, said businesses may need encouragement when they first consider high school interns. "There was some anxiety, some pushback, they didn't really know if it would work," he said. "The kids are young. Can they be successful working in an internship? IBM here had never done it before."

But once the students started working, the doubts evaporated. "When they show up and are willing to be eager and curious about things, and they show up on time and can write a professional email, that translates to fans," he said. The school has now become concerned that they will not have enough students to fill all the internships IBM is offering.

Many business partners find insights from their interns to be downright profitable. Johnstown P-TECH students built a website that doubled business for Jim Law, owner of Frozen Parts in Fultonville, NY, which sells replacement parts for ice cream freezers. He hosted several paid interns for 2 or 3 hours a week, and would have hired them full-time, if they had stayed in town.

"They were 14 and 15 years old, and thinking like a 35-year-old in the business world," he recalled. One student asked why parts of sinks he sold had to be made of metal. "A light went on," he said. "I said, 'they don't.'" One student came up with a company logo that charmed him, and he continues to use it. He heard she is now a doctor.

"I have nothing but high marks for all the students they sent to us," said Law, who used to visit the school a dozen times a year, always with several gallons of ice cream to share.

Gabrielle Madison, who runs Community Relations for the media company Thomson Reuters in Texas, said P-TECH is a way for the company to "grow talent." She finds the P-TECH graduates more loyal and more adaptable in the workplace than the 4-year college graduates the company usually hires, and the company is exploring expanding the program in Michigan and Minnesota.

SHUDON'S STORY

ShuDon Brown, a Brooklyn P-TECH graduate, learned about taking initiative when she was supposed to work on motherboards and hardware questions in her junior-year internship. She realized it was not a good fit for her interests and asked her supervisor, Mike Sava, if she could work on databases, which he agreed to.

Later, Sava mentioned that he had a house in upstate New York with horses. It was a eureka moment for ShuDon, who loved horses and had always dreamt of owning some.

"I suddenly saw that my dream didn't have to stay a dream," she said. "In that moment, Mike gave me a gift he probably has no clue about—he gifted me a vision of my life beyond what a young Black girl in Bed-Stuy thought she could have."

ShuDon earned her high school diploma and her associate degree with honors in 4 years, went on to get her bachelor's degree in 2, and just completed her master's degree while working full-time for IBM.

She is now a supply chain professional for the company in Raleigh-Durham, NC, and is pursuing her PhD in leadership studies.

Another IBM mentor at a later internship, Jason Mudd, had given her extra work when she asked, wrote letters of recommendation for her, and then welcomed her on board when she was hired full-time at IBM. He has since advised her to join various after-work clubs to broaden her network, given her tips on how casual to be on casual Fridays, and clued her in to other unwritten rules of the business world she might not have known otherwise. The clubs have led her to mentor a high school student who visited IBM.

JOEL'S STORY

When Joel Duran first worked as a summer intern for IBM as a junior, helping match students to internships, it was a big deal for him to meet people in corporate America who embodied his goals. In his neighborhood, East New York, it felt like everyone wanted to be a drug dealer or a rapper, he said.

"It was hard to find peers who had the same aspirations and ambitions as I did," he said. "I knew I wanted to get out of that situation."

Joining people who worked 9 to 5 in technology showed him what was possible.

"I could do that too," he said. "When you see so many students from P-TECH transitioning to corporate America at an early age, seamlessly, because you're exposed to it so early, you feel you can do this as well."

At an event senior year, when students were preparing their résumés, Joel met an IBMer named Sean, whom he still speaks with. They hit it off and would talk about what was going on in their lives. At the time, Joel had a close friend who had passed away, and he was able to talk to Sean, who had experienced a similar loss and gave good advice.

"I lost a few friends, coming from that neighborhood, I guess you could say it's expected," Joel said. One died in a sports accident, and another died in a car accident after leaving a college party.

Sean invited Joel to the IBM offices during his summer internship to learn web development as an add-on to his regular internship, and he provided perspective when Joel was considering colleges. One of Joel's main aims in going to college was to get out of his house and neighborhood, and he did not want to be held back by large student loans. Sean, who had grown up middle class and gone to an Ivy

League school, where he met super-wealthy classmates, was able to share his insights with Joel.

"Sean was a very interesting individual," Joel said. "You could make assumptions of who he is, but when you actually speak to him and get to know him, he really is a very deep individual, very complex. It teaches you not to judge people, and that anyone you see who is not from your background, you can't assume because they've got money, they don't know struggle. In reality, everyone has struggle."

Through college at SUNY Albany, which he completed in five semesters, Joel did several more internships with IBM, which hired him full-time. He is working with the Federal Emergency Management Agency as a technology consultant, answering help desk questions on flood plains and risk management. He does not know what his ultimate career goal is, but he knows that what he is doing now feels productive and can help him get closer.

Joel tries to mentor other young people, including his cousins and siblings. He tells them he was not the brightest student, but he put in the work. He knows how many times he failed in order to get where he is. Consistency is critical, he tells them. Trying again and again was the key to escaping East New York.

Recently, he spoke to a friend from his old neighborhood, who told him he was the only person she knew to get out.

"It feels like a black hole sometimes, which is unfortunate to say, but a lot of your peers, the people you grow up with, stay in the same situations, predicaments, and circumstances," he said. "It's definitely depressing."

As far as he is concerned, P-TECH people do not get enough credit for all the hours they put in. "Those interactions tell you people care about you and they want you to be successful," he said. "Everything going on in that little building is pretty special. They're actually changing lives. There's beauty in the struggle."

REAPING THE BENEFITS

When Amalik Morille was a senior at the Brooklyn P-TECH, Charlotte Lysohir, the school's IBM liaison at the time, approached him to see if he was interested in an internship, which he had missed the year before. He googled the woman he would be speaking with.

"That's when I realized just how lucky I was in that situation because Doris Gonzalez was the corporate citizenship head of both North and South America," he said. "Working with someone that high up, on the first shot? Wow, damn, thank you Charlotte!"

He did not feel nervous in that first interview. His desire to provide for his family—his mother, brother, and grandmother—trumped any nervousness he might have felt.

"That's just something you throw out the window, when you have people depending on you," he said. "In my mind, I was like, there's no way I don't have this, so let me just be me. In doing so, it went well."

He waited a week to hear how he had done, and remembers getting the call from Gonzalez with his start date.

"My reaction was immediate tears," he said. "I don't cry for much, and my mother and grandmother came out of the room asking what happened. I said, 'I got the job!'"

His mission: working at 590 Madison Ave., IBM's former headquarters, to create a marketing plan for the CUNY/IBM Watson Case Competition, in which all the CUNY schools would be using AI to address problems in neighborhoods and the city Department of Education. Amalik made great connections and enjoyed the "down-to-earth" people he worked with.

"You do a combination of hard work and skill displayed and a little bit of luck, and it humbles you, but it also gives you a sense of pride," he said. "It's good to know that there are genuine people like that in corporate America."

He knew he was right for the job, "because I had people behind me, pushing me, encouraging me," he said.

Tobias Soul of the P-TECH in Ballarat, Australia, recalls feeling prepared for his 6-week internship with an airline. "I was never scared to go to my managers, it's what I do here," he said. He and his peers helped build a ticketing system, and they finished a week early, so they were assigned to design an executive dashboard in their last week. A supervisor was pleased with the work and showed it to higher-ups in the design department, which made him feel proud. Tobias, who was home schooled through year 10 of his schooling and has cerebral palsy, enjoyed the independence P-TECH offered, as well as the work experience.

"We were given a lot of responsibility to make our own decisions and carry the consequence like you do as an adult," he said.

School leaders are impressed by how much the internships mean to the students, and the transformation they see afterward. "When I went to their internship presentation, I saw kids talking about projects who didn't say 10 sentences the whole school year," said Bush, of the P-TECH in Baltimore.

She knows an IBM internship will not only look terrific on their résumés but will also solidify the workplace skills they are learning at Carver. "Otherwise, all this stuff is abstract," she said.

"One of the students talked about how important he was to the team, when he was doing his internship—'I couldn't be late to team meetings because the team members were depending on me.' That's never anything people think about," she said, adding with a laugh, "Everyone hates group work."

She said the self-confidence they gained in the internships provided the fuel they needed to finish their associate degrees: "Even if they decided they wanted to go to a university, they knew they could work with professionals now. They could say, I did an internship at IBM. I worked on a team with college interns when I was in high school." It is important to note that these internships are much more than a summer job; they are a continued part of the students' education, directly connecting school to career.

SOCIAL CAPITAL

While one could tally up the price of a 2-year degree, and even the hourly costs of academic help through tutors and perhaps mentors, the professional connections made through a program such as P-TECH are priceless. The students understand this, in part through encouragement by teachers sharing workplace skills.

Business liaisons are very willing to help too. Gabrielle Madison, who runs Community Relations for Thomson Reuters in Texas, knows it is unlikely that all the students she works with at North Dallas High School will join the company, so she has opened up her rolodex to ones who want to take their associate degrees to other fields, connecting them to other P-TECH partners, in commercial real estate, for example.

In the three jobs he has had before and after graduating from the P-TECH in Longmont, CO, Xavier Gutierrez has made connections with inventors, moviemakers, and lifetime IBMers.

"I'd meet people all over the world," he said. "Just in my internship, I met a couple people in India through P-TECH, and Brazil." His teachers encouraged students to reach out via LinkedIn to people they met through work, and to thank them for their help.

"If we were ever looking for a job at IBM, they reminded us we could always reach out and ask those people if they knew of anything," Xavier said.

Akhtar, of the Brooklyn P-TECH, connected to 80 people on LinkedIn in just 3 months, while in Norwalk, CT, P-TECH student Julia Turek developed a hefty network long before she was ready to enter the job market.

"Me and my boyfriend had a competition to get more contacts in LinkedIn," she said. "He's still ahead."

Amalik Morille had always valued connections, from learning as much as he could from his neighborhood. "I grew up towards the end of Crime Heights, when Crown Heights was as bad as it could've been," he said. He saw how people with a college degree but a scant network were not getting anywhere.

"To me the prospect of making connections was always valued over a degree. I mean it was the ride from my neighborhood," he said. "I felt prouder of myself when I got my internship with IBM, more than when I graduated."

TIME TO HIRE GRADUATES

When students graduate from P-TECH schools with associate degrees, school staff and industry liaisons help them either to apply to a 4-year college or to work for their school's industry partners. For those interested in moving directly into the workforce at companies, staff prepare students for job interviews and assist throughout the hiring process. Mentors and managers during internships offer their assistance and connections, and, in IBM's case, the HR department helps as well.

Business partners of P-TECH schools look forward to this stage of the partnership. When Mike Reagan, senior vice president of consulting services at CGI, thinks about the students he will hire from the first cohort in P-TECH New Brunswick, he knows they will have heard presentations about his IT and business consulting company, visited it, and, in some cases, interned there.

"By the time they join CGI, they have an advantage over the other college hires I'm bringing in," he said. "Our onboarding is usually the first 2 to 4 weeks, but they're getting it in bitesize chunks in their high school career."

While Reagan is familiar with concerns that some educators have about corporate involvement in the classroom, he said the district, from the superintendent down to the students, has welcomed his firm and its input about what skills it needs. He said many schools put students through classes merely hoping that employers will be looking for particular talents, but with P-TECH, he can regularly share new information about what his clients need and what he hopes to provide.

He has encouraged other companies to partner with P-TECH, and he speaks frequently about the benefits of homegrown employees. Some states and countries regulate the data, banking, and utilities industries, requiring them to use domestic employees, and some U.S. industries are turning away from offshore hires, realizing that employees in different time zones can cause difficulties in communication and workflow.

He is also glad to be making connections with Middlesex Community College and New Jersey Institute of Technology, the 4-year college that has agreed to accept P-TECH graduates as juniors. In fact, Reagan is working on hiring graduates of those schools even before the first P-TECH students graduate, thinking that such hires will be young, have the degrees his company needs, and will be familiar with the programs P-TECH students will be graduating from. They will be well-equipped to serve as CGI mentors to P-TECH students in the years ahead, he reasons.

Reagan knows that many of the young people who graduate with an associate degree may go on to college instead of applying for jobs, but he will be reminding them that his company pays employees to continue their schooling, up to and including a master's degree.

Inspired by the large number of qualified P-TECH graduates, IBM has established an apprenticeship program that lasts about a year and gives students more avenues of preparation for permanent employment at a Fortune 100 company. The jobs P-TECH graduates enter are on clear career tracks, and many graduates have already been promoted once or twice and are in the position of hiring people themselves.

WHEN COLLABORATORS COLLABORATE

For the past decade, IBM has brought P-TECH schools and their partners together for planning and for learning from one another. In 2011, the staff of the Brooklyn school spent 24 hours at the IBM headquarters to learn more about workplace skills, project-based learning, and creative teaching approaches. As new schools came on board, their staffs all met together as well, and as new schools opened in New York, Connecticut, and Maryland, statewide meetings helped school staff, community colleges, and business partners fine-tune their collaborations.

These efforts helped collaborators plan, solve problems, and trade feedback on how to improve the model and enhance MentorSpace and other tools. PTECH.org, an international online platform developed by IBM, is also helpful for those launching new schools. It provides free assistance for beginning and established principals and teachers, including a timeline of critical tasks during the planning of a new school; guidance on workplace skills valued by employers; help with how to set up mentorships, internships, and visits to colleges and businesses; and advice on creating a "scope and sequence" of courses, so students have time to take the necessary courses, in the right order, to finish their degrees. The site also includes curriculum units where students can earn badges recognized by future employers on topics that include blockchain, AI, cloud, and even quantum computing. In 2019, IBM organized Planet P-TECH, a gathering of schools to share best practices, an indication that the model is becoming more than a reform effort, but a movement.

During the coronavirus pandemic, leaders of all the North American P-TECH schools affiliated with IBM were invited to a monthly call to keep in touch; similar calls have happened in Europe, Asia, and Latin America.

TAKEAWAYS

Schools gain from working closely with businesses and community colleges that want to be involved in the community, as the students gain relationships with engaged adults. Such collaborations work best when each partner has a voice in planning interactions.

Students hoping to pursue specific careers can get inspiration from classroom presentations by workers in various fields, from visiting workplaces, and from interacting with mentors. Interns can grow into more advanced roles, enjoying the challenge and earning a paycheck. They can envision bright professional futures for themselves, and they see themselves belonging in fields of opportunity, even if society has told them otherwise.

Community colleges benefit from well-prepared students who graduate on time, and businesses gain a pipeline of familiar, qualified employees who reflect the broader society.

For districts, partnerships can add a range of resources. The private sector and higher education are logical collaborators with high schools and can offer helpful assets, but to get the largest benefit, staff from all three must be part of planning and decisionmaking, all working for the students. The synergy of these efforts creates success on a larger scale than could be achieved separately.

People interested in learning how to create P-TECH collaborations in their countries, states, districts, or schools, and people interested in entering a partnership on behalf of their school, community college, or business, should visit www.ptech.org.

CHAPTER 7

Conscientious Leadership

Do not go where the path may lead, go instead where there is no path and leave a trail.

—Ralph Waldo Emerson

A genuine leader is not a searcher for consensus but a molder of consensus.

—Martin Luther King Jr.

P-TECH could not have evolved into a worldwide network of collaborative schools without the hard work of leaders in the classroom, main office, school district, college, mayor's and governor's offices, C-suite, White House, and beyond.

On the high school level, there is a particular style of principal leadership that requires optimism, deep commitment to equity and collaboration, and a willingness to fail at first, adapt, and keep going. Community colleges and business partners have worked with great determination to nurture and strengthen the model and further its growth.

Outside the school-based collaborations, leadership looks like cooperation and open-mindedness, as various sectors learn each other's languages and priorities, and then figure out how to corral varied interests in one direction. Crucial for the cause, the heads of cities, states, and nations have quickly and boldly signed on to the new model, spoken about it publicly, and have worked to create new partnerships.

For the model to become sustainable, the support of IBM has been crucial. Other large corporations, governments, and labor organizations, similarly, could contribute their time and expertise to ensure the spread of educational innovations.

SCHOOL LEADERSHIP: PRINCIPALS

In a 2009 report,[1] New Leaders for New Schools determined that an effective principal accounted for a 25% increase in student performance. Principals were second only to high-quality teachers in having a positive role in boosting student achievement.

When examining the traits of principals who successfully transformed their schools, the research group Public Agenda found that these principals had an explicit vision for change, did not get bogged down in obstacles, and moved forward effectively in cooperation with their faculty to execute their vision.[2]

Like any principal, a P-TECH school leader has to listen well, respect and motivate teachers, and collaborate with staff, parents, and other community members. He or she has to keep up with student data, understand standards and course content, know how to run a building, and stick to a budget. It is a complex job in any school. Beyond that, P-TECH principals must master the links between high school and community college, ensuring that students meet and master all the requirements to be college ready and, eventually, to graduate. A P-TECH principal needs to make sure that high school teachers engage effectively with the college faculty and must also cultivate productive relationships with their industry partners. This requires becoming familiar with the mindset, habits, pace, and vocabulary of the business world, understanding the resources that may be available and how to access them. This is a complex mission, but one that can truly benefit students.

Perhaps most importantly, every P-TECH principal believes each student can succeed regardless of income level, race, ethnicity, or prior educational achievement, and he or she commits to supporting them. The principals also listen to their teachers, believe the teachers will succeed in the mission, and back them up accordingly.

P-TECH'S FOUNDING PRINCIPAL

Rashid Davis has always lived within walking distance of the schools where he has worked. He walks through his students' communities, he said, to remind himself to keep a sense of urgency: "That's my fear, that we're moving too slow."

He knows that when some of his students get their paid internships, there is much rejoicing but also worry that their new income might jeopardize their family's food stamps. Some graduates who get job offers cannot keep living with their family, as their income might take away their eligibility for public housing. In a city with pricey real estate, they face harder calculations than any they mastered in the classroom.

On the 25-minute walk from his home in the Bedford-Stuyvesant section of Brooklyn to his school in Crown Heights, he sees evidence of the 40% unemployment rate for men of color. He thinks of what his students, predominantly young men of color, see when they walk home, and the difficulties faced by the women in poor neighborhoods. "I walk around purposefully every single day, to be able to fight my own limitations," he said.

Davis's impatience with the status quo has shaped his 25-year career in education. "I've been fortunate to be really engrossed in innovation since the early 2000s," he said, at his desk at P-TECH. "That's why I'm really a pain in the ass to a lot of people, because I'm constantly evolving."

Near his diplomas from Pace, Fordham, and Teachers College, Columbia University, behind his desk hangs a blanket from Morehouse College, his undergraduate alma mater, with its motto, *Et Facta Est Lux*—"And there was light." The words thread their way through the story of how he came to run P-TECH. His careful study of data and his strong desire to use proven techniques to prepare students for bright futures have guided the school from its inception.

"The more you know, the more you can get yourself out of darkness," he said.

P-TECH's teachers provide the strongest testimony of Davis's leadership powers.

Joan "Mama" Casey admires how he trusted the staff. "You have to have the staff involved; you have to have the staff having a say in what is happening," she said. "He trusts you. He doesn't run into the classroom and watch all day. He trusts you to do what he expects you to do, and therefore if you love your craft, it means you will try literally any and every thing to make sure your kids do well. We have that here."

Stanley Kaminsky, a professor from his master's degree program at Fordham University, which gave Davis its first-ever lifetime achievement award, said Davis stood out as insightful.

"He was able to implement ideas and ways to change things without upsetting the quality of what was good already," Kaminsky said. "If you make too many quick changes, things start bouncing off the walls and the ceilings. . . . He was able to find that middle ground of providing some comfort, and some stress or discomfort, for positive change, all focused on what students need to achieve."

He also noticed in Davis a trait that is very hard to teach: the art, rather than the science, of educating and leading.

"The art is interpersonal relations," Kaminsky said. "He seems to have understood well the art of leadership, and the ability not just to persuade, but to convince and work along with other people and have them work with him. That's harder to teach, and he seems to have that package."

Seifullah, one of the first math teachers at the Brooklyn P-TECH, considers Davis a mentor, and she appreciated his view that teachers who model a willingness to fail and try again are teaching their students, by example, how life and learning work. Davis encouraged her to try so many different teaching techniques, and she never felt at risk of being written up as a troublemaker.

"I made a ton of mistakes, and if he would let me know, I didn't feel my job was in danger or that I had been reprimanded disrespectfully," she said. One of her favorite features of the P-TECH model was the way it encouraged staff as well as students to try a difficult challenge, fail, try again with support, and succeed.

Seifullah also admires how Davis has turned P-TECH into an incubator of sorts, nurturing a significant number of teachers-turned-principals, including Seung Yu, the founding principal of the Academy for Software Engineering and principal of Stuyvesant High School; Cindy Casseus, now principal of P.S. 298; and four of P-TECH's assistant principals.

"He does a really phenomenal job at creating leadership," Seifullah said. In the school's third year, Davis asked her and another teacher to lead a team of teachers to work with students who did not have enough credits to start college. She very much enjoyed the work.

"At that point, I wasn't thinking about opening a school," she said. "I was meeting with friends planning a dream school, and I invited Rashid to one of those meetings. He nominated me for that process to propose a school."

Now the principal of the Highland Park Community School, a middle school in East New York focused on STEAM (the A is for Arts) and project-based learning, she aims to treat her teachers the way Davis treated her. "I try to support them and give them the creative freedom I had, from Rashid," she said.

Holding high expectations for staff has its downside of course—a nurturing principal has to spend a lot of time hiring and training replacements.

"I definitely could be working easier at P-TECH if I did not en-courage mentees to grow and accept or pursue school-building lead-ership positions," Davis wrote in a blog post.[3] "Yet, it was necessary for me to help them with their growth as others have helped me to grow."

Kaminsky also admires Davis' knack for turning teachers into principals. "I told him and still tell all the others, thank you so much for helping to form future school leaders, not just to run schools well, but because we have to replace ourselves," he said. "If we don't do that, we're remiss, and all your hard work goes down the tubes."

Zakiyyah Ali, a former teacher in P-TECH Brooklyn who went on to pursue a doctorate in education, was among many of the people Davis has encouraged to aim for promotions. She remembers telling him that, after a year teaching for him, she was offered a job at New York University to study violations of student civil rights. He asked her why she was still sitting in front of him, and said "How do you expect to grow if you never challenge yourself? Girl, get out of my office and go take that opportunity."

Most of all, Ali admires how Davis's work helps students from poor families excel in school. "The last time I checked, being poor didn't mean your brain didn't work," she said. "Davis is shining the light on it, and I love that."

LEADERSHIP IN OTHER P-TECH PRINCIPALS

In the P-TECH in Norwalk, CT, founding principal Karen Amaker's vision requires teachers to push the envelope consistently. "When we meet, I tell them I'm challenging you to do one thing differently," she said. When they ask if they can try an experiment by the end of the first quarter, she says absolutely not—try the next 2 weeks. "We'll have a reflection meeting to talk about your ideas," she tells them. "I'm pushing you. Our kids deserve nothing less."

She too wants her staff to take on leadership roles, if they wish.

"I'm not always going to be around," she said. "I do hope they want to move up, if they want to start P-TECH schools or further the P-TECH mission. And I would love to see students come back to teach, in 2 or 3 years, to have P-TECH graduates who may have earned a degree in software engineering, then come back to teach special edu-cation or science."

She has a vision of P-TECH in its own building, with a "maker space" where an observer would not be able to tell the students from the teachers, as they would be learning from and teaching each other.

"For me, P-TECH really means turning education on its ear," she said. "Absolutely anything is possible."

SUPERINTENDENTS

With 18 P-TECHs, Dallas Schools Superintendent Michael Hinojosa has more such schools in his city than any other, and more than 70 businesses partners. One of them, Toni DeGuire Parker, IBM's Bridge to Employment program manager in Dallas, is proud of her city's philosophy: "Anything anybody else can do, we're going to do just as big if not bigger." In Dallas, where 90% of the public school students are non-White, one of every eight high school students in 2020 was attending a P-TECH program.[4]

Schools wanting to join the model apply to the state education agency and receive planning grants from the district. P-TECHs have to renew their applications each year to make sure they are maintaining the program properly. Dallas County Promise, an offshoot of the national College Promise program once cochaired by Dr. Jill Biden, is a nonprofit group that provides tuition assistance, coaching, and advising. It pays for Dallas P-TECH students' associate degrees and partners with 4-year colleges and universities. In true Texas fashion, the Dallas schools accept cohorts of 125 students per year, larger than average.

Six central office staff people work full-time on the model schools, which are smaller schools within existing ones. Each new school has a dedicated assistant principal/P-TECH administrator, college counselor, and workplace learning coordinator. There is also a citywide advisory board that includes business partners, district leadership, community stakeholders, and leaders of Dallas College.

Dallas P-TECHs cover a variety of career paths, including business administration, law enforcement, public health, energy management, logistics, hospitality management, personal computer support, and early childhood education. During the pandemic, AT&T, Accenture, Pepsi-Co/Frito-Lay, and others provided students with virtual internship opportunities. Other business partners include Bank of America, FedEx, Texas Instruments, Microsoft, Dell, PricewaterhouseCoopers, and, of course, IBM.

Sixty-eight percent of the city's P-TECH students have graduated with their associate degrees in just 4 years, and as of late 2020, a partner in one of the schools, Thomson Reuters, has hired two dozen graduates. They owe much to Dr. Hinojosa's leadership.

Don Haddad is the superintendent of the St. Vrain Valley School District in Longmont, CO, near Boulder. A former national Superintendent of the Year, he has been a strong P-TECH advocate from the very beginning, and it helped him address the district's 45% high school dropout rate for Latinx students. In his conversations with students, some had told him they did not plan on finishing high school, as they wanted to start working as soon as possible, to contribute to supporting their families.

"P-TECH has helped students across the district to understand the importance of a high school degree, and now a college degree. And it's made a huge difference," Dr. Haddad said. With four P-TECHs and two more opening in the fall of 2021, the district, where most students are Latinx and eligible for free lunch, has reached a 90% high school graduation rate for Latinx students. Haddad attributes this largely to P-TECH, calling it "the most systemic and transformative reform in education" he has seen in his career.

At the initial P-TECH school in Longmont, 110 students earned IBM internships, and 70 interned for other industry partners. IBM provided 132 mentors to the district.

COLLEGES

David Levinson, an early supporter of the model, was the president of Norwalk Community College in Connecticut when P-TECH launched in 2014. Following Governor Cuomo's lead in New York, then governor Dannell Malloy had pledged to replicate P-TECH statewide and cover college tuition costs out of state funds, but budget problems prevented that. Dr. Levinson agreed to fund the costs out of his own budget. He consistently championed the program across the state and encouraged other higher education leaders to embrace it.

"P-TECH is a truly innovative and effective way of increasing college readiness and college completion rates," Levinson said. "I'd encourage all our leaders in higher education to embrace it."

By 2018, SUNY embedded the program in all 30 of its community colleges. Johanna Duncan-Poitier, SUNY's Senior Vice Chancellor for Community Colleges and the Education Pipeline, remembers attending an orientation in Schenectady, where P-TECH students were telling 8th-graders about the opportunities at the school, and how it changed their lives.

"You could see there were more students who wanted to be a part of this than there were slots available," she said. "They saw, for many of them—and the parents definitely—this as the only chance."

Duncan-Poitier, who had worked at the state education department when P-TECH was launched under Commissioner John King 4 years earlier, said unlike city students, who see successful businesspeople on the streets and subways, rural students may live in isolation, and they see success in terms of very low-skilled work.

"A lot of colleges in rural areas didn't just adopt P-TECH, they embraced it. They see it as access to experiences students didn't even know were in their reach," she said. "It's life-changing."

The community college presidents think the P-TECH partnerships help non-P-TECH students as well, opening up closer relationships with businesses that lead to internships.

"It impacts the entire environment," she said. "Kids talk to other kids, and become part of a culture of success," so a P-TECH graduate's brother or sister, who might not have planned on college, can now see it as a real possibility.

Duncan-Poitier admires the model's high graduation rate, particularly for students who are behind when they start high school and are at risk of dropping out. It has also helped in her mission of reducing the number of SUNY students who need remedial classes. She has enjoyed watching P-TECH partners meeting together, and having trouble guessing who was a teacher, student, professor, or businessperson.

"K–12 educators speak one language, about what's important to them, testing, and the Regents testing standards," she said. "Community college educators are worried about persistence, graduation, the readiness of the students or the lack thereof."

Businesspeople, meanwhile, talk about needing to hire a skilled workforce. She remembers pitching the program to GlobalFoundries executives who doubted they could allow high school students to play on their million-dollar semiconductor manufacturing machines. "By the end, they had these students coming in who were as good if not better than some of the people working there before," she said. "They saw their value."

Over time, she saw how the representatives of the different sectors had learned each other's language, with school superintendents speaking as eloquently about what was important to IBM, Tesla, or Regeneron as the business representatives could.

She wants to see the model expand further across New York State to help more students become ready for college. SUNY's current chancellor, Jim Malatras, is another strong advocate of the program, having exhibited strong leadership in helping Governor Cuomo and IBM launch its spread across the state.

Duncan-Poitier still bristles when critics say some students should just save taxpayer money and skip college, but she feels that when skilled jobs are going unfilled, the future economy depends on having as educated a population as possible.

"At the end of the day, we can't afford to have disposable people," she said.

MOVING BEYOND THE SCHOOL COLLABORATION

No P-TECH school will be successful without a skilled and effective principal, a dedicated superintendent, a college president who buys in to the model, and engaged business partners. But the vocal support of other leaders in other sectors, especially at the highest levels, has been critical to spreading the model widely.

While the initial plan had been instigated by a mayor, a CEO, and a school chancellor, P-TECH owes a great deal to a significant network of leaders in government. First up was then Mayor Michael Bloomberg, who not only helped launch the program but was willing to cover half the cost of City Tech college tuition and urge CUNY to cover the other half.

Bloomberg shared his enthusiasm about P-TECH with Rahm Emanuel, the mayor of Chicago at the time, who visited him shortly after taking office to discuss innovations in New York City that might work in the Second City. Right after their meeting, as he walked onto the streets of the Upper East Side, Emanuel took out his cellphone and called IBM's CEO, Sam Palmisano, urging his help in opening five such schools in Chicago.

Within the hour, Litow got his call. Palmisano indicated that he wanted to be as responsive and helpful as possible to the mayor, and asked what would be involved. Litow made it clear that it was definitely possible to extend the model into Chicago, but that Emanuel would need to understand that he would have to guarantee that tuition costs would be covered, as Bloomberg had done, and urge collaboration and support both from the school district and the colleges. Meeting Chicago's goal of five new schools would involve lining up four additional industry partners and support from higher education. Palmisano asked Litow to lead a meeting with Emanuel and John Tolva, the city's chief technology officer, who coincidentally had been on Litow's team at IBM. Emanuel declared himself "all in," then promised to recruit other companies, community colleges, and the head of Chicago Public Schools. By October 2011, a month after the Brooklyn school opened, IBM selected Chicago for a Smarter Cities challenge grant providing pro bono services worth $400,000 to lay the groundwork for opening up to five schools.

At the time, a new high school was about to open on Chicago's South Side, named for Sarah E. Goode, who was born a slave and who was the first African American woman to sign for a U.S. patent, for her design of the precursor to a Murphy bed. Emanuel committed to putting a new P-TECH in that building, and the Goode STEM Academy opened in 2012, enrolling 463 students by its second year.

BEYOND CITIES

It would have been limiting for P-TECH to be seen as just an urban school solution. Broader replication of the model would require leadership at the state level to expand to smaller cities, suburban districts, and rural areas. Based on the number of 9th-graders at the first Brooklyn school passing their Regents exams and deemed college ready by the end of their first year, the team at IBM felt ready to replicate the model sooner than expected. While some education experts would have advocated waiting for a few classes of students to graduate, P-TECH was designed as a plug-and-play model to be replicated inexpensively, without requiring changes to union rules or to the way districts operated. P-TECH's architects were convinced the model would help students excel, and soon, so expanding was imperative.

It was time to ramp up the assembly line, while continuing the test drives. The initial year's success in Brooklyn would need to be sustained and increased as students hit 10th grade, while the model would spread, with the help of consistent leadership. The funding and regulating of education in the United States are, overwhelmingly, state functions, and governors have great power—along with a bully pulpit—to advance school improvements, if they choose. In the past, few have. While Jim Hunt of North Carolina was proud to call himself the "Education Governor" at the turn of the previous century, putting education reform in the center of his platform, few of his peers have followed suit. As controversy swirled around the Common Core, charter schools, and school choice, politicians—governors in particular—rarely focused on education, making the leadership of a handful of exceptions so noteworthy.

States had several reasons to adopt the model and open P-TECH schools. For one, many were already paying for early college courses for high school students, for financial aid for their community college students, and for the $2.6 billion in remedial courses and staffing some students required. Tuition for P-TECH students was a sound investment, as they needed no remedial courses. If states negotiating for a P-TECH program wanted to fund college classes only through grade 12, they were declined. The model, and its students, relied on the carrot of the free associate degree at the end—not just classes or credits, but a résumé-leading credential in a job-rich discipline. It was central to the mission.

Case in point is Governor Cuomo's vow to expand P-TECH in every economic development region of the state, aiming to open 10 new schools in 2014. The Business Council of New York State actively encouraged its members to become business partners. In advance of releasing his budget, Cuomo praised the model: "Linking our secondary and higher education institutions to the economic development of the region is a logical connection that will greatly improve our workforce and help students find jobs directly out of college.[5]

When New York's request for proposal attracted an impressive number of applications, he found funding to launch 16 of them, with planning grants and with all tuition costs covered. Of the 500 students who entered those schools in 2014, 199 have completed their college degrees, and another 140 completed at least 1 full year of college credit toward their 2-year degrees. Within 6 years, there were 50 P-TECHs across New York State.

One school opened in Newburgh, the city with the state's highest crime rate and a poverty rate of 31%.[6] When Lt. Governor Kathy Hochul visited it, she saw the unique approach teachers were taking focused on problem solving. In a session with a group of 9th-graders, she asked one girl to name one thing she had learned through the program. The girl responded that she had learned how to do an "elevator pitch" and then explained to the lieutenant governor how to prepare such a pitch, to explain a project in the clearest, quickest way. Hochul has since described herself as "a P-TECH champion."

Shortly after the launches in New York State, then Connecticut Governor Dannel Malloy expressed interest in the model when talking to U.S. Secretary of Education Arne Duncan, who gave him Litow's cellphone number. Duncan had visited the Brooklyn P-TECH twice, once with then President Obama. After a meeting at the governor's residence with business and education leaders, Malloy urged them to get on board. In his 2014 State of the State address, Malloy described his desire to open a P-TECH: "Let's offer students this experience, and help put them on a path to a great job."[7] A collaboration grew, and a P-TECH school in Norwalk opened within roughly 6 months.

Soon after, Connecticut's Education Commissioner at the time, Stefan Pryor, who was instrumental in the Connecticut launch, moved to work for then Rhode Island Governor Gina Raimondo as Secretary of Commerce, having asked the principal of Norwalk High School to speak at his pre-appointment hearing. At Pryor's urging, Raimondo also called Litow to hear more about P-TECH, and after a face-to-face meeting, she convened a group of education and business leaders at the capitol to hear the benefits of the program. At these early meetings, IBM was able to invite its local client companies, which were often receptive to joining partnerships. Thanks to Raimondo's initiative, eight P-TECH schools opened across the state.

Several governors, including Connecticut's, were close to rejecting the model, until they could be assured it had the backing of teachers. Once they heard from Randi Weingarten about her support for the model, they joined in. She also spoke to leaders in Australia on behalf of P-TECH. Ernest Logan, head of the American Federation of School Administrators, the principals union, helped win over several principals, and he provided steady support for Davis during the early days of his school's launch.

Whenever a school district, mayor, principal, college, or business leader expresses interest in creating a P-TECH school, they are asked to make contact with the governor's office as well, as this has proven to be the most seamless route to expansion.

FEDERAL LEADERSHIP

In 2015, after the tragic death of Freddie Gray in police custody, and the resulting civil unrest in Baltimore, leaders including then President Obama looked to bring positive improvements there to diminish the violence and allay tensions. Both then Secretary of Labor Tom Perez, who had visited a Chicago P-TECH, and then Education Secretary Arne Duncan we just mentioned that reached out to Litow regarding creating a P-TECH school in downtown Baltimore.

After visiting the Brooklyn flagship school, Ronald J. Daniels, president of Johns Hopkins University, also wanted to bring P-TECH to Baltimore. (It helped that his invitation had come from his board member and Hopkins alum Sam Palmisano.) Litow made it clear to the cabinet members that if they all wanted more than a single school, they would need to get Governor Larry Hogan on board. In this effort, the governor's key staff member, Keiffer Mitchell, who had served in elected office in Baltimore, was particularly influential. In quickly embracing the idea, Hogan became the first Republican governor not only to support the model but also to play a leadership role in advancing it. He helped open two schools in Baltimore, one focused on health careers with Johns Hopkins as the business partner, and he also garnered legislative support to expand the model further. There are now eight model schools in Maryland. Hogan's sustained leadership was critical to the model's success.

To be sure, Obama's support of P-TECH in his 2013 State of the Union address and during his visit to Brooklyn later that year, meant a great deal to the students and staff in Brooklyn and raised the school's profile significantly. Soon after his visit, he unveiled Youth CareerConnect, a $100 million competitive grant program for 25 to 40 high schools to work with employers and colleges.

P-TECH AROUND THE WORLD

The U.S. education system has deep roots in Europe, as the basic structure of schools, apprenticeships, and college preparatory coursework spread westward to the colonies. More recently, some U.S. school districts have adopted the IB program, created in Geneva, or Singapore math, when that country led the charts in international math and science tests. P-TECH is rare as an education innovation that began in a distressed U.S. neighborhood and achieved traction internationally, in both developed and developing nations, with schools operating in 28 countries. Although many foreign early adopters may have heard about P-TECH through the Internet, much of the credit for the model's dissemination goes to IBM, a global company with offices across more than 170 countries.

Palmisano's successor, Ginni Rometty, CEO of IBM from 2012 to 2020, was committed to P-TECH's growth, and she repeatedly urged the company's general managers abroad and senior executives domestically to consider introducing the P-TECH model to their top government leaders. The local corporate social responsibility team, along with the government relations, communications, marketing, and other teams, were in charge of following up, and IBM was usually willing to be the first industry partner, as it developed a global network of P-TECHs. In their annual reviews, employees were awarded for their success in promulgating the model schools.

In one example, the Moroccan Minister of National Education and Vocational Training, Rachid Benmokhtar Benabdallah, read an online article about P-TECH, and then asked to visit the Brooklyn school while on a state visit in 2016. Upon his return home, the IBM teams on the ground in Morocco and South Africa, the headquarters of IBM's efforts across Africa, engaged with leaders from the Ministry to start a school in Casablanca.

Next, IBM's citizenship team and local nonprofits in Australia introduced Litow and government leaders to discuss P-TECH. When then Prime Minister Tony Abbott visited President Obama at the White House in 2014, he included the Brooklyn school in his itinerary. The Australian version of community colleges involves a 1-year program, but the P-TECH model was able to spread to 14 schools, slightly modified accordingly.

At the urging of Rometty, IBM invited P-TECH students to speak at many high-profile events for company leaders and clients. In 2016, for example, three P-TECH graduates hired by IBM joined her on stage to speak to the company's 250 top senior executives in Florida, and when she was invited to the White House along with German Chancellor Angela Merkel, she asked that two P-TECH alums join them.

Rometty also worked with the larger U.S. business community via the Business Roundtable to encourage her peers to participate in the P-TECH model and to work toward reform of career and technical education (see next chapter). In a 2018 interview, she described P-TECH to *New York Times* columnist Thomas L. Friedman: "The graduation rates are four times the average, and those getting jobs are at two times the median salary." In addition, she spoke about workforce development at the 2018 National Governors Association meeting, where then Governor George Hickenlooper and Governor Hogan spoke about the successful launching of P-TECHs in their states.

She discussed the model at a GoodTech conference in France with French president Emmanuel Macron. In 2020, he asked the Ministry of Education to issue a request for proposals that would create an additional dozen schools across France, building on the five already running.

The model attracted interest from a wide range of businesses, large and small. Of the nearly 250 open schools IBM is the partner or co-partner in 64 of them globally, just over a quarter. Even companies that have competed with IBM, such as Microsoft, are convinced of the importance of creating a pipeline from school to college to career.

Rometty made it clear that spreading P-TECH across the globe was a very high priority linked to educational and economic growth in the communities where IBM did business. She even coined the phrase "new collar jobs," the kinds of positions that were growing in the technology sector that P-TECH graduates would be prepared for. She believed the school model, with its ability to address racial inequality and the digital divide, as well as transform IBM's hiring practices, was directly connected to the company's success and central to her legacy.

After Rometty's retirement in 2020, Arvind Krishna took the helm of IBM. Often when CEOs change, a company's societal commitments do as well, but it is encouraging that Krishna has joined his predecessors in supporting P-TECH.

"From Brooklyn to Chicago, from Dallas to Baltimore, these schools are creating real opportunities and real jobs for young people today," he wrote to Congress in June 2020, describing policy recommendations to advance racial equity. "We should scale them nationally."[8]

CHAPTER 8

Opening a School

As explained in the previous chapters, the 6-year high school model offers students many benefits and addresses many thorny problems for high schools, community colleges, and businesses, with takeaways for education and business leaders and staff. But how exactly does a P-TECH school move from the model's first local proponent to the last day of its first year?

Across the federation of such schools, currently numbering close to 250, programs have taken from 6 to 11 months in the planning stages.

The first New Jersey schools took root after Litow asked for and got help from former Obama chief of staff Denis McDonough, who contacted the newly elected governor, Phil Murphy, about the model. Murphy's education aide, Cary Booker (the brother of Senator Cory Booker), put together a meeting with education leaders. They later visited the Brooklyn P-TECH.

Soon after, Murphy, a Democrat, announced planning grants available for districts in which a certain percentage of the students qualified for free or reduced lunch, following a familiar pattern. In Maryland, the state legislature had established a statewide P-TECH program, including planning grants, with schools needing to reserve half their seats for low-income students;[1] in Rhode Island and Colorado as well, districts were asked to craft schools particularly for at-risk students.

In every case, the new schools opened in what felt like a hurry, but even in a pandemic, it was completely possible. This chapter tells the story of how, after winning one of three planning grants[2] in November 2018 from the New Jersey Department of Education, P-TECH New Brunswick was able to open its doors 7 months later and complete its first school year. Spoiler alert: It involved not just "building the plane while flying it," but, in the face of the pandemic, sewing the parachute while using it.

THE STUDENT

When Johnce (pronounced JOHN-say) Cruz was little, all he wanted for Christmas was Legos. Not sports equipment, not games, just piles of plastic bricks. He would look at the instructions for a particular set and cast them aside, assembling the spaceship or fancy vehicle just from looking at the picture. When, as an 8th-grader, he heard about New Brunswick's new engineering high school, he rushed to sign up. Johnce, whose parents immigrated from the Dominican Republic, had not been accepted in the district's other special program, Health Sciences Technology High School, which required an entrance test and high grades, but he was more interested in engineering anyway. He liked the feeling of taking things apart and inventing things with the pieces. He could picture himself doing that as a grownup too.

The night of the lottery, he, his mother, and one sister gathered in the district's adult learning center, which offers English classes and help getting high school diplomas, to watch as administrators pulled numbered balls from a barrel to choose the school's first class. Of the 84 students who had applied, only 40 would be chosen.

"I was nervous," said Johnce, who wears an attentive expression and often a green beanie hat. "I didn't know if I'd be called or not." But his number and that of his good friend came up, and he was so excited he had to wipe away a tear or two. His mother, Esmerelda Gomez, saw his face and started to cry as well. She was glad entry to the school was not based on scores, she said through a translator. She was impressed that everyone had a chance.

THE SUPERINTENDENT

Many of New Brunswick's students need better chances, and the district's superintendent, Aubrey Johnson, was working hard to provide new opportunities for them. The city of 55,676 has a poverty rate of 34.2%,[3] and all its students qualify for free or reduced-price lunches. While the city is the home of Rutgers University, the Robert Wood Johnson University Hospital, and pharmaceutical giants Johnson & Johnson and Bristol-Myers Squibb, the schools have struggled, with only 11% of students at New Brunswick High School performing at grade level in math. Johnson said of 700 incoming freshmen, only 450 will typically graduate. He has been searching for ways to motivate high school students to stay in school and advance into careers with growth potential.

For years, New Brunswick was considered an "Abbott District," on the list of the state's poorest 31 districts, which were given more state money after courts ruled that they were unconstitutionally underfunded. It remains on the list of poorest districts, with the state covering the costs of new and renovated buildings.

When he taught and served as a principal in Paterson, another impoverished district, Dr. Johnson, who wears his hair close-cropped and, on busy days, sneakers with his suits, would try to convince students why it was important to come to school—it would help their careers and give them more opportunities in the future. But those were abstract reasons, and he found it hard to motivate them, from within or without.

The son of Panamanian immigrants, he knew firsthand the importance of keeping, even hoarding, motivation. He grew up in East New York, a tough section of Brooklyn, and throughout his childhood would volunteer at his mother's private school, learning the craft of teaching while most of his peers were goofing around. When he got in a fight his first day at Samuel J. Tilden High School, Rev. Al Sharpton's alma mater, his mother promptly enrolled him in the private Rhodes School, requiring an hour-and-a-half daily subway commute. The Manhattan school was the inspiration for J. D. Salinger's *The Catcher in the Rye*.

As one of a couple students of color there, Johnson straddled two worlds, feeling connected to neither. He realized he had to work to help his community, so he taught during his high school summers at his mother's school in Queens.

From there, Johnson aimed to get into Northeastern University, but his guidance counselor told him he would not do well in such a large school. His mother believed in him and encouraged him to go, and he flourished. He prevailed again the next time someone disagreed with his dreams—his academic dean advised him to go into communications, but he had set his sights on a career in business.

Not long after college, he pivoted from doing entrepreneurial work at his father's auto glass company, back to his passion of teaching, and he worked his way up into leading a school, then a district, taking the helm of the New Brunswick schools in 2015. He was struck by the community's desire for better schools and its history of authoritative leadership, which may have stifled some creativity. He wanted to give teachers and principals the flexibility to experiment, and if they failed, to learn from their failure and move forward. His desire to motivate staff and students sometimes put him in unusual positions, such as duct-taped up on a hallway in the Lord Stirling Elementary School, where students had been promised they could stick their school leaders on a wall if they read every day for a month. His smile was quite broad as he and the principal and vice principal gave out low fives, their feet a foot or so above the floor.

When he saw the state's request for proposal in 2018 for 6-year model high schools in the STEM fields, the gist of the idea appealed to him, particularly the way the model aligned a high school, free community college, and industry partners.

"To me, that was a big, good shift for our students, an opportunity for our students to go to school and apply what they were learning, through college, and an employer," he said.

In a district where 90% of the students are Hispanic or Latino, and 8% are Black,[4] Johnson liked the way the model promotes equity, choosing students by lottery instead of requiring high test scores for entry to the rigorous program. Johnson's pet peeve is to see model schools working only with students who are already achieving and well-supported—schools that cream the top of the entry pool had better succeed, he said. P-TECH would have to prove it could work well for all students.

"I love it, because once you're admitted, it's our job to find support for every student to be successful, and get potential access to college and industry," he said. The school would not require extra funding from the district, because many of its costs come from the existing budget and from state per-pupil funding. Johnson decided to pull together a team to apply for the state's $300,000 planning grant.

It took the committee 3 weeks of typing on a Google document to complete the grant proposal to create the school, with the help of the ptech.org resource pages. These included step-by-step implementation plans and how to develop a steering committee. The district had enrolled some students in the mechanical engineering program at Middlesex County College earlier, so Johnson met with the president, Mark McCormick, who valued the idea of another partnership, this time leading to a full degree in electrical or mechanical engineering technology. The school found space in an industrial section of town, sharing a driveway with the state Department of Children and Families, in a building that had welcomed other district children while their schools were being renovated.

The district's facilities director knew some local engineering companies, and the plan fell together. Eventually business partners signed on—CGI, the Canadian tech firm; the construction firm Jingoli & Sons; and Cornerstone Building Brands, based in North Carolina, with a strong local presence. New Brunswick, Paterson, and Burlington City each won grants to open the model schools.

THE PRINCIPAL

Michael Fanelli, the principal at the Health Sciences Technology High School, had been on the outer edge of the earliest planning conversations, as he had advice to offer after creating internships for his 200 students at Robert Wood Johnson University Hospital. "I threw my two cents in, and I'm not smart enough to shut up," he said. At the time, he was happy where he was, not actively looking for a new job.

At 50, with almost 3 decades in education, "it's not the time you birth a child," said Fanelli, who is diligent and self-deprecating. But he admitted every administrator dreams of starting a school from scratch. A history teacher by training, he compared himself to the Romans, without original ideas, but adapting others' ideas and improving on them. Johnson admired Fanelli's experience in vocational education and working with industry partners.

"When he applied, I was like, 'This is a steal,'" the superintendent recalled.

As plans developed, Johnson came to appreciate the model's flexibility and how students in the first P-TECH school in Brooklyn had graduated from the program at their own speed. He grew more excited when he learned that Middlesex County College charges only $125 per student for its courses, and that the New Jersey Institute of Technology would agree to accept his graduates' credits and admit them as juniors, if, like most P-TECH students, they want to get a bachelor's degree. These options played in to his philosophy that students should have a great deal of power over their education, telling teachers how they want to learn, where they want to study, or when they feel ready for a midterm, for example.

"I wish I had this when I was in school, a high school, college, and business working together," Johnson said. "It puts you in a position to make the students marketable. . . . The building has me excited."

SUMMER

As the clean, empty hallways filled up, there was more to feel revved up about. All the students attended the summer bridge program, learning computer-based design for engineers, in which they earned college credit, and taking English classes with help from Middlesex County College professors. They received middlesexcc.edu email addresses, took a tour of the campus, and hosted students visiting from China. Student attendance hovered around 98%, despite the distractions of summer.

On August 29, a week before the first day of school, Fanelli gathered his new staff in a circle in the student center, once a big empty room, now resembling a corporate conference center, with high tables for group projects, white boards, and tasteful green touches courtesy of instructional technology supervisor Carla Segarra, who liked how the color stood out from the usual corporate or schoolhouse palette. It was different, like the school, she figured.

"I'm finally the oldest person on the staff," Fanelli said, looking around the room. "Is anyone CPR certified?"

He reminded the nine teachers and support staff that he had asked them each one important question—describe a time when you'd fallen down and failed, and then gotten back up again. He chose them, he told them, for how they would create a school culture.

"Teachers are by nature perfectionists. If you're perfectionists, we need to talk"—perfectionist to perfectionist, it turns out. Some of his biggest struggles ahead would come from wanting to have everything planned out and nailed down, in a year when that goal would be especially elusive.

"If you're trying something in your classroom that you're not sure of, let me help," he told them, peppering his conversation with mentions of scrapping with previous bosses. Fanelli, who had screened about 220 people for these jobs, said he felt like a king around a round table, having found the holy grail of staff.

"Not one of you sitting here, would I rather have someone else," he said. "I can't tell you how happy I am with you all here. After 20 years in administration, I wouldn't take another group."

The stakes, he told them, are high. "You are in the forefront of changing things, not just here but in education," he said. "Kids will rise to the level of expectation we give them. Do you believe every kid can learn? If you said no, you're not here. That's the basis of the whole model. Beyond trying to change kids' lives, we're trying to change the entire community. We're trying to move people out of poverty."

In a brief tour of the school, he explained it was impossible to hear anything in the cafeteria, with its 30-foot ceilings, and showed them classrooms he and other administrators had scoured for supplies—the last school here had left a ream of paper and four pens.

"We're not a school that's existed," he said. But it would likely all come together in time.

He showed them the bulletin board of the group photo of "your cherubs"—40 students, 10 girls, three English as a Second Language students, seven in special education, only seven performing at grade level in math—and he reminded them that research shows pronouncing their names correctly helps create strong bonds. He wanted them out in the hall during the 2 minutes allotted for changing classes, time he thought was longer than necessary, and, as another step toward a welcoming school climate, he asked them to put a sign on their doors with their names, hometowns, hobbies, pets, and favorite quotes and photographs. His own featured a hearth, his girlfriend, the Phillies, Star Wars, Tolkien books, and that quote from Margaret Mead: "Never doubt that a small group of thoughtful committed citizens can change the world; indeed, it is the only thing that ever has."

He concluded the meeting with a promise: "If we get to a point where you're in a situation with a parent, a kid, or an administrator, and you say this is why I did it, why it's right for my kids, you will have my support. Later we can talk about how we should've done it this way or that way. We're here for kids," he said. "I will protect each and every one of you if it's right by the kids."

There were some high-octane surprises as the school opened, starting September 5, when Governor Murphy attended its first day. He told the staff and students that when he talks to leaders of innovative companies looking to settle in New Jersey, their priority is the talent pipeline of future employees.

"With P-TECH, they will see that we are filling our pipeline with tremendous and diverse talent," he said.

Board of Education member Emra Seawood, attending the ribbon-cutting, said she was glad to see students starting such a rigorous program. "They need to be challenged, because I believe we don't challenge our students enough," said Seawood, who had served on the board since 1997.[5] "Their capacity is limitless."

That day, Johnce was both nervous—"maybe I didn't look good enough or felt like I didn't fit in for a couple seconds"—and excited.

He had never changed schools before, so seeing all the new faces and new teachers felt weird at first. But he had enjoyed P-TECH's summer bridge program.

"I felt good, like an adult, being exposed to college teachers," he said. The academics were challenging, but he felt he could manage. "It requires effort and determination."

Near the end of the first week of school, students in Nicole Grafanakis's English class, which focuses on the soft skills needed in the workplace, were watching TED talks and practicing 2-minute presentations on a topic of their choice. Soon after, they would produce five-slide PowerPoint presentations. At first, they were amazed at how long 2 minutes lasted. Grafanakis was glad to hear one student, Diego, say the class felt "like family," as the students became more comfortable speaking in front of each other.

A first-time teacher with a graduate degree from the College of New Jersey, Grafanakis said she sometimes wished she had other English teachers in the building to run things by—to ask how far along their classes were in a certain book, what they are learning on a given day—but she knows she can speak to others at New Brunswick High School, and she is enjoying the 1:4 staff-to-student ratio. At midday, she confessed that she had not glanced at her phone since 7:30 A.M. "I'm attached to my phone. That's how you know I'm enjoying it," she said. "I literally have not looked at it all day."

Johnce was already impressed by how engaged his teachers were. "I appreciate them," he said. "They put in a lot of effort for us, and we have to pay them back with the same effort, doing all the work." His mother was pleased that he had been showing off his design projects at home, as he had never shared his schoolwork before.

"He's always been a good student, but not as engaged or excited," she said. They live right across the street from his old school, and she said he would drag his feet in the morning until its doors opened, then reluctantly head in. This year he wakes up before 6:00 A.M. and gets himself ready for the bus. Meanwhile, the quality of his eye contact seemed to have quadrupled in a month, probably thanks to Grafanakis's class.

AUTUMN

When meeting with the school's business partners later in September, Fanelli explained that 82% of young people learn about careers from their families and no one else. In New Brunswick, only 7% of grownups have bachelor's degrees or higher.[6] For first-generation Americans and first-generation college students—most of his students—it is important to learn about opportunities their families have not had. "We need to make them aware of things they don't even know they don't know," he said.

At the lottery, Fanelli told partners, a parent had pulled him aside to make sure a student in special education could be part of the school. When he was speaking to a group of middle school students about P-TECH, one asked if the school was open to kids who got in trouble a lot in middle school. A Spanish-speaking mother approached him, with her daughter translating. The girl said her mother wanted to know if the daughter could still apply even if she does not speak English very well.

"That was one of my goosebumps moments," Fanelli said. "Each of those times I was able to say to parents, if you live in New Brunswick and have an 8th-grade student interested in the STEM field, we got you. It's a fantastic opportunity. We don't just have you for high school, but for college, and we're going to make sure you end up in a place where you can make a life for yourself."

In late October, leaders from the companies partnering with the school met with the staff to learn more about their mentoring roles, and how to identify the skills entry-level employees need, so the high school and community college could guide students in a straight line to the job market.

"If we continue training them for the same job today as we did 5 years ago, we're doing them a disservice," Fanelli said. "Four, 5 or 6 years from now, I hope you're all here in a cage match fighting for our students because you all want them."

Mike Reagan, vice president at CGI, had his HR director fly in from Tennessee to meet with Fanelli. The company had never considered hiring people with just an associate degree, but they were able to realign their requirements.

Meanwhile, the school's college partner was working hard to be ready for younger-than-usual students.

THE STEERING COMMITTEE

On November 21, the administrative team had one of its monthly check-in meetings, with about 10 district administrators and Fannelli around a table at the Board of Education offices. They talked about how early on, too many students had been failing classes, and some had acted apathetic, with some of the girls torn between schoolwork and taking care of younger siblings or keeping house for their working parents. At Johnson's suggestion, the staff had created an after-school program for everyone 3 days a week using funding from an unfilled math teacher position, among other budgetary magic. After school on Wednesdays, students all worked together, not in their smaller academic groups based on their needs at the moment, and everyone explored STEM topics. They coded a robotic finch, played with Ozobots (small spherical robots), and got creative with building blocks.

Reporting back on the results, Fanelli said at first, he had worried that the extra hours would be a burden for students, but they proved him wrong. "They just walked in and sat down as if it was lunch," he said. The program gave students time to finish their homework or get extra help before going home to their responsibilities. He described a student who had been worried about her grades, but now knows she can finish her schoolwork at school, and then focus on her family.

"Not only is she taking care of the house, but also the academic needs of her younger siblings," he said. "She's literally filling a paternal role. I said to her, 'You just outreach to one of us, we'll create time, I'll stop the world to find time for you.'"

Fanelli, whose other favorite quote is "the most dangerous phrase in the English language is 'we've always done it this way,'" was pleased with how the culture of the students and staff had improved with after-school support. "I'm watching their grades improve, the teachers are seeing, ok, it's working," he said.

There was talk of a staff member who had predicted the program would not work, and discussion of professional development sessions to shore up morale. Jamie Gulotta, the district math supervisor, spoke about five students receiving extra help with math. When the superintendent learned that students, whom he knew by name, could make up work they had done poorly in, he clapped and declared himself happy, though he acknowledged that if retakes were allowed in P-TECH but not at New Brunswick High School, others might complain. He said he would like other principals to emulate the close attention the new school has been giving its failing students.

"Can we push the ones who are excelling?" asked Johnson, whose questions often began with those three words. Three students, Fanelli said, were looking to accelerate, perhaps by taking an additional class. The principal told them they could save themselves time and money by getting more college credits sooner, but that idea is still very abstract to them, until they can start getting paid, ideally through internships with business partners in a few years.

Johnson, who admits some consider him a micromanager, had questions about every agenda item: Can we push students who are struggling in science? Are the parents aware of what we're doing? Can you put videogames in the curriculum? Often, the group answered that such improvements were underway.

What challenges are we facing now as a group? Johnson asked. What do we need to be ahead of moving forward?

In the beginning, Johnson's relationship with Fanelli was more about discussing what was getting accomplished. It was instructive to watch their relationship grow, as the two hard-driving leaders made critical decisions.

"Over time, through some of our conversations, it was more 'don't worry, you're safe, you're good,'" Johnson said, adding he encouraged Fanelli to let him know if he could help untangle any red tape to build the program.

Fanelli said his boss helped him worry a little more about some things, a little less about others. "Our relationship has evolved in that we're more just trusting each other's communication and understanding that communication," Fanelli said.

Near the end of the meeting, each administrator picked three students to mentor. Then, Keira Scussa, assistant superintendent for curriculum and instruction, wished aloud for a P-TECH Friendsgiving the following week, with everyone bringing in a dish. She offered to cook a turkey, Fanelli called apple pie, Segarra called pumpkin, and the superintendent worried again that other schools would feel jealous of the new school. Gulotta floated the idea of "P-TECH, Pizza and Pi(e)." Johnson warned against home-cooked turkey, which could become contaminated or cause allergic reactions—salmonella! Peanut oil! On this matter alone, no action steps were assigned.

A 4-minute drive away, at P-TECH, the students were getting ready to meet their mentors. They had created dream résumés for applying to the partner companies, and Johnce reported a 4.1 GPA (he was at 3.7 at the moment, held back with a B– in algebra). They had also worked on revitalizing old pinewood derby cars, those 5-ounce (and no heavier) race cars Cub Scouts engineer to reach the highest speed. Engineering teacher Victor Alegria's personal woodworking machines could set off smoke alarms, Johnce explained, so the teacher brought a batch of used wooden cars for them to refurbish and race.

A few days later, the Tuesday before Thanksgiving, 20 banquet tables and 70 folding chairs graced the cafeteria, with nontoxic, cafeteria-roasted turkey displayed with fixings. ("The woman can move mountains," Fanelli said as an aside, in disbelief, about Scussa.) At the Friendsgiving celebration, Johnson got a tour from his three mentees of their hallway bulletin boards, as they practiced explaining their best work, for when they would meet their mentors in December.

"I told them, don't take this lightly," the superintendent said. "Every time you speak, you're interviewing, even from 9th grade." The corporate mentors are always looking for promising future employees, he said, "so always talk up, be engaged, and be part of the process."

Meet the Mentors Day, December 13, offered an opportunity for students to explain their projects. Fanelli, who'd arrived at 6:50 A.M., huddled with the teachers about "enforcing a strict no-hoodie rule." Two kids sitting together needed to be separated, in the name of professionalism, and there was a small lack-of-tablecloth crisis.

The students and their mentors visited activity tables, including 3D tic-tac-toe, played with green and red plastic cups in three sizes, with larger cups able to commandeer the spots of smaller ones.

Johnce explained his hallway bulletin board to his mentor, Connor Paladino, community outreach coordinator of Jingoli. He showed computer-generated plans for a classic Thunderbird, including an "exploded view" of its separate parts. Johnce's classmate, Norberto, described a drawing he had made of various adventures in his life, including "swallowing a battery" when he was a year old. He also showed the person-of-the-year magazine cover they had been assigned to draw. It was a picture of himself captioned, "Man Finds a Solution for Global Warming."

WINTER

After the new year, the students visited the Wall Street offices of CGI. Only three had ever been to New York City before, about an hour away by train. One student, Anita, crossed herself several times in preparation for her first elevator ride. As Johnce warily peered down from the 15th floor windows, one of his friends jokingly pushed him from behind, and he reported a near heart attack. But after hearing from new CGI employees about their first year on the job, and practicing brainstorming in small groups, they felt more at home, and they left with CGI coffee mugs and other swag.

Teachers were starting to notice some of the special benefits of the P-TECH model. Gina Bruno, who teaches social studies at P-TECH after having worked at New Brunswick High School and high schools in Jersey City and Palisades Park, was impressed with one noticeable difference in P-TECH students.

"I've taught first period every year for the last 9 years of my life, and first period is usually just a very long attendance-taking," she said. "P-TECH kids are on time, rarely absent, and when they're absent, they come in and ask, 'What did I miss?' That's not normal."

Throughout the year, the staff had often used the Silicon Valley boast that they were building the plane while flying it. Then came mid-March, when New Brunswick schools closed due to the COVID-19 pandemic. As Fanelli explained, "In middle of the flight, they told us we had to jump, and we've been building our parachute while we're falling."

New Brunswick had lined up Internet connections for all its students, and teachers provided live and prerecorded online lessons. P-TECH students were already somewhat comfortable with the technology, but all their spring fieldtrips were canceled, including visits to Middlesex Community College.

SPRING

After a few weeks, Johnce reported having adapted to online learning fairly well. At first, no one was sure if school would open up quickly, but he got used to joining video calls, which made school easier, and he was able to help his 18-year-old sister get online as well.

"Work kind of overlapped on top of more work, with something new always being posted, so sometimes it can become overwhelming," he said in mid-May. But teachers had recently started posting a schedule to help students keep track of assignments, and they were signing students in to new software for three-dimensional game design. Alegria had students design their own face shields as an engineering project. Johnce used a takeout container for his.

The week before school closed, he had made the baseball team, but the season evaporated. P-TECH would be holding online gym classes over the summer, to help students rack up credits, but Johnce didn't like being so sedentary in the meantime. The only silver lining, Johnce said, was having his parents and two sisters home all day.

May 20 was supposed to be the red-carpet moment. Next year's 40 incoming freshmen were to pick up their personalized laptops, ogle the robots in the engineering classroom, soak up high expectations, and hear from current students about their work. And their first day of the summer program, they would be going to Middlesex County College.

Instead, thanks to the pandemic, a couple dozen 8th-graders and parents jumped on a video call, with some listening to a Spanish translation. They heard Dr. McCormick, the college president, tell them he was looking forward to them walking across his stage at graduation, and Joseph Jingoli, head of the construction firm Jingoli & Sons, tell them he hoped they would consider working for him afterward.

Fanelli reminded them they had been chosen to graduate with free associate degrees in engineering, and with that, they could get jobs paying $45,000 to $55,000 a year. They would be taking four classes a day, 80 minutes each, with an average class size of 13. Soon, they would be taking Engineering Design for college credit, English, math, biology, world history, Spanish, a workplace skills seminar, and a computer course designed for engineers.

When his computer screen suddenly went dark, it was a matter of seconds before he popped up in another square on the call. He had accidentally unplugged his computer but had a backup running.

"Ten days removed from 8th grade, you'll be with a college professor in a college preparatory class," he said.

RESULTS

Despite the upheaval of the pandemic, P-TECH New Brunswick staff point to meaningful milestones. All but one P-TECH student passed the math course, and only two Fs were given as final grades all year. (Students will be able to make up those courses.) Attendance was a whopping 99.98, and Johnson said students had earned a total of 117 college credits in their engineering design class.

As in most schools, some students disappeared during online school, or showed up on video calls with their cameras off, which made it harder to keep building the school's team spirit. Fanelli, known for his after-hours emails, recalled sending out a tutoring invitation to a student at 11:30 P.M. When she accepted it, he hopped on to a Google meeting with her right then and asked her where she had been. She sleeps late, she explained. He tried to convince her to wake up for online classes, and she was able to finish up the year successfully, despite her preference for a normal teenager sleep schedule.

Johnson was pleased about how many chances students had to interact with engineers, and how, after the female students had seemed hesitant to speak up in front of their peers, the program brought in more female engineers and mentors to encourage them. He also felt the frequent meetings helped administrators look at student outcomes without blaming students.

"We asked, what can we do differently for them to succeed, and put the onus on ourselves," he said.

Johnce said he is looking forward to next year's classes and meeting his new teachers. He can remember only one moment of panic for the year, right when online classes started, and he feared his grades would go down.

"I think I was overreacting," he said—he got all As. "I'm trying to keep that throughout all the years."

Fanelli said Johnce works hard, wants to be in school, and has strong support at home, which is a magical combination. Gulotta, the math supervisor, chose to mentor Johnce as one of her three students and had checked in with him throughout the year. She had worked with him in 7th grade when he struggled a bit in math, but she could see his potential. While he had seemed unsure about his math skills then, he is completely confident now, she said. "If I am correct, he had some of the best grades in his Algebra class this year," she said. "He is achieving the potential that I always saw in him, and, more importantly, he exudes the confidence that he can."

Fanelli has missed the company of his students dearly, and he is proud of his young staff for being fearless and adaptable.

"I want everyone to fall down, get mucky and clean themselves off in front of everybody, and say it's ok, and do it better next time," he said, in echoes of August. "That's what Dr. Johnson has done for me in our time together. He knows I like to plan and have it all done."

While at times the regular meetings at the Board of Education offices were stressful for Fanelli, with his colleagues noticing a few weapons-grade eye rolls, he chalks that up to his wanting to be too well-prepared, in an environment where plans changed frequently. By the end of the year, he realized the school owed a lot of its successes to Johnson's intense involvement with the school and the way he encouraged staff to look at problems from different perspectives and to innovate without fear of failure. Fanelli knows that is not the norm of how central administrators treat school staff, and he found it incredibly freeing.

"Even though I'm 51, I feel 22," he said, with such an opportunity to create a new way of challenging and supporting students. "This is the way it should be." And Johnson clearly recognizes the importance of empowering his school leaders. Or, as he put it, chuckling, "If I don't feed the principals, they're going to eat the teachers."

When Fanelli first came to the district from the county vocational school in 2017, Johnson ended his districtwide leadership meeting with a visit from the senior class president, who spoke about her experiences in the district and her hopes for the future. When she finished, Johnson told the staff, "And it's your job to make sure all those things can happen."

"This is probably the most student-centered administrator I've known," Fanelli said, and his own staff has advanced that philosophy as well.

"Honest to God, what they've done, I couldn't be prouder of all those people. I did a good thing. I hired a bunch of Type A people who just want to go out there and do it," he said. "They don't understand 'no,' and they will find a way." It has been a joy for him to watch them put the students first, and he hopes they all return in September.*

"I think the thing I'm proudest of is," he said, pausing to compose himself, "those kids want to be there. That to me is the most important thing."

---

*They did.

CHAPTER 9

Lessons for Broader Reform

As it grew, the P-TECH model incorporated lessons learned from the history of school reform. A look back at how businesses and funders have worked with schools in the past and at how many education improvement efforts over the past 50 years have hit roadblocks, informed those who were developing and spreading the P-TECH model at the same time.

School reform has too often become a battleground, involving charter schools, school choice, vouchers, standardized tests, teacher evaluations, standards, and high school admissions requirements. Division among school stakeholders has, too often, damaged chances for reform's success and expansion. The lessons of history lead to one conclusion: For reform to work, there must be early agreement among school leaders, teachers, parents, civic groups, unions, and business and government leaders. These constituencies were all involved in creating and shaping the P-TECH model.

The mere involvement of businesses in education has been questioned, at times for good reason. In the case of P-TECH, IBM made its investments with the student foremost in mind and designed the model in a way to benefit stakeholders in the classroom and beyond. The results have been encouraging and make a strong case for the further expansion of P-TECH schools.

At the federal level, regulatory changes can open up opportunities for forming new model collaborations at lower cost, and additional funding can help more talented and hardworking young people succeed academically, earn a college degree at no cost, and enter careers in growing fields that need them. As the nation struggles to recover from the COVID-19 pandemic and seeks to address its history of racial and socioeconomic inequities, we see P-TECH as not just a model, but a movement.

OVERVIEW OF EDUCATION REFORMS

American history has seen very modest changes to schools. High school became mandatory, junior high became middle school, kindergarten became full day, pre-K spread slowly, while penmanship, civics, and geography were eclipsed by personal finance and computer science. But if students from 1890 traveled through time to 2020, school would feel far more familiar than a mall or an Apple store. Unlike other sectors that have been totally transformed by technology and a range of competitive forces, our schools have changed very little.

In the early 1900s, business leaders gathered with the goal of improving the nation's education system and created the General Education Board. Thanks to the Rockefeller family's initial investment of $129 million—$3.9 trillion in today's dollars—this old-school moonshot helped open 912 public high schools in the south in just a dozen years,[1] helped eradicate hookworm, created the county extension service, and supported schools for training Black teachers "in the methods of industrial schooling."[2] Like P-TECH, it focused on real-world skills and "industrial education," and it aimed to address discriminatory practices that left Black farmers unschooled in soil management.

Indulge us for a second and read the vision of the reformers, from the Board's Occasional Papers,[3] published in 1913:

> We shall not try to make these people or any of their children into philosophers or men of learning, or men of science. We have not to raise up from among them authors, editors, poets or men of letters. We shall not search for embryo great artists, painters, musicians nor lawyers, doctors, preachers, politicians, statesmen, of whom we have an ample supply. . . . The task we set before ourselves is very simple as well as a very beautiful one, to train these people as we find them to a perfectly ideal life just where they are. . . . So we will organize our children into a little community and teach them to do in a perfect way the things their fathers and mothers are doing in an imperfect way, in the homes, in the shops and on the farm.

In short, the rich are not like us. But they think they know what is good for us.

With the passage of the Smith Hughes Act in 1917, the nation solidified its approach to Career and Technical Education, which evolved from colonial America and its apprenticeship system borrowed from

Europe. The act created vocational education opportunities for students aged 14 and up. Starting with about 200,000 students, "voc ed" grew by the 1950s to serving about 3 million students. The employers involved in vocational programs and the skills taught there were largely restricted to manufacturing and the trades, hence the term "trade schools."

In the first half of the 20th century, John Dewey advocated for experiential education linking theory to actual practice, and his philosophy is a guiding light for reformers who want to encourage students to excel at solving real-life problems, to learn to think critically in their college studies and professional lives, and to learn the communication skills that will help them thrive. He is, arguably, P-TECH's patron saint.

Throughout most of the nation's history, education philosophy and reform related solely to White students. Even after the 1954 *Brown v. Board of Education* Supreme Court decision that struck down school segregation, schools continued to offer one set of services to White students and another to students of color, until the passage of the Civil Rights Act enforced the court's decision. Ever since, while schools may be somewhat more integrated in some states, progress has been glacial, and opportunity gaps between White and non-White students continue to grow.

When the Soviet Union launched its Sputnik satellite in 1957, the United States woke up to the need for improved science instruction, but federal interest did not last.

Attempts to integrate schools via court-ordered busing met with mixed success, and the courts filled up with lawsuits over inequitable funding formulas for school districts, particularly those based on property taxes.

The 1983 "Nation at Risk" report[4] led to a push for higher secondary school graduation rates, with a focus on more rigorous academic programs and higher standards. Career and technical education receded from the spotlight and came to be considered a dumping ground for underachieving students. Civil rights organizations, such as the Urban League and the National Association for the Advancement of Colored People (NAACP), denounced the system and pointed out the injustice of relegating students of color to inferior schools funneling into low-wage jobs.

As in Rockefeller's time, America's business leaders continued to be concerned about the nation's education system. In the 1980s, they started "join a school" and "adopt a school" measures, providing sporting goods, musical instruments, or donations, and involving employees in tutoring or other community service efforts. While often beneficial, such programs did not yield significant or scalable benefits.

In the 1990s, facing rising enrollments and overcrowded classrooms, some districts began experimenting with alternatives to larger, more impersonal high schools, where students fell through the cracks, particularly in big cities. Joseph Fernandez, the New York City schools chancellor from 1990 to 1993, worked closely with his deputy, Litow, in expanding the model of small schools to create innovative options for students.

The Bill and Melinda Gates Foundation latched on to the importance of the reform and provided school districts with $650 million, part of their $2 billion effort to improve high schools.[5] Decades after the movement began, an evaluation performed by MDRC demonstrated the effectiveness of the small schools movement, and yet it also became controversial, creating concerns that opening new small schools was often coupled with closing unsuccessful schools and diverting some of the best students from traditional schools. The most successful small schools, the Gates Foundation found in the end, held high expectations for students to go to 4-year colleges, were not selective in admissions, served students who were poor and would be the first generation in their families to attend college, and often were charter schools with extended school days.

In the mid-1990s, another group of powerful business and political leaders gathered with the goal of improving America's schools. They hoped to build momentum behind ideas such as rigorous curriculum and standards-based reform and accountability, favored by the teachers unions, principals unions, and governors from both sides of the aisle. Yet by 1995, just over 10 states had any form of an educational standard, and most were very weak.

In March 1996, the CEO of IBM at the time, Louis Gerstner, organized a group of CEOs and governors who, along with the National Governors Association, brought together then President Bill Clinton and a governor and business leaders from every state to a National Education Summit. The summit, at IBM, breathed new life into the standards movement, leading to a Common Core of educational standards of what math, science, and language arts skills students should know in each grade. It aimed to ensure that high school graduates were ready for college and the workplace.

The Common Core State Standards (CCSS) Initiative was announced in 2009, sponsored by the National Governors Association and the Council of Chief State School Officers. Starting in that year, the Gates Foundation contributed hundreds of millions of dollars to the effort. The standards were a very valuable idea, but their implementation created discord. People disagreed about whether and what tests should be used to measure attainment of the standards, parents and teachers pushed back against too many standardized tests, and when some states wanted to tie teacher pay to their students' test scores for accountability, they met vehement criticism from millions of educators.

Within a decade, the consensus around standards-based reform began to crumble. According to Mike Cohen, former White House aide to President Clinton and head of Achieve, the group created by CEOs and governors to assist in achieving higher standards, while the idea made imminent sense, CCSS's implementation was severely flawed. Linking student test scores to teacher evaluations alienated both teachers and parents. And while CCSS firmly made states in control of the standards process, some on the right labeled it a federal takeover, and some on the left considered it a victory for testing advocates. Governors from both parties began to jump ship, and business leaders, whose support was vital to sustaining the movement, slid out of view. Even though many states that eschewed CCSS ended up with education standards that strongly resembled it, the movement is now considered a case study of how *not* to reform education.

In the meantime, the No Child Left Behind Act of 2002, signed by President George W. Bush, with bipartisan support from Senator Ted Kennedy and others, aimed to increase school accountability, yet it alienated many crucial constituencies with its focus on standardized tests and teacher evaluations.

Similarly, deep divisions arose in the battle behind school choice and charter schools. Initially, as with CCSS, many divergent educational interest groups united behind charter schools and enhanced school choice, which empowered parents with vouchers to use at schools they wanted their children to attend. Albert Shanker, the leader of the American Federation of Teachers, was a strong supporter of charters and school choice, as were many civil rights organizations. And yet, very quickly, the implementation of these reforms alienated stakeholders. Charter schools were criticized for screening admissions, refusing access to students with disabilities, diverting funding away from public schools, and shredding collective bargaining protections for teachers. Charter advocates believed their critics were opposed to innovation and reform.

As the 2008 recession hit, public funding for education declined, and charters and choice became divisive issues in political campaigns at the national, state, and local levels.

In many districts, it became an insult to call someone a reformer, even though the need for school innovation is indisputable. Creating sustainable, widespread solutions for problems in education is far more difficult when scarce funds, equity, and labor practices are at stake.

As the United States began to recover from the recession, good new jobs required higher levels of education. According to Anthony Carnevale, the labor economist at Georgetown University, over 90% of new jobs required a postsecondary degree, while jobs requiring a high school diploma or less were disappearing and paid lower wages.

Meanwhile high school graduation rates increased, but college completion rates made only modest gains, and students of color and low-income students fared poorly. Businesses needed the nation's schools and colleges to address the skills crisis, which affected their bottom lines. A 2021 McKinsey survey found almost nine out of 10 business leaders were facing skills gaps now or expected them in the next 5 years.[6]

Funding disparities between high-wealth districts and low-wealth districts and schools grew, with few and illusory remedies. Racial disparities, including those caused by admissions screening, continued largely unabated. Overall, schools were underfunded and had trouble recruiting and retaining teachers. Education cuts that left teachers earning prerecession wages and forced some public schools to close one day each week led to teacher strikes in nine states in 2018–2019.[7]

ANOTHER WAY TO CREATE CHANGE

P-TECH schools grew out of this history, from which certain points shone clearly.

The battles over charter schools, school choice, and the CCSS produced a divisive environment, putting up barriers to certain students, and leading many to believe change is impossible. Therefore, buy-in from a big tent of constituents is crucial to success. Key stakeholders must be engaged early on as supporters, or else they become adversaries. Nothing is quicker to bring a school reform effort to a screeching stop than the group that was left out of the planning. With an understanding of what actually works, teachers, principals, and superintendents can see how change is possible, sustainable, and scalable. That knowledge in itself is empowering.

While P-TECH's spread was certainly easier because of dedicated corporate leaders commanding a giant network of boots on the ground, the model's other business partners number in the hundreds, with more joining monthly. We envision new reforms working well by spreading through other large networks, such as teachers unions, state education departments, and community college coalitions, particularly if new programs meet the needs of multiple constituencies.

For meaningful reform to work and spread widely, we believe there are certain nonnegotiable requirements:

- It needs to grow from the philosophy that every student can succeed.
- It needs to elevate equity, to address school segregation and structural racism that harm students who are not White and well-off.
- It should be available to all, without barriers to entry.
- It should provide students with a supported education that prepares them well for college and existing entry-level jobs with growth potential.
- It should be easily replicable and affordable.
- It must require no changes to local regulations.
- A broad coalition must be involved in its planning.

BUSINESS OUT OF THE CLASSROOM?

Educators, social critics, and the general public have at times expressed discomfort with businesses becoming involved in the classroom. No one wants product placement in the curriculum, or a company taking away liberal arts in favor of instruction in widget making. Despite John D. Rockefeller's largesse toward the General Education Board, many remember him for proclaiming, "I don't want a nation of thinkers, I want a nation of workers." The profit motive has no place in main offices of schools, as seen in some low-performing charter schools, and in the predatory practices of for-profit colleges, which have for decades defrauded vulnerable groups such as low-income and homeless students and returning veterans, leaving them with worthless degrees and mounds of debt.

IBM's executive innovators were cognizant of such potential negative impressions of corporate involvement in the schools, and they worked hard to collaborate with educators and stakeholders, listening to them describe their needs and goals. While some corporations might have pushed for curriculum changes or insisted that only the highest performing students attend the schools they supported, such stances are counterproductive.

The company's contributions, all of them in-kind, amount to $3 to $5 million a year, over 10 years. They have included one liaison for each of the 64 schools IBM partners with; four or five central support staff; the costs of paid internships at IBM and some smaller companies; and, in some schools, additional tutoring, including 24/7 assistance during the pandemic. Mentors provided volunteer hours, and numerous employees helped organize worksite visits and host gatherings such as Planet P-TECH.

In addition, IBM created three online platforms for P-TECH. MentorPlace supports mentoring, and ptech.org provides educators starting a P-TECH school with examples of project-based learning curriculum, advice on recruiting students and mentors, and ways to assure high school classes prepare students well for college courses. It also includes a complete workplace learning course developed by Eric Berngen, a former Chicago P-TECH teacher and industry liaison. The free Open P-TECH platform, created by former Newburgh liaison Cliff Archey, is available in 10 languages to any teachers and students, and it helps students gain a wide range of technical skills and certifications while also helping teachers gain fluency in the material. The latter cost $3 million (not including related salaries) and was refined for wider use during the pandemic.

Such investment in the schools pales in comparison to what several philanthropic entities have donated in support of educational reform. In the 1990s, the Annenberg Foundation gave $500 million to schools that eschewed testing and used innovative ways to determine student competencies. Starting in 2000, the Bill and Melinda Gates Foundation invested $2 billion in improving high schools, and over 20 years, the Eli and Edythe Broad Foundation invested $4.5 billion to support charter schools, award top performers, and prepare principals and superintendents to attract, train, and prepare nontraditional leaders.

As for Facebook cofounder Mark Zuckerberg's $100 million donation to the Newark schools in 2010, too much of it went to outside, pricey consultants who did not know the city well and failed to listen to the parents, teachers, students, and local residents who had the most at stake in the schools.[8] In Newark schools, any ideas, no matter how worthwhile, will not survive with just private-sector funding. If the goal is structural change involving budgets and regulations, more partners must be involved from day one.

All four of these efforts had substantial resources behind them, granted to individual school districts or nonprofits. But funding school reform through foundations, often characterized as "checkbook philanthropy," has several pitfalls. Even the largest charitable contributions are dwarfed by the size of the federal, state, and local education budgets. Charitable grants are usually time-limited—they run out. Some critics view them as the wealthy's attempt to buy success; unions often view them with distrust. In addition, when priorities and staffing change and when enthusiasm flags, efforts fade away. If results disappoint, funders rightly move on to support the next promising initiative. The system does not give them incentives to stay with one reform for the long haul.

Conversely, with the P-TECH model, Fortune 100 corporations, 650 other business partners, and hundreds of schools and community colleges have a clear stake in its growth and replication. While there are some cash contributions, in-kind investment demonstrates partners have "skin in the game." Community college tuition is the main expense the model requires, and there are numerous ways to fill that relatively modest budget line.

It works in the interests of all the community colleges and business partners to continue supporting their partner high schools. The colleges are rewarded with prepared students who graduate on time, and the businesses can grow their own talent for jobs they are struggling to fill. The companies are not asked to write checks to participate. They are asked for mentoring, hosting site visits, and creating internships, each of which has some benefit to the partner as well. The win-win-win aspects of the model will help it continue to succeed and spread.

In new communities, after political leaders helped smooth the way for the model's expansion, it faced a variety of challenges—how to transport students between high school and college in spread-out districts, how to coordinate a large number of corporate partners in areas where a chamber of commerce was sponsoring a school, and keeping business partners engaged when they faced deadlines, personnel changes, or budget challenges.

Yet as the number of schools expands, so does their influence. The principles of P-TECH have started to spread organically through

P-TECH teachers such as Jamilah Seifullah, who founded the Highland Park Community School in Brooklyn, or through Michael Dardaris, who moved on from leading a P-TECH school to become the senior director of career readiness education at Stride, the national online schooling firm. His former business teacher, Michael LaMastra, joined the Career and Technical Education team at the New York State Department of Education.

The challenge now is to make sure that a decade of success, with nearly 250 schools across 28 countries, increases its momentum. As then President Barack Obama said when he visited the school in 2013, this innovative pathway from school to college to career must be made available not to some students but to all students. To that end, there are some specific actions that must be taken by leaders at the federal, state, and local levels to make sure that the promise of P-TECH continues.

HIGHLIGHTS FROM THE COLLABORATIONS

Here is a sampling of encouraging results from a variety of P-TECH schools[9] in alphabetical order by city:

- Carver High School, Baltimore, MD: 90% attendance compared to the district rate of 76%; 97% of 11th-grade students on track to earn their high school diploma in 3.5 years; 69% expected to graduate high school and college in 4 years.
- Cy-Tech in Baton Rouge, LA: 93% of 9th-graders complete at least one college class, and 89% of 10th- and 11th-graders meet college-ready benchmarks.
- W. H. Adamson Collegiate Academy in Dallas, TX: 100% of students are non-White and eligible for free or reduced-price lunch, and 100% of 11th-graders are college ready.
- Skyline High School, Longmont, CO: 95% of high school freshmen pass at least one college course; average college GPA of 3.09; 42% of first class finished high school and their associate degrees in 4 years.
- Newburgh, NY: 94% attendance rate compared to 89% districtwide.
- New York State: No P-TECH student has taken a single remedial class, compared to 50% of their peers in public community college.

- Norwalk, CT: 100% high school graduation rate, compared to 90.4% in the district; college pass rate of 91%.
- Paterson, NJ: For year 3, there were 253 applicants for 60 spots at PANTHER Academy.

Although many of the P-TECH schools are less than 6 years old, many of P-TECH's business partners have started to bring on board the students they helped nurture in high school and college:

- IBM has hired nearly six dozen P-TECH graduates, Tesla over a dozen, and GlobalFoundries a half dozen.
- Thomson Reuters hired 24 of its 30 Dallas apprentices into full-time jobs, and they expect to expand to 100 apprenticeships and 85 or 90 full-time hires in 2021.
- In July 2020, IBM created 1,000 additional paid internships, at its own facilities and with other P-TECH partners, a tenfold increase, to diversify its tech talent.[10]
- In the partnering community colleges, no P-TECH student has needed to take a remedial course.
- In the first 16 schools in New York State, the 2-year college graduation rate was 400 percent higher than the national average for low-income students and students of color.

It is also important to understand that while the majority of schools are very successful, not every P-TECH school is an unequivocal success. While the goal is for every school and every student to succeed, a very small number of schools have had problems, and while many have improved, some have not. One of the schools in New York State, Adirondack P-TECH, is no longer accepting new students and phasing out, due to a revolving door of principals and failure to provide adequate transportation for students to attend college courses. Of the five schools that opened in Chicago, one had difficulty getting the industry partner to deliver on its commitments to provide students with mentoring, paid internships, and other support.

Of course, no school reform will be 100% successful. A quarterback who completed 60% of his passes would still be on the road to a Heisman Trophy. With well over 90% of P-TECH schools thriving, a few schools with problems are hardly evidence of a faulty model. They do indicate, however, that intervention when problems emerge must be part of an effective replication plan.

NEXT STEPS FOR EXPANSION

The challenge now is to build on a decade of P-TECH's academic success and vigorous expansion. We envision a time when any student who wants to follow a supported pathway from school to college to career can do so, close to home. When the model moves from hundreds to thousands of schools, a distinct possibility once leadership and resources are available, it will require work to make sure the quality of the program remains high. IBM can continue to play a role here, but districts will need to devote staff to provide oversight, technical assistance, and ongoing support. For P-TECH to expand, leadership at the federal as well as state level will be essential.

Some specific actions must be taken by leaders at the federal, state, and local levels to make sure this happens. Funding and grant support, as well as innovative uses of Perkins funding, Pell grants, and college work-study programs, can help spread opportunity to tens of thousands more students.

P-TECH students can benefit from three main federal programs: Pell grants and the College Work Study Program (CWSP) help low-income students afford higher education, and the Carl D. Perkins Vocational and Technical Education Act provides funding for career and technical education. All three need increased funding, as they have not seen substantial increases for decades, and all need modifications to create better opportunities for young people.

The Pell grant program, which provides tuition support for low-income college students, had a budget in 2019 of about $27 billion, less than it received a decade earlier. Legislators should expand the grants' eligibility requirements, not only to address the college affordability crisis for high school graduates but also to include students who are taking college courses while on the high school registers. This will ease the cost for states and school districts and serve more students, including those in P-TECH schools.

CWSP, which costs the government about $1 billion a year, also needs significantly more funding, as well as reforms in how the money is spent. In Work Study, federal funds pay approximately 70% of a college student's wages, usually on campus, in cafeterias, and in libraries. Hourly wages are close to the federal minimum wage, averaging about $7.75 per hour. The jobs provide virtually no career skills, compared to P-TECH internships at companies such as IBM, which pay $15 per hour for students in high school and can lead to professional advancement. Providing more federal funding, allowing more off-campus work linked to career opportunities (perhaps through P-TECH partnerships), and asking employers to contribute a larger share of wages would help reduce student college expenses and prepare them better for the job market.

Further expansion of P-TECH will also be eased by adding federal funding under the Perkins Act, which is currently budgeted at only $920 million, not all of which was spent. It would be far more effective at $3 to $5 billion.

The act was reauthorized in 2018, and the regulations guiding the funding were revised to reflect better the needs of the job market, in ways that encourage the spread of the P-TECH model.

IBM and Litow engaged a range of collaborators from education, business, labor, and civil rights organizations and began an effort to encourage Congress to embed some of the core principles of P-TECH into the reauthorization of the Perkins Act. While the Corporate Citizenship department led this effort, it relied heavily on IBM's government relations team and the consistent leadership and support of the company's CEO at the time, Ginni Rometty, and other senior executives.

Congress passed the act in 1984 to provide federal support for vocational education, in response to 1983's "Nation at Risk" report by the U.S. National Commission on Excellence in Education. That study found that America's schools were falling behind those in other nations and led to a range of federal actions to reform the education system.

The act was amended in 1998 and again in 2006 to encourage more diversity, inclusion, and links to academics, but it largely continued to fund vocational education efforts on a per capita basis. In 2010, the Department of Education released a Career and Technical Education blueprint, calling to reform Perkins and connect funding to labor market information, but it was not adopted. Litow realized that this effort would not be successful without the core elements of P-TECH—connecting school to college to work. Any such efforts needed to be bipartisan and supported by a wide range of stakeholders.

The nation's vocational programs did not link to labor market data, so they could not prepare students for the highest quality jobs, skilled ones with higher wages and career opportunities. Students needed experiential training in growing, not shrinking, fields. Vocational education needed input from employers, and it needed to flow directly to higher education, a concept that met resistance at first, appearing too new. But P-TECH was beginning to prove this was possible, and students around the country could benefit from that insight.

In 2012 and 2013, Litow drew up a set of core principles based on the philosophy that went in to the P-TECH model:

- A link to labor market data, so programs would focus on preparation for high-wage and high-potential jobs
- Business/employer engagement in program design
- A focus on experiential learning, including paid internships, along with classroom education, so students could get work experience while in school
- A link to postsecondary education, recognizing that a high school diploma is not a satisfactory end
- An effort to establish performance metrics

These core elements became the rallying cry to bring together a broad coalition of organizations, including the U.S. Chamber of Commerce, the Business Roundtable, and state and local Chambers of Commerce, plus labor organizations such as the American Federation of Teachers, civil rights groups such as the Urban League and NAACP, colleges and universities, cities, states, school districts, and student organizations such as Young Invincibles, whose support had been critical to the passage of the Affordable Care Act.

It was crucial that civil rights groups be part of the coalition, as for decades, many of them rightly believed that vocational education was a warehouse for African American students, where they would get an inferior education, training for low-skill jobs, and few chances to obtain employment afterward. Many of them hesitated to join the coalition until they learned it supported a direct link to a college degree and job opportunities. The memory was fresh of then President Barack Obama visiting and supporting a vocational school in Crown Heights, where all the students were non-White, on track to get associate degrees and high paying jobs. Ultimately more than 400 groups signed on to support the basic principles.

Litow remembers joining Randi Weingarten, the president of the American Federation of Teachers, in a visit to Senator Bob Casey of Pennsylvania to ask for his support of the Perkins reform. The senator, a Democrat, remarked that it was the first time that a labor leader and a business leader were on the same page about anything. That comment reinforced the importance of a united front—it was far easier for a politician to agree to a proposal if he or she saw that it had broad-based support.

"If people are not engaged and part of an effort from the beginning, they start sinking it," Litow said. "That's how it works. That is the wrong way to do anything. You have to remove the barriers, not construct them."

Going forward, Litow and Ned McCullough in the IBM government relations office in Washington, D.C., began to meet and work with the coalition and congressional leaders on both sides of the aisle.

Rometty was vocal in support of the revised law, explaining on CNBC, "For the first time on record, the number of job openings in the United States is larger than the number of Americans who are unemployed and actively looking for work."[11] She described P-TECH schools to the Business Roundtable, saying, "In our view, these are just the sorts of programs we think the Perkins Act will soon be well positioned to support on a national level."[12]

Only five members of Congress voted against the reauthorization of the Perkins Act when it first came to the floor. It took another year or more to get the Senate on board, but, in 2018, the reauthorization passed with significant bipartisan support. The bill included an appropriation of an additional $275 million. The bill's guidance on how the money will be spent, with common sense and accountability, can help improve career and technical education across the country, but the stakeholders will need to remain vigilant and engaged.

Conclusion

Oscar, Akhtar, Joel, Amalik, Xavier, Irann, Mariana, Selah, Keira, Tobias, Johnce, ShuDon, Kelly, and David are defying the odds and succeeding. They are proving the naysayers wrong. P-TECH put them in the driver's seat, and they are staking out bright futures on their own terms. They found a high school and college, aligned with a business, offering high expectations, rigor, and intensive support, to help them soar. Every student deserves such an opportunity.

As shown in the previous chapters, P-TECH is an innovative school model that broke the mold of a traditional high school and tore down the barriers between school, college, and career. But it goes far beyond one effective, innovative school. It spread rapidly across the globe. Harvard Business School professor Rosabeth Moss Kanter called P-TECH "the fastest scaling school model in America." *The National Journal* called it "the reinvention of the American high school."

We believe more than high school is in need of reform. We can use lessons from the high school to college to career model to innovate and collaborate to improve schools from pre-K through middle school as well. There are already worthy ideas ripe for innovation.

For decades, researchers have found significant benefits for children with longer school days and longer school years. Advocates have argued strenuously for such changes, only to be told they are too expensive. Tens of thousands of nonprofit organizations serve students after school, on weekends, and over vacations, paid for by local and state governments, private donations, and families. What if those organizations and their funded staff operated out of our schools? What if those services were fully integrated into our classrooms?

Just as P-TECH brought together schools, colleges, and business partners, this kind of effort could unite schools, local and state governments, nonprofit groups, and philanthropists to organize, deliver, and fund an effective longer school calendar. It could integrate arts, music, sports, needed health and mental health services, tutoring, and social services, with a goal of improving achievement in the schools.

All those stakeholders, as well as parents, teachers, home school associations, and school leaders, must be at the table to discuss what they need and what they can offer. Goals must be set and monitored, incentives for participation must be clearly agreed upon, and, above all, students must be the top priority. Delivered effectively, such a program would be cheaper than the status quo and have great benefits to the broader community with better prepared, better cared for, and more engaged students with brighter futures.

Moving forward, even previously divisive issues, such as school choice, charter schools, standards, and accountability, could be totally reinvigorated if all the relevant decisionmakers met together and focused on areas where their interests aligned.

A barrier to expanding school choice or charters is the fear that they will divert funding from public schools or undermine hard-won teacher rights. Those are valid concerns, so let's build into the design funding and protections for teachers, and provide a seat at the table to everyone concerned. Not everything is negotiable, of course. The rights and needs of all students, regardless of income or race, must be the focus of any reform.

For those who want to help create excellent schools, support must go beyond writing checks. IBM was able to move from providing "spare change to real change," Kanter writes. This is what is needed, and it is possible.

Public education is the lifeblood of our democracy. If our schools fail, our economy fails. Our students' achievement is eventually connected to every issue of consequence our country will face, including racial justice, public health, closing the digital divide, income equality, and economic empowerment.

Successful reforms such as P-TECH must be spread as far as possible, but that is not enough. We need a Marshall Plan approach to improving our schools at every grade level, and we must think and act big. Guided by the lessons learned at a small school in Crown Heights, we must tackle the broader issues of school improvement and do so now. Innovation is not only possible but also in the best interests of our students. They deserve nothing less.

Afterword

Since the doors of the first P-TECH school opened 10 years ago, it has grown from one small school in Brooklyn to a global movement.

When we talk about P-TECH, the outcomes that matter most are the middle-class milestones, which are the prizes realized from working hard in high school, college, and the workplace. We're talking about the experiences and opportunities that can change generations, and I'm going to be unapologetic about it—the goal can't be just a high school diploma, it's college completion. The definition of success in this high school is a completed college degree, and it really gets to the crux of equity. It's about changing zip codes and about opportunities that go beyond the zip codes.

One of my favorite statistics here is the number of students hired by IBM who were low performers in middle school. They were told they could never graduate from college. They couldn't imagine they would not only complete a college degree but also be earning a competitive salary at a Fortune 100 company in a high-growth career before they were out of their teens. But that's the message we send to our P-TECH scholars every day. We believe in you, and you can succeed. You will succeed—all of you.

At P-TECH Brooklyn, we had more Black male college graduates than the best community college in New York State. Our overall college completion numbers are more than 400% higher than the national average, even though many of our students start high school way behind.

I'm thinking about Michael Blanchett, who had a stutter and an Individualized Education Plan (IEP). We now have the 46th President of the United States, Joe Biden, who has had to overcome stuttering. About 15% of our students have an IEP. In many schools, students like Michael often struggle to graduate high school. Other schools might have written him off. We recognized him as someone who could earn a competitive college degree and work at IBM. Michael achieved both and that's where he is now.

Here's how we do it. We narrow the focus. We assess early and often, and we get better results. I said early on, if you really meet students where they are and allow them to move at their own pace, you're creating a culture that could change outcomes.

I would rather you struggle through the rigor, and the trying to get it, and pass that college algebra course the second time you take it. But then you've got it. You've passed it. I said early on, fail early, fail often, but keep moving. That right there is a book in itself.

Our successes came from changing structures and changing culture. We changed 9th grade intentionally to increase reading and math levels, which form the basis for STEM studies. It's about how you use your time and how you create a culture where relationships matter and achievement is valued. When students are college ready, their pictures go up on the walls in our hallways, large as life. Amanda Crawford became a state track champion and posed for hers with her grandmother, and she went on to get her bachelor's degree. We're a family, and we know our families are deeply involved and proud of their kids' success.

These students aren't just college ready. They are well on their way to bachelor's degrees and beyond. One's working on her PhD. All six of our valedictorians and salutatorians left high school with a STEM degree. If you can make sure your valedictorian is leaving high school with a 2-year college degree, they have a far better chance of completing a 4-year degree.

Our business and college partners have joined this family, building a scaffold of attention and assistance. The more adults who work and network with our students, the more they are blown away by their brains and creativity. The more relationships P-TECH graduates have, the more power they have to pursue their dreams.

More students are waiting for schools that inspire and empower them, and they can't wait for months or years. I tell our nation's leaders, don't give up on any young person, for any reason. Look at what all students can achieve with this opportunity.

And I tell my students, P-TECH is the new 1%. How many Black males under 21 have a debt-free college degree and are working at a Fortune 100 company? If you ask me, every school should be P-TECH.

—Rashid Ferrod Davis

Notes

Chapter 1

1. Obama, B. *State of the Union Address.* (2012). https://obamawhitehouse.archives.gov/the-press-office/2013/02/12/remarks-president-state-union-address

2. Chen, G. (2014, October 31). White Students Are Now the Minority in U.S. Public Schools. www.publicschoolreview.com/blog/white-students-are-now-the-minority-in-u-s-public-schools

3. Jan, T. et al., (2020, June 13). As Big Corporations Say "Black Lives Matter," Their Track Records Raise Skepticism. www.washingtonpost.com/business/2020/06/13/after-years-marginalizing-black-employees-customers-corporate-america-says-black-lives-matter/?arc404=true

4. Litow, S. (2019, June 19). Does College Matter? Of Course. www.shankerinstitute.org/blog/does-college-matter-course

5. REACH NY. (2020, December). *Aiming Higher: How Improving Post-secondary Equity and Attainment Will Put New York State on the Path to a Bright Future.* https://newyork.edtrust.org/wp-content/uploads/2020/12/Aiming-Higher.pdf

6. Nadworny, E. (2019, March 13). College Completion Rates Are Up, But the Numbers Will Still Surprise You. www.npr.org/2019/03/13/681621047/college-completion-rates-are-up-but-the-numbers-will-still-surprise-you

7. Centers for Disease Control and Prevention. (n.d.). COVID-19 Hospitalization and Death by Race/Ethnicity. www.cdc.gov/coronavirus/2019-ncov/covid-data/investigations-discovery/hospitalization-death-by-race-ethnicity.html

8. Iacurci, G. (2020, May 14). 40% of Low-Income Americans Lost Their Jobs Due to the Pandemic. www.cnbc.com/2020/05/14/40percent-of-low-income-americans-lost-their-jobs-in-march-according-to-fed.html

9. National Student Clearinghouse Research Center, High School Benchmarks. (2020). *National College Progression Rates.* https://nscresearchcenter.org/wp-content/uploads/2020_HSBenchmarksReport.pdf

10. Pulliam, J. D., & Van Patten, J. J., *History of Education in America*, Pearson, 2006.

11. Deutschman, A., & Fefer, J. D. (1992, August 10). Why Kids Should Learn About Work. https://money.cnn.com/magazines/fortune/fortune_archive/1992/08/10/76725/

12. Civic and the Everyone Graduates Center at the Johns Hopkins University School of Education. (2019, June 11). Building a Grad Nation: Progress and Challenge in Raising High School Graduation Rates. www.americaspromise.org/2019-building-grad-nation-report

13. Litow, S. (2013, November 19). Preparing Today's Students for Tomorrow's Jobs: Improving the Carl D. Perkins Career and Technical Education Act, November 19, 2013, p. 17. www.govinfo.gov/content/pkg/CHRG-113hhrg85479/html/CHRG-113hhrg85479.htm

14. Litow, S. (2019, May 6). An Inconvenient Truth: The Road to Retirement Means Working Longer. www.cnbc.com/2019/05/06/an-inconvenient-truth-the-road-to-retirement-means-working-longer.html

15. Litow, Does College Matter?

16. Tough, P., *How Children Succeed: Grit, Curiosity, and the Hidden Power of Character*, Houghton Mifflin Harcourt, 2012.

17. Litow, Preparing Today's Students.

18. Gordon, E. E., *Future Jobs: Solving the Employment and Skills Crisis*, Praeger, 2013, p. 3.

19. CareerBuilder's New Talent Crunch Study Explores the Impact of the Skills Gap and Vacancies on Revenue and Turnover. (June 27, 2012). http://press.careerbuilder.com/2012-06-27-CareerBuilders-New-Talent-Crunch-Study-Explores-the-Impact-of-the-Skills-Gap-and-Vacancies-on-Revenue-and-Turnover

20. P-TECH. (n.d.). General Information. www.ptechnyc.org/domain/23

21. Tammany Hall. (2021, January 22). https://en.wikipedia.org/wiki/Tammany_Hall

22. Baker, K. (2002, March 23). The Courthouse That Graft Built. www.nytimes.com/2002/03/23/opinion/the-courthouse-that-graft-built.html

23. Paul Robeson High School Students in New York Campaign Against Closing, 2009–2011. (n.d.). https://nvdatabase.swarthmore.edu/content/paul-robeson-high-school-students-new-york-campaign-against-closing-2009-2011

24. Medina, J. (2008, March 28). Student Stabbed at Crown Heights School. https://cityroom.blogs.nytimes.com/2008/03/28/student-stabbed-at-crown-heights-school/

25. Williams, T. (2007, February 26). A Team Feared by Rivals Now Sits Idle, and Angry. www.nytimes.com/2007/02/26/nyregion/26robeson.html

26. Ibid.

27. Mendoza-Moyers, D. (2019, April 27). P-Tech Program Seeks to Bridge New York's Education, Skills Gap. www.timesunion.com/business/article/P-Tech-program-seeks-to-bridge-New-York-s-13796066.php; plus internal correspondence.

28. Frequently Asked Questions—P-TECH.org. (n.d.). www.ptech.org/resources/faqs/

29. Litow, S. (2018, September 14). A School Model That Delivers Equity and Access for All. www.crainsnewyork.com/op-ed/school-model-delivers-equity-and-access-all

30. CitizenIBM. (2019, October 9). Rashid Davis—Reflections from the Founding P-TECH Principal. www.youtube.com/watch?v=tb70t9acQsU

31. Abdul-Alim, J. (2017, June 4). P-TECH Ready to Put Partnerships to Test. https://diverseeducation.com/article/97373/

32. Young, J. (2021, January 22). Pandemic Does Not Slow P-TECH Program. www.observertoday.com/news/page-one/2021/01/pandemic-does-not-slow-p-tech-program/

Chapter 2

1. Gershenson, S., Holt, S. B., & Papageorge, N. (2016). Who Believes in Me? The Effect of Student–Teacher Demographic Match on Teacher Expectations. *Economics of Education Review 52*: 209–224. https://doi.org/10.1016/j.econedurev.2016.03.002; Hunt, T. (2019, September). Alumnus Finds Continued Success with Innovative P-TECH School. https://gse.news.fordham.edu/blog/2019/09/04/alumnus-finds-continued-success-with-innovative-p-tech-school/

2. The College Board. AP for All—NYC: Education. (2019, September 20). https://professionals.collegeboard.org/testing/states-local-governments/partnerships/nyc/ap-all

3. Statewide High School Graduation Rate Shows Continuing Gains. (2014, December 18). www.nysed.gov/news/2015/statewide-high-school-graduation-rate-shows-continuing-gains

4. Rosenthal, R., & Jacobson, L. (1968). Pygmalion in the Classroom. *Urban Rev 3*: 16–20. https://doi.org/10.1007/BF02322211

5. Tenenbaum, H., & Ruck, M. (2007, November 2). Are Teachers' Expectations Different for Racial Minority Than for European American Students? *A Meta-Analysis Journal of Educational Psychology 99*(2): 253–273.

6. de Boer, H., Timmermans, A., & van der Werf, M. (2018). The Effects of Teacher Expectation Interventions on Teachers' Expectations and Student Achievement: Narrative Review and Meta-Analysis. *Educational Research and Evaluation 24*(3–5).

7. Alvidrez, J., & Winstein, R. (1999). Early Teacher Perceptions and Later Student Academic Achievement. *Journal of Educational Psychology 91*(4): 731–746.

8. Boser, U., Wilhelm, M., & Hanna, R. (2014, October 6). The Power of the Pygmalion Effect: Teachers' Expectations Strongly Predict College Completion. https://cdn.americanprogress.org/wp-content/uploads/2014/10/TeacherExpectations-brief10.8.pdf

9. Davie, S. (2016, January 19). Teachers' Bias Can Limit Students' Future. www.straitstimes.com/opinion/teachers-bias-can-limit-students-future

10. MetLife. (2009). *The MetLife Survey of the American Teacher: Collaborating for Student Success; Part 2: Student Achievement*. www.metlife.com/content /dam/metlifecom/us/homepage/about-us/newsroom/MetLife_Teacher _Survey_2009_Part_2.pdf

11. Boser, Power of the Pygmalion Effect.

12. PsycholoGenie. Psychology Behind the Golem Effect and Consequences of the Same. (2013, May 24). https://psychologenie.com/psychology -behind-golem-effect

13. Baldwin, J. (1979, July 29). If Black English Isn't a Language, Then Tell Me, What Is? https://archive.nytimes.com/www.nytimes.com /books/98/03/29/specials/baldwin-english.html

14. Text: George W. Bush's Speech to the NAACP. (2000, July 10). www .washingtonpost.com/wp-srv/onpolitics/elections/bushtext071000.htm

15. Dee, T. (2005). A Teacher Like Me: Does Race, Ethnicity, or Gender Matter? *American Economic Review 95*(2): 158–165.

16. Rubie-Davies, C., Hattie, J., & Hamilton, R. (2006). Teacher Expectations of Students. *British Journal of Educational Psychology 76*(3): 429–444. www.ecs.org/clearinghouse/01/05/51/10551.pdf

17. van den Bergh, L. et al. (2010). The Implicit Prejudiced Attitudes of Teachers: Relations to Teacher Expectations and the Ethnic Achievement Gap. *American Educational Research Journal 47*(2): 497–527.

18. McKown, C., & Weinstein, R. (2008). Teacher Expectations, Classroom Context, and the Achievement Gap. *Journal of School Psychology 46*(3): 235–261.

19. Papageorge, N., & Gershenson, S. (2016, September 15). Do Teacher Expectations Matter? www.brookings.edu/blog/brown-center-chalkboard /2016/09/16/do-teacher-expectations-matter/

20. Cohen, G. L., & Garcia, J. (2014). Educational Theory, Practice, and Policy and the Wisdom of Social Psychology. *Policy Insights from the Behavioral and Brain Sciences 1*(1): 13–20.

21. Boaler, J. (2013). Ability and Mathematics: The Mindset Revolution That Is Reshaping Education. *FORUM 55*(1): 143–152.

22. Canning, E. et al., (2019, February 1). STEM Faculty Who Believe Ability Is Fixed Have Larger Racial Achievement Gaps and Inspire Less Student Motivation in Their Classes. https://advances.sciencemag.org /content/5/2/eaau4734

23. Ibid.

24. Cottrill, C. (2019, August 24). Column: Fighting Bias in Programs for Gifted Students. www.tampabay.com/news/perspective/column-fighting -bias-in-programs-for-gifted-students/2273427/

25. The Education Trust. (2020, January). *Inequities in Advanced Coursework: What's Driving Them and What Leaders Can Do*. https://s3-us-east-2.amazonaws .com/edtrustmain/wp-content/uploads/2014/09/08183916/Inequities-in -Advanced-Coursework-Whats-Driving-Them-and-What-Leaders-Can-Do -January-2019.pdf

26. Gershenson, S., and Papageorge, N. (2018). The Power of Teacher Expectations: How Racial Bias Hinders Student Attainment. *Education Next* 18(1): 64.

27. Barshay, J. (2020, March 30). Bright Black Students Taught by Black Teachers Are More Likely to Get into Gifted-and-Talented Classrooms. https://hechingerreport.org/bright-black-students-who-are-taught-by-black -teachers-are-more-likely-to-get-into-gifted-and-talented-classrooms/

28. U.S. Department of Education. (2016, May 6). REPORT: The State of Racial Diversity in the Educator Workforce. www.ed.gov/news/press-releases /report-state-racial-diversity-educator-workforce

29. National Center for Education Statistics. (2020, May). Racial/Ethnic Enrollment in Public Schools. https://nces.ed.gov/programs/coe/indicator_cge .asp

30. National Center for Education Statistics. (2020, May). Characteristics of Public School Teachers. https://nces.ed.gov/programs/coe/indicator_clr.asp

31. Papageorge, Do Teacher Expectations Matter?

32. Jones, M. A. (2017, October 5). Study Proves Black Teachers Have a Significant Impact on Black Students. https://theundefeated.com/features /study-black-teachers-have-significant-impact-on-black-students/

33. U.S. Department of Education. (2014, September). Teacher Attrition and Mobility: Results from the 2012–13 Teacher Follow-Up Survey, First Look. https://nces.ed.gov/pubs2014/2014077.pdf

34. Boser, U., Wilhelm, M., and Hanna, R. (2014, October). The Power of the Pygmalion Effect. www.americanprogress.org/issues/education-k-12 /reports/2014/10/06/96806/the-power-of-the-pygmalion-effect/

35. College for America. (2018, October 3). Addressing the College Completion Gap Among Low-Income Students. https://collegeforamerica.org /college-completion-low-income-students/

36. Shapiro, D., et al. (2017, April). *A National View of Student Attainment Rates by Race and Ethnicity—Fall 2010 Cohort* (Signature Report No. 12b). National Student Clearinghouse Research Center. https://nscresearchcenter.org /wp-content/uploads/Signature12-RaceEthnicity.pdf

37. Jussim, L., & Harber, K. (2005, February 1). Teacher Expectations and Self-Fulfilling Prophecies: Knowns and Unknowns, Resolved and Unresolved Controversies. *Personality and Social Psychology Review* 9(2): 131–155. https:// doi.org/10.1207/s15327957pspr0902_3

38. Leonhardt, D. (2016, November 4). Schools That Work. www .nytimes.com/2016/11/06/opinion/sunday/schools-that-work.html

39. de Boer, Effects of Teacher Expectation Interventions.

40. Spiegel, A. (2012, September 17). Teachers' Expectations Can Influence How Students Perform. www.npr.org/sections/health-shots/2012/09/18 /161159263/teachers-expectations-can-influence-how-students-perform

41. Rumley, E. (2019, April 6). Super Bowl Champion Victor Cruz Joins 60 Paterson Students Destined for New P-Tech High School for "Signing

Day." www.tapinto.net/articles/super-bowl-champion-victor-cruz-joins-60
-paterson-students-destined-for-new-p-tech-high-school-for-signing-day

42. Office of Equity and Access. (2017, October 6). AP for All. https://
oea.nyc/apforall

43. Mattingly, J. (2019, September 3). Richmond High School Students
See Improved Performance on Advanced Placement Tests. https://richmond
.com/news/local/richmond-high-school-students-see-improved-performance
-on-advanced-placement-tests/article_ce2dedac-dfa5-536b-99b0
-51a88d39f3b2.html

Chapter 3

1. The Nation's Report Card. (2019). Results from the 2019 Mathematics and Reading Assessments. www.nationsreportcard.gov/mathematics
/supportive_files/2019_infographic.pdf

2. Deputy Commissioner Dr. Kimberly Young Wilkins to District Superintendents, Superintendents of Public Schools, School Administrators, November 18, 2019, New York State Education Department. Equitable Course
Access Guidance, www.nysed.gov/memo/essa/equitable-course-access
-guidance (cf. https://nces.ed.gov/programs/coe/indicator_coi.asp)

3. Garcia, E. (2020, February 12). Schools Are Still Segregated, and
Black Children Are Paying a Price. www.epi.org/publication/schools-are-still
-segregated-and-black-children-are-paying-a-price/

4. Spencer, K. (2015, July 30). Even after Neighborhoods Integrate,
Many Students Attend "Apartheid Schools." www.theatlantic.com/politics
/archive/2015/07/even-after-neighborhoods-integrate-many-students
-attend-apartheid-schools/432435/

5. Warner, J. (2018, May 4). "A Nation at Risk" and the Re-Segregation
of Schools. www.insidehighered.com/blogs/just-visiting/nation-risk-and-re
-segregation-schools

6. Killen, M. (2019, Fall). Developing Inclusive Youth. *American Educator*
43(3): 8–12. www.aft.org/sites/default/files/ae-fall2019.pdf

7. Bohrnstedt, G., et al. (2015). School Composition and the Black–White
Achievement Gap. U.S. Department of Education, Washington, DC: National Center for Education Statistics. https://nces.ed.gov/nationsreportcard
/subject/studies/pdf/school_composition_and_the_bw_achievement_
gap_2015.pdf

8. Johnson, R. C., Long-Run Impacts of School Desegregation & School
Quality on Adult Attainments, NBER (working paper 16664, January 2011,
revised August 2015).

9. Warner, "A Nation at Risk."

10. Arundel, K. (2020, October 29). Disappointing 12th Grade NAEP
Prompts Calls for Curriculum, Funding Improvements. www.educationdive
.com/news/naep-results-leads-to-calls-for-improvements/587981/

11. Warner, "A Nation at Risk."

12. U.S. Government Accountability Office. (2016, April). *Report to Congressional Requesters, K-12 EDUCATION, Better Use of Information Could Help Agencies Identify Disparities and Address Racial Discrimination.* www.gao.gov /assets/680/676745.pdf

13. Berwick, C. (2018, October 26). 3 Promising Models of School Integration. www.edutopia.org/article/3-promising-models-school-integration; U.S. Department of Education. (2016, July). *The State of Racial Diversity in the Education Workforce.* www2.ed.gov/rschstat/eval/highered/racial-diversity /state-racial-diversity-workforce.pdf

14. Morgan, I., & Amerikaner, A. (2020, February 20). Funding Gaps 2018. https://edtrust.org/resource/funding-gaps-2018/

15. EdBuild. (n.d.). 23 Billion. https://edbuild.org/content/23-billion

16. Rice, J. (2003). Teacher Quality: Understanding the Effectiveness of Teacher Attributes. www.epi.org/publication/books_teacher_quality_execsum_ intro/

17. Douglas-Gabriel, D. (2019, July 14). How Student Debt Hinders Teacher Diversity. www.washingtonpost.com/education/2019/07/09 /how-student-debt-hinders-teacher-diversity

18. Dilworth, M. E., & Coleman, M. J. (2014). *Time for a Change, Diversity in Teaching Revisited.* www.nea.org/sites/default/files/2020-05/Time_for_a _Change_Diversity_in_Teaching_Revisited_%28web%29.pdf

19. Murphy, M., & Zirkel, S. (2015). Race and Belonging in School: How Anticipated and Experienced Belonging Affect Choice, Persistence, and Performance. *Teachers College Record 117*(12): 1–40.

20. Fiddiman, B., Campbell, C., & Partelow, L. (2019, July 9). Student Debt: An Overlooked Barrier to Increasing Teacher Diversity. www.americanprogress .org/issues/education-postsecondary/reports/2019/07/09/471850/student-debt -overlooked-barrier-increasing-teacher-diversity/

21. Grissom, J. A., Rodriguez, L. A., and Kern, E. C. (2017, March). Teacher and Principal Diversity and the Representation of Students of Color in Gifted Programs: Evidence from National Data. *The Elementary School Journal 117*(3). www.journals.uchicago.edu/doi/abs/10.1086/690274?journalCo de=esj

22. Gershenson, Holt, and Papageorge, Who Believes in Me?

23. Papageorge, N., Gershenson, S., & Kyung, M. K., Teacher Expectations Matter, NBER (working paper 25255, November 2018). www.nber.org /papers/w25255

24. Egalite, A., Kisida, B., & Winters, M. (2015, January 31). Representation in the Classroom: The Effect of Own-Race Teachers on Student Achievement. www.sciencedirect.com/science/article/abs/pii/S0272775715000084

25. Griesbach, R. (2018, July 10). With Man Up, a New Memphis Teacher Prep Program Is Training, Mentoring Men of Color. https://tn.chalkbeat .org/2018/7/10/21105428/with-man-up-a-new-memphis-teacher-prep -program-is-training-mentoring-men-of-color

26. Papageorge, Gershenson, & Kyung, Teacher Expectations Matter.

27. Why America Lost So Many of Its Black Teachers. (2019, July 9). *The Economist.* www.economist.com/democracy-in-america/2019/07/08/why -america-lost-so-many-of-its-black-teachers

28. Will, M. (2020, December 3). 65 Years after "Brown v. Board," Where Are All the Black Educators? www.edweek.org/ew/articles/2019/05/14/65 -years-after-brown-v-board-where.html

29. Reckdahl, K. (2020, October 21). Two Percent of Teachers Are Black Men. A City Is Trying to Recruit More. https://hechingerreport.org/two -percent-of-teachers-are-black-men-a-city-is-trying-to-recruit-more/

30. Correspondence from Education Trust, November 20, 2020.

31. Thompson, O., School Desegregation and Black Teacher Employment, NBER (working paper 25990, June 24, 2019). www.nber.org/papers/w25990

32. Will, 65 Years after "Brown v. Board."

33. Amber, M. (2018, May 4). The Rise and Fall of Black Teachers and Principals in U.S. Public Schools Since Brown v. Board. https://commons. trincoll.edu/edreform/2018/05/the-rise-and-fall-of-black-teachers-and -principals-in-u-s-public-schools-since-brown-v-board/

34. Jacinto, A., & Gershenson, S. (2019, March). The Intergenerational Transmission of Teaching. www.iza.org/publications/dp/12201/the -intergenerational-transmission-of-teaching

35. Long, C. (2020, March 11). A Hidden History of Integration and the Shortage of Teachers of Color. www.nea.org/advocating-for-change/new -from-nea/hidden-history-integration-and-shortage-teachers-color

36. Why America Lost So Many of Its Black Teachers.

37. Will, 65 Years after "Brown v. Board."

38. Ingersoll, R., & Merrill, L. "The Changing Face of the Teaching Force," in *The American Public School Teacher*, eds. D. Drury and J. Baer. Harvard Education Press, 2011.

39. Email correspondence with founder Dr. Patrick Washington, March 25, 2021.

40. DATAUSA. (n.d.). Teacher Education. https://datausa.io/profile/cip /teacher-education

41. U.S. Department of Education, *State of Racial Diversity.*

42. Moss, J. (2016, Summer). Where Are All the Teachers of Color? www.gse.harvard.edu/news/ed/16/05/where-are-all-teachers-color

43. National Center for Education Statistics. (2020). *The Condition of Education, Racial/Ethnic Enrollment in Public Schools.* https://nces.ed.gov/programs /coe/pdf/coe_cge.pdf

44. U.S. Department of Education, *State of Racial Diversity.*

45. Ibid.

46. Allegretto, S., & Mishel, L. (2018, September 5). The Teacher Pay Penalty Has Hit a New High: Trends in the Teacher Wage and Compensation Gaps through 2017. www.epi.org/publication/teacher-pay-gap-2018/

47. Massachusetts Department of Elementary and Secondary Education. (n.d.). School and District Profiles. https://profiles.doe.mass.edu/general/general.aspx?topNavID=1

48. Dilworth & Coleman, *Time for a Change*.

49. Pathways2Teaching®. (n.d.). www.pathways2teaching.com/

50. Dallas Independent School District. (n.d.). P-TECH and Early College Programs: P-TECH/ECHS by Campus. www.dallasisd.org/Page/42563

51. Grundy, C. (n.d.). ST. VRAINNOVATION: Future-Ready Graduates. http://magazine.svvsd.org/future.html

52. U.S. Department of Education. (2004, November). *Alternative Routes to Teacher Certification*. www2.ed.gov/admins/tchrqual/recruit/altroutes/report.pdf

53. Perkins, B., & Arvidson, C. (2017). The Association between a Community College's Teacher Education Program and the 4-Year Graduation Rates of Black and Hispanic Teacher Education Students. *Community College Journal of Research and Practice 41*: 8.

54. Our Mission. Golden Apple. www.goldenapple.org/mission

55. Golden Apple Accelerators Program. www.goldenapple.org/accelerators

56. Moroney, M. (2020, June 24). There Aren't Enough Black Teachers in the U.S.—and We Desperately Need to Change That. www.popsugar.com/family/why-we-need-more-black-teachers-in-america-47543451

57. Weingarten, R. (2019, July 11). Democracy in Education, Education for Democracy. www.aft.org/press/speeches/democracy-education-education-democracy

58. Gill, J. (2017, August). *State Action: Strategies for Building the Teacher Pipeline*, Council of Chief State School Officers. https://ccsso.org/resource-library/state-action-strategies-building-teacher-pipeline

59. U.S. Department of Education, *Alternative Routes*. www2.ed.gov/admins/tchrqual/recruit/altroutes/report.pdf

60. Ingersoll & Merrill, "The Changing Face of the Teaching Force."

61. White, L. (2019, September 4). Bill Would Expand Minority Teacher Loan Program. www.wpr.org/bill-would-expand-minority-teacher-loan-program

62. Gill, *State Action*.

63. Dixon, D., & Griffin, A. (2020, February 5). If You Listen, We Will Stay. https://edtrust.org/resource/if-you-listen-we-will-stay/

64. Email correspondence with founder Dr. Patrick Washington, March 25, 2021.

65. Dixon & Griffin, If You Listen.

66. The Education Trust–New York. (2017, October). *See Our Truth*. https://seeourtruth-ny.edtrust.org/wp-content/uploads/sites/4/2017/10/See-Our-Truth.pdf

67. Will, 65 Years after "Brown v. Board."

68. DeRuy, E. (2016, November 7). The Burden of Being a Black Teacher. www.theatlantic.com/education/archive/2016/11/the-challenge-of-teaching -while-black/506672/

69. Sun, M. (2018, July–September). Black Teachers' Retention and Transfer Patterns in North Carolina: How Do Patterns Vary by Teacher Effectiveness, Subject, and School Conditions? *AERA Open* 4(3): 1–23. https:// journals.sagepub.com/doi/pdf/10.1177/2332858418784914

70. Will, 65 Years After "Brown v. Board."

71. Goldring, R., Gray, L., & Bitterman, A. (2013, August). Characteristics of Public and Private Elementary and Secondary School Teachers in the United States: Results from the 2011–12 Schools and Staffing Survey (NCES 2013-314). Washington, D.C.: National Center for Education Statistics, U.S. Department of Education. https://nces.ed.gov/pubs2013/2013312.pdf

72. Dilworth & Coleman, *Time for a Change.*

73. Barnum, M. (2018, July 25). Black Teachers Leave Schools at Higher Rates—But Why? www.chalkbeat.org/2018/7/25/21105406/black-teachers -leave-schools-at-higher-rates-but-why

74. Weingarten, R. (2019, April 18). The Freedom to Teach. www.aft.org /freedomtoteach

75. U.S. Department of Education Office for Civil Rights. (2014, March). Civil Rights Data Collection, Data Snapshot: Teacher Equity. www2.ed.gov /about/offices/list/ocr/docs/crdc-teacher-equity-snapshot.pdf

76. U.S. Bureau of Labor Statistics. (2021, January 8). E-16. Unemployment Rates by Age, Sex, Race, and Hispanic or Latino Ethnicity. www.bls.gov /web/empsit/cpsee_e16.htm

77. Kaiser Family Foundation. (2020, October 23). Poverty Rate by Race/ Ethnicity. www.kff.org/other/state-indicator/poverty-rate-by-raceethnicity/? currentTimeframe=0&sortModel=%7B%22colId%22%3A%22Location%22 %2C%22sort%22%3A%22asc%22%7D

78. Gramlich, J. (2020, August 27). The Gap Between the Number of Blacks and Whites in Prison Is Shrinking. www.pewresearch.org/fact- tank/2019/04/30/shrinking-gap-between-number-of-blacks-and-whites -in-prison/

79. Pathways in Technology Early College High School, www.facebook. com/PathwaysInTech/

80. Hardy, D. (2015, November 24). How Race and Class Relate to Standardized Tests. https://thenotebook.org/articles/2015/11/24/how-race-and -class-relate-to-standardized-tests/ for Philadelphia figures; Chang, A. (2018, June 14). The Fraught Racial Politics of Entrance Exams for Elite High Schools. www.vox.com/2018/6/14/17458710/new-york-shsat-test-asian-protest   for New York City figures.

81. Shapiro, E. (2019, March 18). Only 7 Black Students Got into Stuyvesant, N.Y.'s Most Selective High School, Out of 895 Spots. www .nytimes.com/2019/03/18/nyregion/black-students-nyc-high-schools.html

82. Tweet from Rashid Davis, January 24, 2012, https://twitter.com /rashidfdavis/status/1353377554091151365?s=20

83. Kirp, D. (2016, October 29). Nudges That Help Struggling Students Succeed. www.nytimes.com/2016/10/30/opinion/nudges-that-help-struggling -students-succeed.html

84. Citywide Engagement for Student Recruitment—P-TECH.org. (n.d.). www.ptech.org/case-study/citywide-engagement-for-student-recruitment/

85. Stevens, K. B. (2019, April 22). The Socioeconomic Achievement Gap Hasn't Budged in Half a Century. Now What? www.aei.org/publication/the -socioeconomic-achievement-gap-hasnt-budged-in-half-a-century-now-what/

86. Dallas Independent School District. (n.d.). P-TECH and Early College Programs/Who Can Apply? www.dallasisd.org/Page/41446

87. Dynarski, S. (2018, July 19). *Evidence on New York City and Boston Exam Schools.* www.brookings.edu/research/evidence-on-new-york-city-and -boston-exam-schools/

88. Reeves, R., & Schobert, A. (2019, July 31). *Elite or Elitist? Lessons for Colleges from Selective High Schools.* www.brookings.edu/research/elite-or-elitist -lessons-for-colleges-from-selective-high-schools/

89. GOODE STEM ACADEMY HS: Academic Progress. (n.d.). www .illinoisreportcard.com/School.aspx?source=trends&Schoolid=150162990250861

90. Jan, et al., As Big Corporations Say "Black Lives Matter."

91. Son, H. (2020, August 10). Banks and Tech Giants Including JPMorgan and Amazon Pledge to Hire 100,000 Minority and Low-Income New Yorkers. www.cnbc.com/2020/08/10/banks-and-tech-companies-including -jpmorgan-google-and-amazon-form-new-york-jobs-council.html

92. Cheng, C. (2020, December 10). Merck CEO Ken Frazier and Ginni Rometty Start Groundbreaking Initiative to Give 1 Million Black Americans without College Degrees "Family-Sustaining" Corporate Jobs by 2030. www.businessinsider.com/ken-frazier-ginni-rometty-launch-oneten-to-hire -black-workers-2020-12

93. Fuller, J., & Raman, M. (October 2017). Dismissed by Degrees. www.hbs .edu/managing-the-future-of-work/Documents/dismissed-by-degrees.pdf

94. Blair, P., & Ahmed, S. (2020, June 28). The Disparate Racial Impact of Requiring a College Degree. www.wsj.com/articles/the-disparate-racial -impact-of-requiring-a-college-degree-11593375171

95. Blair, P. Q., et al., Searching for Stars: Work Experience as a Job Market Signal for Workers without Bachelor's Degrees, NBER (working paper 26844, March 2020). www.nber.org/papers/w26844.pdf

96. Dixon, D. (2020, December 7). 5 Ways State Leaders Can Support Teacher Diversity. https://edtrust.org/the-equity-line/5-ways-state-leaders -can-support-teacher-diversity/

97. The Education Trust. (2020, May 24). 5 Things to Advance Equity in Access to Strong and Diverse Educators. https://edtrust.org/resource /5-things-to-advance-equity-in-access-to-strong-and-diverse-educators/

98. The Education Trust, *See Our Truth*.

99. Rhode Island Board of Education. (n.d.). Rhode Island's Strategic Plan for Public Education: 2015–2020. www.ride.ri.gov/Portals/0/Uploads/Documents /Board-of-Education/Strategic-Plan/RIStrategicPlanForPK20Education.pdf

100. Ian Rosenblum phone conversation, December 4, 2020.

101. See https://leginfo.legislature.ca.gov/faces/billStatusClient.xhtml?bill_id =201720180SB807.

Chapter 4

1. Shapiro, D., et al. (2018, February). *Completing College: A State-Level View of Student Completion Rates* (Signature Report No. 14a). https://nscresearchcenter .org/wp-content/uploads/NSC_Signature_Report_14_StateSupp.pdf

2. Adelman, C. (1999). *Answers in the Tool Box: Academic Intensity, Attendance Patterns, and Bachelor's Degree Attainment*. https://files.eric.ed.gov/fulltext /ED431363.pdf

3. Chen, G. (2010, February 18). Why Do 60% of Community College Students Need Remedial Coursework? www.communitycollegereview.com/ blog/why-do-60-of-community-college-students-need-remedial-coursework

4. Lifton, K. (2010, February 11). About 1 in 5 Students Need Remedial Help in College. https://wowwritingworkshop.com/about-1-in-5-students -need-remedial-help-in-college/

5. Scott-Clayton, J., Crosta, P. M., & Belfield, C. R., Improving the Targeting of Treatment: Evidence from College Remediation, NBER (working paper 18457, October 2012), www.nber.org/system/files/working_papers/w18457 /w18457.pdf

6. Center for American Progress. (n.d.). Remedial Education Costs U.S. Students $1.3 Billion Annually, New CAP Analysis Finds. https://nlci.org /remedial-education-costs-u-s-students-1-3-billion-annually-new-cap -analysis-finds

7. Community College Research Center. (n.d.). Community College FAQs. https://ccrc.tc.columbia.edu/Community-College-FAQs.html

8. Scott-Clayton, Crosta, & Belfield, Improving the Targeting of Treatment.

9. Carnegie Math Pathways. (n.d.). Frequently Asked Questions. https:// carnegiemathpathways.org/faq/

10. Adelman, C. (1999, June). Answers in the Tool Box: Academic Intensity, Attendance Patterns, and Bachelor's Degree Attainment Executive Summary. www2.ed.gov/pubs/Toolbox/Exec.html

11. Quinton, S. (2014, December 11). The Race Gap in High School Honors Classes. www.theatlantic.com/politics/archive/2014/12/the-race-gap -in-high-school-honors-classes/431751/

12. Education Commission of the States. (2016). 50-State Comparison, Advanced Placement: All High Schools/Districts Required to Offer AP. http:// ecs.force.com/mbdata/MBQuestRT?Rep=AP0116

13. Grosserode, S. (2019, November 21). AP for All? New York State Pushes Greater Student Diversity in High-Level Courses. www.lohud.com /story/news/education/2019/11/21/new-york-advanced-courses-minority -students/4241779002/

14. Perna, L. W., et al. (2015). Unequal Access to Rigorous High School Curricula: An Exploration of the Opportunity to Benefit from the International Baccalaureate Diploma Programme (IBDP). *Educational Policy 29*(2): 402–425. https://files.eric.ed.gov/fulltext/EJ1054288.pdf

15. Theokas, C. (2013, June 5). Finding America's Missing AP and IB Students. https://edtrust.org/resource/finding-americas-missing-ap-and-ib -students/

16. The Education Trust. (2020, January). *Inequities in Advanced Coursework: What's Driving Them and What Leaders Can Do.* https://s3-us-east-2. amazonaws.com/edtrustmain/wp-content/uploads/2014/09/08183916 /Inequities-in-Advanced-Coursework-Whats-Driving-Them-and-What -Leaders-Can-Do-January-2019.pdf

17. Civil Rights Data Collection. (n.d.). 2015–16 State and National Estimations. https://ocrdata.ed.gov/estimations/2015-2016

18. Education Trust, *Inequities in Advanced Coursework.*

19. Ibid.

20. Ibid.

21. Education Commission of the States, 50-State Comparison.

22. Ford, J., & Triplett, N. (2019, August 22). E(race)ing Inequities: How Access to Advanced Placement Courses Breaks Down by Race. www.ednc .org/eraceing-inequities-how-access-to-advanced-placement-courses-breaks -down-by-race/

23. Goldberg, N., & Chapman, B. (2019, February 27). Record Number of NYC Students Took AP Exams in 2018: Mayor de Blasio. www.nydailynews. com/new-york/education/ny-metro-nyc-record-ap-exams-20190226-story. html

24. Richman, T. (2019, July 22). Thousands of Baltimore Students Have Lacked Access to Advanced Placement. That's about to Change. www .baltimoresun.com/education/bs-md-ap-class-expansion-20190722 -jeujgzgus5cm7lj4ehczb2t2wi-story.html

25. Roegman R., & Hatch, T. (2016, February). The AP Lever for Boosting Access, Success, and Equity. *Kappan Magazine 97*(5). www.tc.columbia.edu /ncrest/publications--resources/0031721716629653.pdf

26. Mathews, J. (2019, November 23). The Power of Changing Your Mind (or How a Teacher Came to Believe in His Students). www.washingtonpost. com/local/education/the-power-of-changing-your-mind-or-how-a-teacher -came-to-believe-in-his-students/2019/11/22/db620816-0b39-11ea-97ac -a7ccc8dd1ebc_story.html

27. Mathews, J. (2019, September 22). The Best Little Schoolhouse in Oregon, and How It Got to Be That Way. www.washingtonpost.com/local

/education/the-best-little-schoolhouse-in-oregon-and-how-it-go-to-be-that
-way/2019/09/17/418b3264-d5b3-11e9-9343-40db57cf6abd_story.html

28. Peinado, E. (n.d.). AP for All. http://magazine.svvsd.org/AP.html

29. Email communication from Greg Stephens, June 24, 2020.

30. College Board. (2017). Pre-AP for All Planning Guide. https://pre-ap
.collegeboard.org/pdf/preap-all-guide.pdf

31. www.change.org/p/college-board-create-advanced-placement-courses-in
-african-and-african-american-history?utm_content=cl_sharecopy_22936108
_en-US%3Av8

32. Tugend, A. (2017, September 7). Who Benefits from the Expansion of
A.P. Classes? www.nytimes.com/2017/09/07/magazine/who-benefits-from
-the-expansion-of-ap-classes.html

33. More Blacks Are Competing in Advanced Placement Programs, But
the Racial Scoring Gap Is Widening. (2008). *Journal of Blacks in Higher Education*. www.jbhe.com/features/59_apscoringgap.html

34. Newsweek International Insight. (2017, April 19). International
Baccalaureate—Setting the Standard in Excellence. www.newsweek.com
/insights/best-ib-schools-usa-2017

35. Perna, L. (2015). Unequal Access to Rigorous High School Curricula:
An Exploration of the Opportunity to Benefit from the International Baccalaureate Diploma Programme (IBDP). *Educational Policy 29*(2): 402–425.

36. Gordon, M., VanderKamp, E., & Halic, O. (2015). International Baccalaureate Programmes in Title I Schools in the United States: Accessibility, Participation and University Enrollment. www.ibo.org/globalassets/publications
/ib-research/title-1-schools-research.pdf

37. Gordon, VanderKamp, & Halic, International Baccalaureate Programmes.

38. Moody, J. (2020, April 21). U.S. News Releases 2020 Best High
Schools Rankings. www.usnews.com/education/best-high-schools/articles
/us-news-ranks-best-high-schools

39. Barshay, J. (2020, March 30). Research on Early College High
Schools Indicates They May Pay for Themselves in the Long Run. https://
hechingerreport.org/research-on-early-college-high-schools-indicates-they
-may-pay-for-themselves-in-the-long-run/

40. Berger, A., et al. (2013, September). Early College, Early Success:
Early College High School Initiative Impact Study. American Institutes for
Research. www.air.org/sites/default/files/downloads/report/ECHSI_Impact
_Study_Report_Final1_0.pdf

41. Henneberger, A. K., Witzen, H., & Preston, A. M. (2020, May 7). A
Longitudinal Study Examining Dual Enrollment as a Strategy for Easing the
Transition to College and Career for Emerging Adults. *Emerging Adulthood*.
https://journals.sagepub.com/doi/full/10.1177/2167696820922052

42. Friedmann, E., et al. (2020, January). A Leg Up on College: The Scale
and Distribution of Community College Participation among California High

School Students. Wheelhouse, The Center for Community College Leadership and Research. https://education.ucdavis.edu/sites/main/files/ucdavis_wheelhouse_research_brief_vol5no1_online.pdf

43. Berger et al., Early College, Early Success.

44. Fink, J., Jenkins, D., & Yanagiura, T. (2017, September). What Happens to Students Who Take Community College "Dual Enrollment" Courses in High School? https://ccrc.tc.columbia.edu/media/k2/attachments/what-happens-community-college-dual-enrollment-students.pdf

45. Edmunds, J., et al. (2012). Expanding the Start of the College Pipeline: Ninth-Grade Findings from an Experimental Study of the Impact of the Early College High School Model. *Journal of Research on Educational Effectiveness* 5(2): 136–159.

46. Kirst, M. W., Venezia, A., & Nodine, T. Ramp-Up to College in California: A Statewide Strategy to Improve College Readiness and Comprehensive Dual Enrollment. www.mtsac.edu/president/cabinet-notes/Dual%20Enrollment-Ramp%20Up%20to%20College.pdf

47. Rosen, R. (2020, June 5). Bridging the School-to-Work Divide. www.mdrc.org/publication/bridging-school-work-divide

48. American Academy of Arts and Sciences. (2017). *The Future of Undergraduate Education: The Future of America.* www.amacad.org/sites/default/files/academy/multimedia/pdfs/publications/researchpapersmonographs/CFUE_Final-Report/Future-of-Undergraduate-Education.pdf

49. Addis, S., & Withington, C. (2017). Improving High School Graduation Rates among Males of Color. https://dropoutprevention.org/wp-content/uploads/2017/11/rwjf-ndpscn-moriah-ImprovingGradRatesMalesofColor-2016.pdf

50. P-TECH. (n.d.). Hands-On Learning as One Key to Student Learning. www.ptech.org/case-study/hands-on-learning-as-one-key-to-student-learning/

51. www.oneida-boces.org/PTECH

52. Education Trust, *Inequities in Advanced Coursework.*

53. Deputy Commissioner Dr. Kimberly Young Wilkins to District Superintendents, Superintendents of Public Schools, School Administrators, November 18, 2019, New York State Education Department. Equitable Course Access Guidance, www.nysed.gov/memo/essa/equitable-course-access-guidance

54. Education Trust, *Inequities in Advanced Coursework.*

Chapter 5

1. Dorman, J., Havey, N., & Fagioli, L. (2020, Spring). Bridging the Gap: Summer Bridge Programs as an Effective Strategy for Improving Minority Student Academic Attainment in Community Colleges. *Journal of Applied Research in the Community College* 27(1): 65–80.

2. Girls Not Brides. (2019, June 21). Bangladesh—Child Marriage around the World. www.girlsnotbrides.org/child-marriage/bangladesh/

3. P-TECH. (n.d.). Chicago Academy and the Early College Success. www.ptech.org/case-study/chicago-academys-approach-ensures-early -college-success/

4. Anderson, D. (2020, August 25). Joppatowne High P-TECH Freshmen Welcomed with Yard Signs, Personal Visit from School Administrators. www.baltimoresun.com/maryland/harford/aegis/cng-ag-ptech-welcome -0826-20200826-rx5nn2fcpre2pkme5b4xqzr5ta-story.html

5. P-TECH, Chicago Academy.

6. P-TECH. (n.d.). The Importance of Family Ties. www.ptech.org/case-study/the-importance-of-family-ties/

7. Hammond, Z., *Culturally Responsive Teaching and the Brain: Promoting Authentic Engagement and Rigor among Culturally and Linguistically Diverse Students*, Sage, 2015.

Chapter 6

1. P-TECH. (n.d.). Northern Borders Academy Skills Mapping Document. www.ptech.org/wp-content/uploads/2018/10/Northern-Borders-Academy -Skills-Mapping-Document.pdf

2. Ibid.

3. P-TECH. (n.d.). Skills Map for Great Southern Tier STEM Academy. www.ptech.org/wp-content/uploads/2018/10/GST-Manufacturing-Tech -SkillsMap.pdf

4. Young, J. (2021, January 22). Pandemic Does Not Slow P-TECH Program. www.observertoday.com/news/page-one/2021/01/pandemic-does -not-slow-p-tech-program/

5. P-TECH. (n.d.). Bosch Diesel—Biggest Employer in the Vysocina Region, Czech Republic. www.ptech.org/case-study/bosch-diesel-biggest -employer-in-the-vysocina-region-czech-republic/

6. Major Influence: Where Students Get Valued Advice on What to Study in College (2017, September). www.insidehighered.com/sites/default /server_files/files/Gallup-Strada_Education_Network-Major-Influence%20 EMBARGOED.PDF

Chapter 7

1. Gates, S. M., et al. (2013, November 30). *Preparing Principals to Raise Student Achievement: Implementation and Effects of the New Leaders Program in Ten Districts.* https://eric.ed.gov/?id=ED561152

2. Teacher Collaboration in Perspective: A Discussion Guide for Teachers and Principals, A joint project of the Spencer Foundation and Public Agenda. (2017). www.publicagenda.org/wp-content/uploads/2019/09/PublicAgenda _TeacherCollaborationInPerspective_ADiscussionGuide_2017.pdf

3. Davis, R. (2018, May 24). After Two Decades, I Still Remain Hopeful for New Equity Narratives. www.linkedin.com/pulse/after-two-decades-i -still-remain-hopeful-new-equity-narratives-davis/

4. Correspondence from Toni DeGuire Parker, January 5, 2021.

5. Governor Cuomo and IBM Announce Public-Private Partnership to Prepare NYS Students for High-Skills Jobs of the Future. (2014, September 29). www.governor.ny.gov/news/governor-cuomo-and-/ibm-announce-public-private-partnership-prepare-nys-students-high-skills

6. Welber, B. (2020, February 4). Hudson Valley City One of "50 Worst Cities to Live In" in U.S. https://hudsonvalleypost.com/hudson-valley-city-one-of-50-worst-cities-to-live-in-in-u-s/

7. Malloy, D. P. (2014, February 6). *State of the State Address.* https://portal.ct.gov/Malloy-Archive/Press-Room/Speeches/Governor-Dannel-P-Malloys-2014-State-of-the-State-Address

8. IBM CEO's Letter to Congress on Racial Justice Reform. (2020, November 9). www.ibm.com/blogs/policy/facial-recognition-sunset-racial-justice-reforms/

Chapter 8

1. Association for Career and Technical Education. (2017). State Policies Impacting CTE: 2017 Year in Review. www.acteonline.org/wp-content/uploads/2013/04/2017_State_CTE_Policy_Review.pdf

2. Governor Murphy Announces P-TECH Education Model for New Jersey. (n.d.). www.nj.gov/governor/news/news/562018/approved/20181127b.shtml

3. U.S. Census Bureau. (2019, July 1). QuickFacts: New Brunswick City, New Jersey. www.census.gov/quickfacts/newbrunswickcitynewjersey

4. Correspondence with Dr. Aubrey Johnson, March 26, 2021.

5. Kratovil, C. (2017, April 27). New Brunswick School Board President Loses Election by One Vote. https://newbrunswicktoday.com/2017/04/27/new-brunswick-school-board-president-loses-election-by-one-vote/

6. National Center for Educational Statistics, District Demographic Dashboard 2014–18.

Chapter 9

1. McElroy, K. (2016, August 15). A Nation of Workers: How Public Education Is Dummying Down Our Labor Force. www.jetsetmag.com/exclusive/business/nation-workers-public-education-dummying-labor-force/

2. Link, W. (2000). Jackson Davis and the Lost World of Jim Crow Education. Albert and Shirley Small Special Collections Library. https://small.library.virginia.edu/collections/featured/jackson-davis-collection-of-african-american-educational-photographs/related-resources/jackson-davis-and-the-lost-world-of-jim-crow-education/

3. Gates, F. T. (1970, January 1). The Country School of Tomorrow. https://archive.org/details/countryschoolof00gate/page/6/mode/2up

4. The National Commission on Excellence in Education. (1983, April). A Nation at Risk: The Imperative for Educational Reform. https://edreform.com/wp-content/uploads/2013/02/A_Nation_At_Risk_1983.pdf

5. Strauss, V. (2019, April 24). How Much Bill Gates's Disappointing Small-Schools Effort Really Cost. www.washingtonpost.com/news/answer -sheet/wp/2014/06/09/how-much-bill-gatess-disappointing-small-schools -effort-really-cost/

6. Agrawal, S., et al. (2021, January 7). Mckinsey: Beyond Hiring: How Companies Are Reskilling to Address Talent Gaps. www.mckinsey.com /business-functions/organization/our-insights/beyond-hiring-how-companies -are-reskilling-to-address-talent-gaps#

7. Campbell, A. (2019, February 13). A Record Number of U.S. Workers Went on Strike in 2018. www.vox.com/policy-and-politics/2019/2 /13/18223211/worker-teacher-strikes-2018-record

8. Russakoff, D. *The Prize: Who's in Charge of America's Schools?* Houghton Mifflin Harcourt, 2016.

9. Email correspondence from IBM including January 2020 final data report, January 25, 2021.

10. Louissaint, O. (2020, July 20). New Paths, New Faces: IBM Offers 1,000 Paid Internships to Diversify Tech Talent. www.ibm.com/blogs /corporate-social-responsibility/2020/07/new-paths-new-faces-ibm-offers -1000-paid-internships-to-diversify-tech-talent/

11. Rometty, G., & Bush, W. (2018, June 22). Congress Must Address the "Skills Gap" and Update Our Education System by Passing the Perkins Act. www.cnbc.com/2018/06/22/congress-must-address-the-skills-gap-and -update-our-education-system-by-passing-the-perkins-act.html

12. Rometty, G. (n.d.). Why the Senate Must Act on Education. www .businessroundtable.org/why-the-senate-must-act-on-education

Index

About the Authors

Stanley Litow is Professor of the Practice at Duke University where he also served as Innovator in Residence. He also teaches at Columbia University. He is a trustee of the State University of New York and serves as an opinion columnist at *Barron's*. He previously served as deputy chancellor of schools for New York City and as president of the IBM Foundation and vice president of Corporate Citizenship and Corporate Affairs at IBM. At IBM, he helped create Pathways in Technology Early College High School (P-TECH), the innovative grade 9 to 14 school connecting school to college to career. He also created the IBM Corporate Service Corps, the private-sector version of the Peace Corps, and the Smarter Cities Challenge to improve how more than 100 cities globally serve their citizens. In addition, he helped develop a virtual supercomputer to aid in research on cancer and AIDS. As deputy schools chancellor, he assisted in the creation of multiple new small high schools. Previously, he served in the mayor's office in New York City as executive director of the New York City Urban Corps and as the founder and executive director of Interface, a think tank and advocacy organization. He has served on Presidential Commissions for two U.S. presidents and on numerous commissions for the governor of New York. He is the author of *The Challenge for Business and Society: From Risk to Reward*.

Tina Kelley is the coauthor of *Almost Home: Helping Kids Move from Homelessness to Hope*, a national bestseller published by Wiley/Turner in 2012. She was a reporter at *The New York Times* for a decade, where she was part of the Metro team that won a 2002 Pulitzer Prize in the Public Service category for coverage of the September 11 attacks. She wrote 121 "Portraits of Grief," which were short descriptions of the victims. Her articles have also appeared in *TheAtlantic.com*, *New Jersey Monthly*, *Orion*, and *People* magazines. During her 20-year newspaper career, she worked at *The Philadelphia Inquirer*, *The Seattle Times*,

203

and *The Seattle Post-Intelligencer*. She also worked with Mr. Litow at the Educational Priorities Panel, writing investigative reports as part of the coalition's efforts to reform the New York City public school system. A graduate of Yale University, she and her husband live in New Jersey and have two children. She is the author of four books of poetry, *Rise Wildly* (2020) and *Abloom & Awry* (2017) from CavanKerry Press, and from Word Press, *Precise* (2013) and *The Gospel of Galore* (2003), which won a Washington State Book Award. Her poems have appeared in *Audubon*, the *Journal of the American Medical Association*, *Poetry Northwest*, *Prairie Schooner*, *The Best American Poetry 2009*, and on the buses of Seattle, WA.